D0875838

TURF WARS

American Politics and Political Economy
A series edited by Benjamin I. Page

TURF WARS

HOW CONGRESSIONAL COMMITTEES CLAIM JURISDICTION

DAVID C. KING

THE UNIVERSITY OF CHICAGO PRESS
CHICAGO AND LONDON

David C. King is associate professor of public policy at the
Kennedy School of Government, Harvard University.

The University of Chicago Press, Chicago 60637
The University of Chicago Press, Ltd., London
© 1997 by The University of Chicago
All rights reserved. Published 1997
Printed in the United States of America

06 05 04 03 02 01 00 99 98 97 1 2 3 4 5

ISBN: 0-226-43623-3 (cloth)
ISBN: 0-226-43624-1 (paper)

Library of Congress Cataloging-in-Publication Data

King, David C.
    Turf wars : how Congressional committees claim juris-
diction / David C. King.
        p. cm.
    Includes bibliographical references and index.
    ISBN 0-226-43623-3 (cloth : alk. paper).—
ISBN 0-226-43624-1 (pbk : alk. paper)
    1. United States. Congress—Committees. 2. Compe-
tent authority—United States. 3. Jurisdiction—United
States. I. Title.
    JK1029.K56   1997
    328.73'0765—dc21   96-53058
                                                   CIP

⊗The paper used in this publication meets the minimum
requirements of the American National Standard for Information Sciences—Permanence of Paper for Printed Library
Materials, ANSI Z39.48-1984.

*This book is for
all my children*

CONTENTS

Figures		ix
Tables		xi
Acknowledgments		xiii
INTRODUCTION		1
1	TURF WARS ON CAPITOL HILL	11
2	THE NATURE OF COMMITTEE JURISDICTIONS	33
3	WHAT HAPPENS WHEN JURISDICTIONS ARE REFORMED?	56
4	PARLIAMENTARIANS AS INSTITUTIONAL GUARDIANS	78
5	ESSENTIAL STRATEGIES FOR STAKING CLAIMS	105
6	FLYING TRAINS AND TURF WARS	121
7	GOVERNING THROUGH FRAGMENTED COMMITTEES	137
	Notes	149
	Bibliography	181
	Index	201

FIGURES

1.1 Jurisdictional ambiguity for a three-committee legislature 16

2.1 Consolidation of committees into House Judiciary Committee, 1794–1996 36

2.2 The common law logic of jurisdictional fragmentation 40

2.3 Commerce Committee activity in its statutory jurisdiction, 1947–1974 49

2.4 Growth of Commerce Committee's common law jurisdiction, 1947–1994 53

3.1 Commerce activity on energy issues that were granted jurisdiction in the 1980 reforms 69

3.2 Commerce Committee activity on issues lost in 1995 reform 74

TABLES

1.1 The Two Steps of Jurisdictional Change 23

2.1 Statutory Jurisdiction of the Senate Finance Committee, 1996 37

2.2 Common Law Jurisdiction, Sample from the 1920 Edition of Cannon's *Procedure* 39

2.3 Statutory Jurisdiction of the House Commerce Committee 46

3.1 Intercommittee Memberships of House Committees Consolidated by the 1946 Legislative Reorganization Act 61

3.2 Jurisdictional Changes in the 1995 House Rules 72

4.1 Overview of the History of Bill Referrals 87

6.1 OLS Model of Prereferral Entrepreneurial Activity on Maglev Trains, 1987–1992 131

6.2 Committee Characteristics and Maglev Bill Referrals 135

ACKNOWLEDGMENTS

This book began when I was a graduate student at the University of Michigan, and I owe a great debt to my friends and teachers there, especially Richard Hall, John Jackson, and John Kingdon. Through their writings, William Morrow, Keith Krehbiel and Barry Weingast have had an important influence on my work, and I hope I can keep learning from them. Frank Baumgartner, David Brady, Steve Brams, John Brehm, Michael Cohen, Roger Davidson, Doug Dion, Bryan Jones, Joel Kaji, Walter Oleszek, Kim Scheppele, Jack Walker, and Richard Zeckhauser made important contributions by asking me questions to which I had, at the time, no good answers.

At the John F. Kennedy School of Government, I am surrounded by wonderful colleagues who are genuinely interested in turf wars and their policy consequences. Michael Terra and Anjali Kataria helped track down references and data. My faculty assistant, Rebekah Freeman, kept me organized. The Institute of Politics gave me a grant to update the book after the 1994 elections, and I am very grateful.

With the Kennedy School's help, I have shared my research with former and current Members of the House, and their insights have been particularly valuable. I especially thank Mickey Edwards and Phil Sharp. I have also interviewed several dozen congressional staffers and lobbyists, and I thank them for sharing their experiences and expertise. For the most part, their names do not appear in these acknowledgments because I promised them all the cover of anonymity, but this book could not have been written without them.

This book is likely to make the House parliamentarians nervous, because I will never understand the intricacies of the House rules as well as they do. To them I say: thank you for indulging me, and I trust they will find my statements of fact far more often right than wrong.

Parts of Chapters 2 and 3 appeared in the March 1994 issue of the

American Political Science Review in "The Nature of Congressional Committee Jurisdictions." I trust that this book completes the story I began there. Of course, I should have completed this book sooner, but I have had so much fun with this project that I never really wanted it to end. John Tryneski and his colleagues at the University of Chicago Press have been tremendously helpful and patient.

I thank my children, Kalyn, Kelsey, Kendall, Cody, and Carson, for being so supportive. Above all, I thank my wife, Kirsten Syverson King. This book has been improved by every moment of her attention to it.

INTRODUCTION

Turf—and the power that goes with it—defines a legislative committee. Jurisdictions are property rights over issues. They distinguish one committee from another; they attract legislators to certain panels, and they set boundaries on what politicians can and cannot do. Pick any twenty pages in the *Congressional Record* or watch an hour of C-SPAN, and you will see telltale signs of jurisdictional intrigues. Who should come up with antismoking proposals? A tax committee? An agricultural committee? A health committee? Should insurance be regulated by a consumer protection or a probusiness committee? On almost every political issue, turf—or *which committees get to decide things*—makes all the difference. That is why turf wars rage on Capitol Hill, not to mention state legislatures and city councils around the country. Most major laws passing through the U.S. Congress during the last decade were shaped, to varying degrees, by intercommittee negotiations over turf. Without exception, every committee and subcommittee chair in Washington plays what insiders call the "jurisdiction game."

In the months between the 1994 elections and Newt Gingrich's (R-GA) ascendancy to the Speakership, House Republicans unveiled ambitious proposals to realign committee borders. By January 1995, sweeping proposals were sidetracked in favor of modest measures largely embracing the good old status quo.[1] Perhaps nothing is more sensitive to committee leaders than their jurisdictions. Trespassers and reformers beware.

When Gingrich's predecessor, Thomas Foley (D-WA), took the Speaker's reigns in 1989, he found turf wars to be his "biggest unexpected headache."[2] It is a headache that is getting worse every year as new policy areas like global change, sex discrimination, and industrial competitiveness become more fragmented among committees. The ju-

1

risdiction game is played so intensely that some panels now employ staffers known as "border cops" to help protect their territories and to plan assaults. If you had called the House Commerce Committee in the early 1990s and asked for "the border cop," you would have been put through to a senior staffer—David Finneghan. Finneghan lost his job when the Republicans swept into office, but a new border cop patrolled his beat.

For individual legislators, the payoffs for winning in turf wars include expanded power, greater prestige, opportunities to make a personal mark on important legislation, and improved services to voters. For the committee system as a whole, however, the relentless pursuit of turf by legislators can undermine the collective benefits that committees might otherwise provide. That is to say, turf wars can cripple a committee system. As with nations and hunting groups, poorly defined boundaries lead to wasteful skirmishes. One issue explored in this book is how legislatures might simultaneously harness the entrepreneurial spirit of the jurisdiction game without debilitating legislatures overall.

What Other Political Scientists Have Said about Jurisdictions

Though it *seems* impossible to talk about committees without talking about where jurisdictions come from and how they might change, political scientists have mostly done just that. Look at any congressional scholar's bookshelf. Only a handful of works emphasizing jurisdictional dynamics have been written by political scientists since World War II, and the focus of those books tends toward congressional reform or agenda setting more generally.[3] Scholarly articles about turf wars have also been rare, though interest has been picking up thanks in large part to a research project at Texas A&M directed by Frank Baumgartner and Bryan Jones.[4] When I began writing this book, I had to answer a nagging question. Maybe, I thought, my colleagues have ignored the jurisdiction game because it is too trivial or too obvious to waste time on it. If so, I was unlikely to uncover anything valuable.

Consequences of turf wars, however, are anything but trivial, which is one reason why committee chairs take turf so seriously. On reading how some other scholars have talked about committee turf, it became clear why jurisdictional *change* has received so little attention. The answer is that, with rare exceptions when Congress "reforms" its committee system, scholars have believed that jurisdictions *do not* change. No less an expert than Nelson Polsby taught us that an important element in the institutionalization of the U.S. House is that "jurisdictions are fixed in the rules."[5] Committee boundaries, some say, are stable facts, and since they do not change, we do not need to pay much attention to them. ("A constant explains no variance.") Jurisdictions (goes one common analogy) are like castle walls: immobile and impressively well fortified. Gary Cox and Mathew McCubbins summed up "the standard view," noting that "the foundation stones of committee autonomy are usually taken to be the seniority system and the fixity of committee jurisdictions."[6]

Roger Davidson and Walter Oleszek take exception to this conventional view, having learned about turf wars while working in the House on the 1974 "Bolling Committee" reform proposals (named after Missouri Democrat Richard Bolling). Oleszek was also an important staffer on the more recent Joint Committee on the Organization of Congress (1993–94). Committee boundaries, write Davidson and Oleszek, "are defined by the rules of each house, various public laws, and precedents," making the House's *written* rules only one source of jurisdictional legitimacy.[7] That is a theme I develop more fully, while placing turf wars in a theoretical framework. Larry Evans and Walter Oleszek are chronicling the jurisdictional changes introduced by House Republicans in 1995, and their account promises to focus our attention on the oft-times rancorous scuffles over turf.[8]

Several generations ago, when members of the American Political Science Association were as likely to be politicians as professors, budding political scientists grew up steeped in the parliamentary practices of the U.S. Congress.[9] Their knowledge was deep, detailed, and historically rich. They were (in the old sense of the word) institutionalists, perhaps too often preferring learned descriptions over theoretically informed generalizations, and too often reporting the rules of institutions while neglecting how individuals behaved in various settings. These early political scientists were equally at home on Capitol Hill and in the ivory tower.

Around mid-century, "behavioralists" eclipsed the old institutionalists. Employing public opinion polls and statistical techniques, this new breed of social scientist focused on individuals—not institutions.[10] Old descriptions of rules and procedures gathered dust. Today, "new institutionalism" places rational-acting individuals, typically modeled with techniques inspired by microeconomics, in specific institutional settings. Institutions constrain and are changed by individuals.[11] The move to understand the interactions of individuals and institutions should be applauded, though it is unfortunate that so much of the old institutionalism goes unread. This book tries to blend insights from both traditions.

By not paying enough attention to the old institutionalism, recent generations of political scientists embraced a mistaken view of jurisdictions. They implicitly accepted an image of turf highlighting a stagnant and misinformed image of the House and Senate rules. The rules manuals have not, until recently, been thought of as dynamic or adaptive documents. "The whole House," writes Arthur Maass, "can and does control the number of committees and their jurisdictions."[12] While it is true that the whole House sets the number of committees, it is simply not true that the whole House controls jurisdictions. Maass's conception (and he is hardly alone) puts too much faith in the written rules, which are indeed passed by floor majorities. How do the rules on bill referrals influence bill drafting strategies?[13] And where do the written rules that outline jurisdictions come from? How do we get legislative rules and procedures (of which those governing turf are a small part)?[14]

Committee borders in the House of Representatives, I will argue, are not stable institutional facts revised primarily when the House goes through occasional bursts of reform (such as in 1946, 1974, 1980, and 1995). Jurisdictions—like many facets of institutions—can be manipulated by political actors. Accordingly, Talbert, Jones, and Baumgartner have documented the use of "nonlegislative hearings" to set the stage for jurisdictional expansions by policy entrepreneurs.[15]

While malleable at the boundaries, committee jurisdictions provide a predictable form and structure to legislative organization. Over the last two decades, students of Congress have become increasingly drawn to the study of legislative organization, and for good reason. An extensive literature on distributive politics has shown how a majoritarian institution (like Congress) with a strong committee system (like Congress) can produce nonmajoritarian policies (like pork-barrel projects benefiting the few at the expense of the many).[16] That is a *distributive theory* view because it assumes that legislators are strongly motivated by distributing resources to friends and constituents. A revisionist literature, based on *information theory*, argues that the committee structure in Congress is a solution to the institution's need to make informed policy choices in an efficient way.[17] A third approach, relying on *strong parties*, has the majority caucus shaping Congress (through rules and procedures) in ways that benefit party supporters.[18] Which theoretical perspective is dominant is important because— applied to turf wars—they make different recommendations for reform. Rarely does a year go by without someone sounding the call for organizational reform, and committee realignments are usually the centerpieces of these proposals.[19]

The strong-parties thesis of Gary Cox and Mathew McCubbins rejects the conventional wisdom of fixed jurisdictions, arguing that turf is under the control of the majority party caucus. Committees are (at least in principle) controlled by the House, which "determines their jurisdictions," and, claim Cox and McCubbins, "the majority party has reshuffled jurisdictional responsibilities several times since the Legislative Reorganization Act of 1946."[20] While the strong-parties thesis is intriguing and helps us think through how legislatures solve collective action dilemmas, the parties have less control over committee jurisdictions than Cox and McCubbins would have us believe. I will argue that most jurisdictional changes happen when bills are referred to committees—not when reforms are brought to the House floor for a vote. Even on those occasions when turf wars are played out on the floor, however, Eric Schickler and Andrew Rich find evidence that "the determination of committee jurisdictions appears to be a matter that is with rare exceptions left to the membership as a whole rather than restricted to the majority party caucus."[21]

Scholars in the distributive politics tradition, chief among them Barry Weingast, have noticed that legislators seek out committee assignments not just because they are (or hope to become) policy experts.[22] Members get on committees to benefit their constituents. They do this by concentrating benefits within their districts while spreading the costs across the country. Since interests are local, and lone parochial interests cannot muster a floor majority, Congress has evolved a committee system that helps build floor majorities to pass bills that are not necessarily preferred by the whole chamber. Committees institutionalize logrolls among parochial interests. The implication is that the process creating committee jurisdictions is driven by narrow, constituency-based interests. If we care about national interests, distributive politics theory should make us dubious about the benefits of having flexible committee boundaries.

Using the information theory approach, which is most closely associated with Keith Krehbiel, one can come up with the opposite conclusion. When a full legislature votes, there is tremendous uncertainty about what their actions (policies) will actually do (outcomes). Committees, utilizing experts, decrease the uncertainty linking policies and outcomes.[23] This view of legislative organization holds out the ideal that committees can provide the best available information to the whole chamber. If turf wars encourage specialists to enter the fray, then jurisdictional change can benefit the whole legislature.

How should we make sense of the three theoretical traditions in light of turf wars? Would the everyday players of the jurisdiction game even recognize themselves as seen through the political science lens? Thankfully, the answer is yes, and the most consistent explanations they give fit within an information theory perspective, as we will see. Of more interest to nonpolitical scientists, however, are three overriding questions: Where do jurisdictions come from? How do they change, and can legislatures adapt when new problems arise?

The Book, Summarized

In the following chapters, I tell the story of how committee turf in the U.S. House of Representatives embraces new (and sometimes old) jurisdictionally ambiguous issues. I sketch the basic argument here, accepting the risk of having the rest of this book ignored.

The theory outlined in Chapter 1 has two steps, one in which rational legislators pursue their individual interests, and a second in which an agent—working for the whole House—responds. First, policy entrepreneurs on committees introduce bills that do not clearly fit within a committee's established borders. The bill has to be referred to a committee within twenty-four hours, and this is done by House employees (called parliamentarians) operating in the name of the Speaker. Entrepreneurial politicians are driven to introduce legislation by any number of motivations, ranging from very narrow parochial interests to the national good. The second step of the theory kicks in when the parliamentarians decide which committee should receive a jurisdictionally ambiguous bill. They use a decision rule called the "weight of the bill," which rewards committees that have established expertise on closely related issues. This second step closely mirrors predictions derived from information theories. I explore a turf war in the House over precedent-setting referrals covering magnetically levitated trains. That case highlights the importance of expertise over distributive politics.

The committee system is a collective good, meaning every legislator benefits from deference to committees and the ways that policies are meted out. Like all collective goods, rational-acting individuals have incentives to undermine the institution. One way they do this is by taking politically useful turf away from other committees, claiming it for their own. Failing that, policy entrepreneurs try staking claims to entirely new issues. The result is jurisdictional fragmentation. The mere existence of fragmentation should lead us to suspect that committee borders are malleable, and this flexibility becomes clearer after distinguishing between two types of committee jurisdictions: statutory and common law.

This is an important distinction, and much of this book flows from it. Statutory jurisdictions are what are written down in formal legislative rules. These rules are voted on by the full House or Senate, and they rarely change except at the margins. For the most part, when political scientists have talked about the stability of committee borders, they have implicitly had statutory jurisdictions in mind. Common law jurisdictions, on the other hand, are granted whenever jurisdictionally ambiguous bills are referred to committees. These referral decisions set precedents that are every bit as binding as those written down in the formal rules. Referral decisions breathe life into committee jurisdictions; and referral decisions are why policy entrepreneurs wage turf wars. A history of the House Commerce Committee grounds the distinction between common law and statutory jurisdictions, and the data for this section are drawn from reviewing summaries of all Commerce Committee hearings published from 1947 through the close of 1994. This amounts to 2,847 bound volumes covering 6,259 days and 863,581 pages of hearings.

Occasionally, Congress passes reform packages promising to "rationalize" and "reinvigorate" committee jurisdictions. Much ink has been spilled trying to explain what happens during these elusive and seemingly important moments of reform. At least with respect to committee turf, however, there is less to these touted "reforms" than legislators would have us believe. The general pattern is that common law jurisdictions, which build up between reforms, become codified into the formal rules. Jurisdictional changes (and perhaps many other forms of institutional change) are incremental. Our emphasis, then, should be primarily on common law (not statutory) jurisdictions, and that gets us focusing on how bills are referred to committees.

Bill referrals are absolutely critical because they establish the precedents that become common law jurisdictions. What happens when jurisdictionally ambiguous bills are introduced in the House of Representatives? Parliamentarians, unelected but long-serving employees of the House, play a crucial role. Formally, according to the rules of most legislatures, the speaker or majority party leader sends bills to committees. In practice, especially on routine issues, the parliamentarians are in charge of bill referrals.

The House parliamentarians are virtually unknown outside of Washington, D.C., but most state legislatures have similar clerks helping arbitrate turf wars. It was not always so. In the House of Representatives, for example, bill referrals were contested by floor majorities throughout most of the 1800s. That proved unworkable, as political factions of the day—not any institutionally focused or collectively stable decision process—handed out turf. In the late 1800s and early 1900s, the Speaker of the House referred jurisdictionally ambiguous bills. As a partisan leader, the Speaker sometimes rewarded friends and punished enemies by parceling turf. Once again the collective benefits that committees are supposed to provide were undermined. Following the revolt against Speaker Joseph Cannon (R-OH) in 1910, the Clerk at the Speaker's Table (later renamed the "parliamentarian") gained considerable power. The goal was to take partisan politics out of what had long been intensely political turf wars. Today, the parliamentarians walk a fine line between being neutral judges and being seen as politically charged employees of the majority party.

The parliamentarians are not necessarily at the top of a hierarchical pyramid. They too have to be sensitive to the political environment around them, as the Senate parliamentarian found out when he was summarily fired by the new Republican majority following the 1980 elections. I argue, however, that in the House the Speaker and majority party, per se, do not control these institutional guardians. It is important to note that when Newt Gingrich took over as Speaker, he fired every partisan (and several nonpartisan) House employee. The parliamentarian, Charles Johnson, survived unharmed, enhancing the office's nonpartisan image. If the parliamentarians seem sensitive to political forces, though, they seem to be most closely associated with the median position of the whole House.

Like judges, the parliamentarians (with sometimes significant input from the Speaker or party leaders) can only award common law jurisdictions when they are confronted with specific bills to refer. Their role is reactive. It is up to political entrepreneurs to present bills for referral, and it is in the details of crafting legislation that the jurisdiction game is at its finest. Whenever possible, entrepreneurs try to claim turf by amending a law that is already in their committee's jurisdiction, because amendments to laws are almost invariably sent back to the original committees. If no suitable host law is found, entrepreneurs build an elaborate foundation of arguments to persuade the parliamentarians that a bill should be sent to their committees.

The most common strategy is arguing that a jurisdictionally ambiguous issue is not ambiguous at all. Rather, one claims, the "new" issue is clearly implied by a history of referral precedents to a committee. When several committees compete for the same issue, the outcome hinges on how firmly the sides establish a link to long-resolved committee boundaries. This is important because the parliamentarians decide referrals using "the weight of the bill." The weight of the bill is analogous to a judge's "weight of the evidence" criterion, though here the weight depends on which committee seems to have the closest jurisdiction to an ambiguous piece of turf. From the parliamentarian's perspective, the process of reviewing memoranda about referral precedents seems impartial and lawyerly. From the politician's perspective, creating those memos and anticipating what the opposition might do makes for all-out war.

If committees compete for referrals and lose, they have lost forever. So while there are potential gains from staking claims, the consequences of losing are extreme. Referral precedents settle an issue once and for all. As a result, most policy entrepreneurs are risk averse, nipping away at the edges of jurisdictionally ambiguous issues instead of trying to swallow up whole issue areas in a single foray. Turf expands incrementally, and this is a guaranteed prescription for fragmentation. How many committees in Congress now work on environmental issues? Dozens, each from their own perspective, and each with its own glacial strategy for encroaching on the few jurisdictionally ambiguous issues that remain.

Is the fragmentation of committee turf a sorry thing? Yes, if one aspires to an efficient and uncluttered legislative process. Yes, if one worries about the duplication of staffs, hearings, and reports. Yes, if one fears the multiplication of special interest groups, each associated most closely with one or another committee.

Do we want less jurisdictional fragmentation? Not if it is an inevitable byproduct of turf wars, which are how legislatures embrace new social and economic problems. Not if, without turf wars, our legislatures will fall ever more out of touch with constituents. Not if fragmentation allows otherwise excluded interest groups access to the political process. With fragmentation, we have to take the bad with the good. On balance, it is better to have legislative structures that live and breathe.

In Chapter 1, I try to persuade the reader that turf wars are worth paying attention to, and I sketch a theory of jurisdictional change. Chapter 2 draws out the distinction between common law and statutory jurisdictions, and we see how the House Commerce Committee expanded its borders since World War II. What happens when jurisdictions are reformed is the subject of Chapter 3, and I argue that jurisdictions change primarily a little bit at a time—not in big chunks during reform periods. The House parliamentarian's role as a neutral judge of turf wars is detailed in Chapter 4. The basic strategies that legislators use to expand turf are outlined in Chapter 5. Chapter 6 shows the two-step theory of jurisdictional change in action through the case of magnetically levitated trains. The final chapter draws lessons about the causes and consequences of jurisdictional fragmentation.

ONE

Turf Wars
on
Capitol Hill

Battle upon battle, Washington's turf wars are usually hidden from public view. On November 24, 1993, a jurisdictional dispute between leaders of two powerful Senate committees spilled onto the front pages of newspapers around the country. One headline read "Senate Chairmen in Tug of War over Health Plan; Two Panels Battle for Jurisdiction—and Power."[1] It is "atomic war," said one aide, while another warned of a "giant spitting contest" between the Finance Committee's chairman, Senator Daniel Patrick Moynihan (D-NY) and Senator Edward M. Kennedy (D-MA), chairman of the Senate Labor Committee.

Spitting contests? Atomic war? The public is more accustomed to the overly formal collegiality we see on C-SPAN. Turf wars make for high stakes politics because committee jurisdictions are malleable at their borders, and change is ongoing.

Committee jurisdictions are akin to property rights, and few things in Washington are more closely guarded or as fervently pursued. Former Speaker Thomas Foley says that no single policy dispute during his tenure ignited the kinds of passions among members that turf wars could inflame. That became perfectly clear during the transition from Democratic to Republican rule in early 1995, when newly anointed committee chairs fought pitched battles to keep their committee boundaries intact.[2] Why fight over committee jurisdictions? These battles are about power and influence in their rawest forms. They are about property rights over public policies. From the Latin words *juris* and *dictio*, jurisdiction literally means the right or authority to make pronouncements that are binding and are backed up by law. "No characteristic of the committee system," writes the Congressional Research Service, "is more critical than its jurisdictional structure—

the way in which it divides and distributes control over policy subjects."[3]

Beginning in early 1995, and under the leadership of Speaker Newt Gingrich (R-GA), House Republicans have remade the organizational landscape of Congress. Committee chairs, now subject to term limits, smaller budgets, and a bevy of Speaker-controlled task forces, have been weakened considerably. Under the new regime, a growing number of important measures have bypassed the committees entirely, though most observers expect committees to continue as the main gateway for public policy.[4] In this new environment, turf is perhaps more important than ever as committee chairs fight to hold onto their power bases.

"Politics," says congressional scholar Richard Fenno, "involves the interaction of private ambition, public institutions, and agenda-setting events."[5] So too with turf wars. One can scarcely talk of politics without at least implicit assumptions about turf. In courts, jurisdiction is "the power to hear and determine a case," and "without jurisdiction, a court's judgment is void."[6] Within legislatures, jurisdictions distinguish one committee from another. They are, in almost every sense, a lawmaker's legislative power base. It is no wonder that committee boundaries are hotly contested.

Chief executive officers of banks and insurance companies have learned a lot about committee jurisdictions lately. In the early 1980s, the House Energy and Commerce Committee (simply renamed "Commerce" in 1995) began expanding its turf to include the regulation of insurance companies, an issue previously left largely to the states. Had insurance regulation been claimed by the House Banking Committee instead, banks would likely be peddling insurance today.[7] Rather, bankers wrestled in the early 1990s with former Commerce Committee chair John Dingell (D-MI), who refused to let them sell insurance. Meanwhile, insurance executives withered under Dingell's glare, wondering what he might have had in store for them. The stakes in health care insurance are higher still, since health care is one of the country's largest—and fastest growing—sectors of the economy.

Should we be heartened or discouraged by the prevalence of turf wars? "Both the committee system and executive agencies," writes political scientist William Morrow, "would be blatantly unresponsive to the demands of changing times if they did not engage in jurisdiction changes based on experimentation to meet the challenges of evolving social problems."[8] That, in a word, is why turf wars should be fought. Since the battles affect us all, we should be enthusiastic spectators.

When turf wars are settled, in most cases with the help of the House and Senate parliamentarians, the treaties determine where future bills will be referred. And that, writes Spencer Rich of the *Washington Post*, is probably the most important outcome of a turf war because, in the long run, jurisdictions mean "attention, power, the ability to influence events, satisfy constituencies, attract support and carry out ideological dreams."[9]

Turf wars are not new. Choose a decade and glance through the *Congressional Record;* every volume is riddled with disputes over bill referrals.[10] And as we will see, toning down crippling warfare over turf was an important institutional development in Congress in the early 1900s. Still, today, throughout the Capitol's corridors, the jurisdiction game is being played by legislators, lobbyists, and congressional staff. One top aide to former House Speaker Foley calls it "the hottest game in town." At root, turf wars involve staking claims to jurisdictionally ambiguous issues. The image to have in mind is not one of well-established kingdoms fighting over the boundaries that separate them. Rather, congressional turf wars are more like land rushes. Think of wagons racing into the Oklahoma territory in 1889. Turf wars are a political scramble among policy entrepreneurs staking claims for their committees.

Anyone who pays taxes, drives a car, visits the national parks, or worries about day care has been touched by the outcomes of fights to control congressional turf. Recent disputes include the regulation of regional phone companies, the fate of the Export-Import Bank, the speed and direction of the General Agreement on Tariffs and Trade, catastrophic health insurance, regulations on the hauling of wastes in empty food containers, drunk-driving legislation, the building of coal-slurry pipelines, the regulation of potentially contaminated seafood, the scope of the Americans with Disabilities Act, and the installation of tighter airport security measures.[11] As if turf wars among *policy* committees are not enough, the House and Senate appropriations committees sometimes authorize on spending bills, making jurisdictions even more muddled.

I do not address turf disputes with the appropriations committees, and I bypass them for a specific reason. House Rule 21(2) prohibits authorizing on an appropriations bill, but the Rules Committee can waive points of order against the violation. (Such a waiver caused a storm of controversy in the 102d Congress, 1st session, over grazing fees on public lands.) Since the House and Senate appropriations committees are prohibited from writing policy, all turf advances that they make are temporary. No binding precedents are set. As a result, committee chairs occasionally bargain with the appropriations committees to "lend" them turf on an issue when authorizing committees fail to report legislation. When that happens, it is not a turf war. It is a clever—and temporary—way to advance legislation supported by the committee of jurisdiction.[12]

I hope this book finds two audiences: political scientists interested in legislative structure, and general readers with an appetite for the subtleties and strategies of Capitol Hill. This is not a "how to" manual for political entrepreneurs. Instead, this book raises and answers questions about how legislatures embrace (or fail to embrace) new issues, and it addresses the consequences of jurisdictional fragmentation in the U.S. Congress.

What are the fundamental characteristics of jurisdictions? How and when do jurisdictions shape policy outputs? What are the basic strategies policy entrepreneurs use to take turf away from a committee or to stake a claim to something nobody else is doing? If committee jurisdictions can expand into new areas, does this mean legislatures absorb new policy problems facing society? Or is the jurisdictional system so rigid that Congress falls out of touch with our real problems? Who are the parliamentarians, and how have they become institutional guardians in the House of Representatives? More important, is jurisdictional fragmentation inevitable, and what might fragmentation mean for the governability of this diverse country? These seven questions drive this book.

Why Worry about Committee Jurisdictions?

It is an article of faith among Congress watchers that committees are important. Woodrow Wilson's dictum that Congress in committees is Congress at work has been repeated countless times, and for good reason. It is true. In the last quarter-century, there has been a flowering of research on committees,[13] and we now know, among other things, a great deal about how legislators seek committee assignments.[14] Yet we know surprisingly little about how jurisdictional boundaries, governing the flow and fate of legislation, come to be drawn in the first place.

Until recently, most political scientists have considered jurisdictions to be static institutional facts. Melissa Collie and Joseph Cooper caricatured the conventional wisdom, saying, "Stories of jurisdictional infighting are legion, and turf protection so pronounced as to have frustrated all but the most minor changes in committee jurisdictions since 1945."[15] Like castle walls, jurisdictions protect the fiefdoms of committee barons. And like castle walls, they do not move easily. Rational choice scholars also typically assume that jurisdictions are fixed, partly because their models are easier to develop if they do not have to worry about turf wars.

The established view is only half true. I will show that committee boundaries evolve through an interplay between policy entrepreneurs on committees and judgments by the House and Senate parliamentarians. While committee jurisdictions look stable in the short run, they are variable in the long run. And variations in committee jurisdictions can have a tremendous impact on legislative outcomes at any particular moment. Turf is important in all legislatures (such as the U.S. Congress, state assemblies, and most city councils) that routinely defer to committee positions.

Imagine a generic legislature with three committees, one each for transportation, health, and agriculture. As is typical in U.S. assemblies, the full legislature usually adopts committee decisions, so the real battleground for changing policy is in the committees. On average, Health Committee members have more expertise on health issues, and they may well represent a few large hospitals in their districts. Agriculture Committee members know the most about farm issues, and they are probably elected from farming-intensive districts. Members self-select onto one of the three committees both because they have some expertise in an area (or want to develop expertise) and because they want to impress their constituents.

When voting on bills in the full legislature, members on the reporting committee look for cues about how to vote. Members on the Agriculture Committee vote "yes" for the health bills, and Health Committee members do the same on agriculture bills. To cynics, committee deference looks like members trading votes—or logrolling—for explicit future favors. On logrolling, the cynics (and economists)[16] are almost always wrong. Explicit vote trades are exceedingly rare in U.S. legislatures. Rather, logrolling is institutionalized through committees and within political parties.[17]

Committee deference is the price we pay for encouraging legislators to specialize in difficult policy areas. The alternative—writing laws in the full legislature is unworkable in complex societies. It has been tried thousands of times in hundreds of legislatures, and it is a prescription for deadlock. Committees, defined and constrained by their jurisdictions, are our best hope. What happens in our three-committee legislature when we introduce jurisdictional ambiguities? Claims are staked; turf wars are launched. Should a bill on "tractor safety" be handled in the Agriculture or the Transportation Committee? Where should "ambulance services" go? And is the problem of "pesticide residues" more appropriately housed in Agriculture or Health? When a bill is sent to a committee, it reflects a "referral decision" or an established set of "rules for referral." As we will see, the most important jurisdictional decisions are made the first time an ambiguity is resolved, because those referral decisions set binding precedents (see fig. 1.1).

To the uninitiated, these might seem like trivial quibbles, but they are not. Take pesticide residues. In 1972, the U.S. House of Representatives faced a similar choice, deciding whether a bill regulating pesticides should go to the Interstate and Foreign Commerce Committee or the Agriculture Committee. By drafting the bill in a clever way, Agriculture won, and environmentalists have been complaining about fertilizer and pesticide companies ever since. The results of that turf war—for better or worse—are as close as your next meal.[18]

One staff director of a House committee describes turf this way: "Jurisdiction boils down to whether you'll have a seat at the table when important decisions are being made. If you're not at the table, you're a nobody."[19] This image of jurisdiction as "a seat at the table when important decisions are being made" is a powerful one. What, for example, would have happened if the landmark 1964 Civil Rights Act never passed? A turf war decided who sat at the table crafting that legislation. The bill was strategically written to confer jurisdiction in the Senate to the Commerce Committee and to the Judiciary Committee in the House. Why? Because without jurisdictional maneuvering, the Civil Rights Act would surely have died in the hands of Southerners on hostile committees.[20] A monumental opportunity would have been lost.

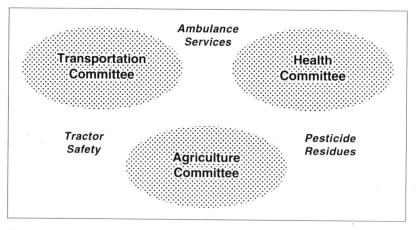

Figure 1.1 Jurisdictional Ambiguity for a Three-Committee Legislature

Most instances of staking jurisdictional claims are not as visible as the 1964 Civil Rights Act, and counterfactual consequences are not so easily traced. Still, turf wars are everywhere. T. R. Reid's widely read *Congressional Odyssey* tells of Senator Pete Domenici's (R-NM) successful expansion of the Committee on Public Works' jurisdiction to include waterway user fees, an issue long locked away in the Committee on Commerce, Science, and Transportation.[21] Stephen Breyer, now an associate justice on the U.S. Supreme Court, had his first successes in Washington staking a claim to airline deregulation for the Senate Administrative Practices and Procedure Subcommittee.[22] John Barry's account of the rise and fall of Speaker Jim Wright was enlivened by jurisdictional battles between John Dingell (D-MI) and Dan Rostenkowski (D-IL).[23] Or, on a local level, the ways jurisdictional ambiguities are settled can shape a town. Should the right to pass judgment on new building projects in a city go to an economic development committee, an environmental management committee, or both? The answer depends, in part, on how similar proposals have been handled in the past. For legislatures big and small, turf wars—the staking of claims to jurisdictionally ambiguous issues—shape our public policies.

The Pervasiveness of Jurisdictional Ambiguities

Ambiguities arise when bills are introduced that do not fit neatly in existing committee boundaries. In the U.S. Congress, all bills—even jurisdictionally ambiguous ones establishing referral precedents—have to be sent to a committee within one day. "Newly recognized legislative issues," writes Charles Tiefer, "offer the greyest of the grey areas, since their newness means they have not been settled conclusively by prior rules or precedents."[24]

Recall our generic legislature. Should ambulance safety be handled in the Transportation or the Health Committee? Ask a lawmaker, and the answer is likely to depend on whether he or she sits on either committee. The process of sorting out these ambiguities often falls to clerks and parliamentarians, whose role is discussed later in this chapter. Jurisdictional ambiguities, and the turf wars they spawn, are pervasive because new issues routinely arise and because long-standing "conditions" become redefined as "problems."[25] When new issues arrive on the political agenda, grey areas between committee boundaries open. Which House committee should handle consumer protection legislation: Agriculture? Banking? Commerce? Judiciary? All four? Where should insurance legislation be referred: Banking? Commerce? Ways and Means? Should child abuse legislation be shaped by the Judiciary

Committee or by the Committee on Economic and Educational Opportunities?

Think about the filing system you have for keeping track of old bills. Dentists' bills go under health. Grocery receipts and restaurant trips go under food. Movies are under entertainment. Mortgage payments are housing expenses, and a new plumbing fixture is a hardware expense. If only the world were so simple. Unexpectedly, and without a folder for such things, you may have to decide where to file the cost of a dinner with friends. Food? Entertainment? It is a jurisdictional ambiguity. They are common in filing systems, and the assigning of bills to committees is essentially a filing system. It is impossible, as students of parliamentary procedure have long noted, to have jurisdictions without ambiguities.

Jurisdictions are ranges of authority; they summarize an important element of political power, but if these centers of power focus on the same old sets of issues in only slightly different ways, then few observers would care. How adaptive is the committee system to "new" issues? Under what conditions do legislatures tackle policy problems that do not fit nicely into preexisting boundaries? There are times when committee systems can and do embrace new problems, such as consumer protection and environmental legislation in the 1970s. Even in the 1990s, a dozen House committees are still jockeying for pieces of environmental turf.[26] The rules of the jurisdiction game help us understand when and why legislatures address some issues and ignore others.

Winning turf wars gives committees the power to act, but some observers say that a committee is power*ful* only to the extent that a final bill differs from what the full chamber would have passed in the absence of the committee. "Committee power," argues Steven Smith, "is observable and important only when the policy preferences of a committee and the chamber differ."[27] Smith's definition is in the distributive politics tradition. One measure of committee power may be this ability to generate policies that the chamber would not have otherwise preferred, but this is not the same as saying that the chamber would have otherwise *passed* a bill preferred by the floor. From conversations with legislators, staffers, and lobbyists, I sense that most political practitioners view committee power in a more "informational" way. Namely, much of a committee's power comes from the likelihood that the legislature would not have been able to pass *any bill,* even a bill reflecting the interests of the floor's median voter, without using the committee as a labor saving device.[28]

No serious students of Congress would argue that the House Commerce Committee is not powerful, even though that panel's membership is heterogeneous and its bills are often close to the preferences of the House. (The same was true of the Ways and Means Committee under Wilbur Mills.)[29] If anything, House Commerce is more powerful today than a generation ago, not because it passes bills wildly at odds with the position of the House's median voter (in fact it does not), but because it handles so many bills on so many issues. The size of the committee's turf, and the committee's willingness to fight turf wars, makes House Commerce the epitome of Washington power.

A history of the House Commerce Committee is reviewed in the next chapter, and it gives insights into the way the jurisdiction game is played. Before turning to the ins and outs of turf wars, however, I sketch the outlines of a theory of jurisdictional change. This is not the kind of theory that my rational choice–modeling friends will recognize, because I solve nothing in closed form. Rather, the theory is a sustained argument spawning a set of testable hypotheses, and I touch on the basic framework of the argument throughout the book.

A Theory of Jurisdictional Change

My view of turf wars turns on a distinction between "statutory" jurisdictions on one hand and "common law" jurisdictions on the other. (Drawing out this distinction is the purpose of Chapter 2.) Statutory jurisdictions refer to the list of issues that are written down in the *House Rules Manual* delineating committee boundaries. They do not change, except during occasional bursts of reform (like in 1995). Statutory jurisdictions are easy to find, footnote, and quantify, and they have garnered most of the attention from scholars.

Common law jurisdictions, in contrast, are more elusive, harder to identify, and have been largely overlooked by congressional scholars. Common law committee boundaries are established by the House parliamentarian when a bill on a new or jurisdictionally ambiguous issue is referred to a committee, setting a referral precedent. Such referral decisions are binding for future bills. I want to suggest that common law jurisdictions are where most of the organizational action is. For example, I demonstrate in Chapter 2 that more than two-thirds of the House Commerce Committee's activity in the early 1990s was on issues that have emerged through "common law" means since 1946. When political scientists ignore common law jurisdictions, then, they overlook a large slice of a committee's agenda. Moreover, most of the changes in statutory jurisdictions cannot be explained without first developing a theory of common law change. Jurisdictions are also set, though only rarely, through "memoranda of understanding" and by brokered agreements between committee chairs.[30] These situations and strategies are discussed in Chapter 5. Common law jurisdictions are, by far, the route most chosen by policy entrepreneurs.

Jurisdictional change is *incremental*, and it grows out of interactions among a small set of *individuals*. In this light, institutional change is not a collective act ratified by a majority of the House of Representatives. It bubbles up from the actions of purposive individuals interacting with institutional "facts" like committee boundaries. Institutional change is ongoing.

Committee systems let legislators divide their labors into specialized, decentralized work groups. The logic behind specialization may be distributive (members may want committees to provide concentrated benefits to their districts while spreading the costs widely), and members' motives may be nondistributive (such as wanting to promote good public policies that benefit the whole nation). The relative importance of distributive and nondistributive motivations is debated by political scientists, but it need not concern us here. More important is that we see the committee system itself as a collective good.[31] Whatever the reasons (distributive or otherwise) for the development of committee systems, as collective goods the benefits derived from committees are available to all legislators (legislators are nonexcludable), and participation in the committee system does not diminish its value (consumption is nonrival).

As collective goods, there are several important characteristics of committee systems. First, though they are decried as places where legislation is too often killed, without the division of labor that committees afford, legislatures would get even less done than they already do. One of the most important purposes of committees is that they make it possible for legislatures to avoid paralysis on the floor as workloads increase. Second, when committees write "Christmas tree bills" in a distributive frenzy, the coalitions supporting those bills tend to be universalistic; all the legislators benefit.[32] Likewise third, when legislatures confront complex issues requiring specialized knowledge, every member benefits from a committee system that diminishes the amount of uncertainty about policy outcomes when they vote.[33] So for both distributive and nondistributive legislation, committee systems are collective goods, and as such they may fall victim to the plight of many collective goods. That is, if they are produced at all, collective goods are inherently unstable.[34]

The instability of a committee system has its roots in the entrepreneurial motivations of legislators.[35] When the turfs of the committees on which members serve do not match their interests, and if the members have institutional assets to prosecute a turf war, legislators try to grab territory that will benefit them. If members could change what their committees do at will, the building blocks of the committee system—self-selection based on jurisdictions, and division of labor into specialized work groups—would be chipped away. As Davidson and Oleszek argue, "[S]elf-interest often prevails over institutional welfare."[36] One long-time Rules Committee aide said there is constant pressure from members seeking short-term political gains to tear down rules that protect the long-run interests of the institution.

> You don't have members who are interested in creating an institution that will exist after them. They're more interested in having an impact, on passing bills. They're only here for a few years, and the institution out-lasts them.

When William Brown retired as parliamentarian in 1994, he left the House with a similar observation. "The House changes from year to year," wrote Brown, "with new Members and staff and circumstances always reshaping this institution; what does not change is the reservoir of intellect and inventiveness which characterizes those who work in the legislative branch."[37] It is that intellect and inventiveness that constantly seeks to change the institution in ways that will promote member goals—sometimes at the expense of the institution. It is the parliamentarian's job to provide continuity and faithfulness to fundamental rules.

Imagine yourself able to design a legislature from scratch. You would likely want a committee system with boundaries flexible enough to embrace social problems as they emerge. And you might also want to keep the committee borders just firm enough to discourage individual legislators (with little interest in "creating an institution that will exist after them") from rearranging turf for their own good at everyone else's expense. Any legislative designer faces this tricky tradeoff. There has developed within the U.S. House of Representatives a *process* of arbitrating jurisdictional claims that protects the committee system as a collective good. Further, the ways turf wars are often resolved enhance the informational efficiency of the legislature.

In developing the House bill referral process, jurisdictional arbitration was intentionally taken out of the hands of floor majorities and out of the hands of party leaders. This contention—that the floor majority and party leaders allow a third party to arbitrate jurisdictional disputes—will be met with skepticism by some readers. The parliamentarian, while not directly controlled by the floor, is ever mindful of the mood of the legislature, and it is unlikely that the parliamentarian will deviate (for long) from the will of the floor's median voter. In Chapter 4, I offer reasons why one might expect the development of a jurisdictional arbiter, and I outline the decision rules used to enhance the committee system's informational efficiency.

It takes two steps—one at the individual level and one at the institutional level—to change committee turf. It is not enough to develop a theory just about policy entrepreneurs or a theory just about institutions. They influence each other. "The legislative environment," writes Wayne Francis, "may be seen as a continuous interplay between institutional structure or procedure and individual adjustment and adaptation."[38] Gerald Gamm and Kenneth Shepsle describe this well, noting:

> Rational man in an institutional and historical setting is not an entirely free agent, but rather is encumbered and constrained by his context. By the same token, institutional context and historical setting by themselves are insufficient as independent, exogenous causes of things; rather they must be seized upon and exploited by institutional agents.[39]

The interplay in turf wars finds committee-based policy entrepreneurs proposing turf changes in the form of jurisdictionally ambiguous bills that have to be referred to a committee. Then an institutional guardian—the House parliamentarian in our discussion—decides which committee or committees will receive new turf. The two steps are summarized in table 1.1.

Step One: Policy Entrepreneurs Try to Expand Their Turf

Policy entrepreneurs stake claims on "jurisdictionally proximate" pieces of new policy turf. The larger a committee's current jurisdictional endowment, the more likely it is that new turf is nearby. The now-defunct District of Columbia Committee's territory was constrained by the 69-square-mile area surrounding the Capitol Building, so the panel's jurisdictional forays were necessarily limited.[40] The Committee on Veterans' Affairs has a jurisdictional endowment limiting how much "hunting and fishing" (to use one staffer's phrase) the committee can do. Likewise, the House Oversight and the House Standards of Official Conduct committees do not provide good bases from which to launch into new issues.[41] With jurisdictions, usually, the rich get richer while the poor get the same old bills. House committees with large and potentially expansive jurisdictions include, among others, Agriculture, Banking and Financial Services, Commerce, Judiciary, Science, Small Business, and Ways and Means.[42]

Merely having a good base from which to build an empire, however,

Table 1.1 The Two Steps of Jurisdictional Change

Step one: policy enterpreneurs try to expand their turf:
  Lawmakers self-select onto committees based on jurisdictions.
  Jurisdictions rarely match legislators' policy and constituency preferences
    perfectly, so they either (a) move to a committee with a better jurisdictional
    match or (b) stay on the committee and try to change its borders.
  Committee and subcommittee leaders are advantaged in turf wars because they
    have resources (primarily staff and procedural prerogatives such as the ability
    to call hearings) that others do not have.
  When policy entrepreneurs get wind of a jurisdictionally ambiguous issue, they
    ask two questions: (a) Can we get into the jurisdiction game on this one.
    (b) Do we want to get into the game? The first question is answered by
    assessing the jurisdictional proximity of the new issue to the committee's
    current turf. The second question depends on the policy goals of the
    entrepreneur and other committee members.
  Entrepreneurs employ bill introduction strategies that lead to incremental
    changes in jurisdiction. If several committees are targeting a jurisdictionally
    ambiguous issue, they each use strategies that link the new issue to their
    current turf, leading to fragmented jurisdictions covering new issues.

Step two: parliamentarians refer jurisdictionally ambiguous bills:
  Left unchecked, policy entrepreneurs wreak havoc on the legislature by
    continually undermining and poaching on other committee's jurisdictions.
    Rules and procedures are how legislatures solve such collective goods
    problems.
  The bill referral process is crucial because when a jurisdictionally ambiguous bill
    is sent to a committee, that establishes a referral precedent, thereby changing
    the committee's common law jurisdiction. Since the early 1800s, the referral
    process has gone through three important stages. By the early 1920s, the U.S.
    House developed a mechanism to award jurisdictions based on informational
    efficiency.
  On jurisdictional questions, the parliamentarian is a neutral arbiter who is not
    directly controlled by the Speaker or the majority party. The parliamentarian
    seems more influenced by the desires of the floor's median voter than by any
    particular faction.
  Parliamentarians award jurisdiction to committees based on jurisdictional
    proximity and committee expertise. They call this the "weight of the bill"
    decision rule, which is analogous to the "weight of the evidence" rule used by
    formal judges.

is not enough. There needs to be a sense on the committee that the jurisdiction needs to change, and the committee needs to be willing to
invest in staff and member expertise. The sense on a committee that
the borders need to change is driven by how good a match there is between the committee's current turf and the interests of its members.
Committees with heterogeneous memberships and homogeneous turf
have the greatest pressures to launch turf wars. Some committee juris-

dictions, like Agriculture, for example, are homogeneous and attract a homogeneous set of members. Other committees, however, attract heterogeneous sets of members, and when these members find the jurisdiction too constraining, they contemplate turf wars.

Committees with large discretionary agendas are advantaged in turf wars, because they are less likely to have regular recurring authorizing bills that sap their energies.[43] The desire for a discretionary agenda was palpable in interviews with members and staffers. One ranking minority member reflected on the inability of then Agriculture Chairman "Kika" de la Garza (D-TX) and Foreign Affairs' Lee Hamilton (D-IN) to prosecute turf wars:

> Agriculture has one or two main bills which are in effect for several years. In the mean time, it lies fallow, having exhausted itself in its main function. Foreign Affairs is even worse. It has two bills, the State Department bill, which it barely passes, and the general foreign aid bill, which almost kills the committee. Either it can't pass it or it dies in the Senate. Failure undermines a committee's reputation in the House . . . Other committees, like Energy and Commerce have, potentially, a lot of time on their hands, and those committees attract members who are interested in policies of national importance. Those members tend to have an interest in playing power politics. And they have a jurisdiction that is big enough, or broad enough, to allow them to push out to other issues.

Policy entrepreneurs are aggrandizers, but they do not try to make jurisdictional claims on any and every issue. When they get wind of a jurisdictional ambiguity they ask two questions: (1) *Can* we get into the jurisdiction game on this one? and (2) Do we *want* to get into the game? The first question is easily dispensed with by deciding whether the committee can make a plausible claim to the parliamentarian that the target issue is close to something that the committee is already handling. For some new issues, like satellite communications was in the late 1950s, there may be only one or two committees that can make such a plausible claim to the parliamentarian. In that case the two House panels were Interstate and Foreign Commerce (with jurisdiction over communications) and Science and Astronautics (with jurisdiction over space). Other subjects, like energy issues in the 1970s, may be wide open to a half-dozen committees.[44]

The first hypothesis, then, concerns jurisdictional endowments and the proximity to an issue. *The probability of policy entrepreneurs arising on committee* j *with respect to jurisdictionally ambiguous issue* k *is related to the jurisdictional proximity between* k *and the issues already considered by* j. That is, lawmakers are more likely to become policy entrepreneurs if the "new" issue is close to something they are already doing. This seems obvious, but it does help clarify why some committees are bevies of entrepreneurs while other panels rarely have anyone contemplating a turf war. The larger a committee's turf, the more issues there are nearby, and the more opportunities potential policy entrepreneurs will have.

Once lawmakers decide that a committee *can* get into the jurisdiction game because of some plausible link to existing activities, they explore whether the new issue is worth pursuing. A second hypotheses is drawn from the heterogeneity of a committee's membership. *The more heterogeneous the set of interests represented by committee members is, the more likely policy entrepreneurs will arise on the committee.* These first and second hypotheses work in conjunction, so that you'd expect the most entrepreneurial activities on heterogeneous committees with turf that is already close to an ambiguous issue. Further, there are opportunity costs associated with launching turf wars because staff attention must be taken off of things that the committee is already doing.

We fill out "step one" of the theory with three more speculations. A policy entrepreneur's tenacity in pursuing a jurisdictionally ambiguous issue is related to (1) *constituency interests in the issue,* (2) *membership expertise and experience within the panel,* and (3) *staff expertise and the opportunity costs of staff commitment to the issue.* These hypotheses were *induced* after carefully observing turf wars and talking with players in the jurisdiction game. Working on other issues in legislative organization, strikingly similar predictions were *deduced* by Tom Gilligan and Keith Krehbiel. More on that later. The underlying assumptions that helped organize my observations on Capitol Hill flow from what motivates legislators, how they select committee assignments, and the powers that committee and subcommittee chairs hold. We turn, briefly, to those assumptions now.

WHAT MOTIVATES LEGISLATORS?

Legislators have a mix of goals, which occasionally conflict with each other. The primary goal is *reelection,* because they cannot pursue their other goals if they are not in office. Still, legislators are not single-minded seekers of reelection. Most have *policy objectives* that are independent of their reelection interests, and some legislators also have a drive to gain *power within the institution.*[45] Committees attract members emphasizing different mixes of these goals. "The opportunity to achieve the three goals," writes Richard Fenno, "varies widely among committees. House members, therefore, match their individual patterns of aspiration to the diverse patterns of opportunity presented by

House committees."[46] Fenno found, for example, that members of the Appropriations and the Ways and Means committees "voiced strikingly similar personal goals" that focus on power and prestige. Members on the Interior and the Post Office committees had "the primary goal of helping their constituents and thereby insuring their re-election," while members of the Education and Labor and the Foreign Affairs committees emphasized "a strong personal interest in and a concern for the content of public policy in their committee's subject matter."[47]

No committees attract members who are motivated solely by one of the three primary goals. Some committees are undoubtedly better at helping members provide distributive benefits to their districts (members of the old Merchant Marines and Fisheries committee, for example, were known to steer harbor enhancement projects to their districts), but all committees afford members some opportunities to pursue all three goals. Transportation and Infrastructure Committee members may well have genuine "good public policy" goals in mind when they push for noise abatement programs along highways in their hometowns. Government Reform and Oversight Committee members, though they cannot report bills to change the status quo, may hold oversight hearings to further their public policy goals. Ways and Means Committee members may write "tax transition rules" into bills that benefit special interests back in their districts—thereby improving their reelection odds.

Because of self-selection onto committees, members only *tend* to emphasize one set of goals over another. As Richard Hall argues, members also self-select what bills they will work on in committees, and they decide how much to participate in the shaping of those bills. These decisions, too, reflect a mix of motivations. Each committee and each bill "evokes" a different (though still roughly predictable) mix of member motivations.[48]

SELF-SELECTION ONTO COMMITTEES

It is well known that members in the U.S. House vie for seats on committees that most closely match their personal interests and the interests of their constituents. Turf is paramount in selecting committees because, as Ken Shepsle wrote in *The Giant Jigsaw Puzzle,* "it is the jurisdictional characteristics which attract the distinctive membership and environmental constraints distinguishing committees from one another."[49] For reasons related to the mix of preferences in their electoral districts, legislators "seek assignments to those committees in which their constituents have an important stake and toward which their own previous backgrounds predispose them."[50] Committee jurisdictions, however, never perfectly match district interests because (1) jurisdictions are narrower than the full mix of district interests, (2) committee size is limited so that members often cannot receive their preferred assignments, (3) assignments are handed out, in part, to create geographic dispersion within a committee,[51] and (4) intercommittee transfers are discouraged by the loss of seniority.[52] Because committee jurisdictions tend to be narrower than the range of interests that members are expected to represent, legislators have two options. They can switch to other committees, which costs valuable within-committee seniority, or they can stay on the committee and try to expand its turf into other areas.

INSTITUTIONAL ASSETS

Not all lawmakers are equal. Legislatures have little oligarchies at their cores. The House Speaker, chosen every two years by a vote of the majority party caucus, has a large influence on the scheduling of legislation and on the appointment of majority party members to committees. Committee and subcommittee chairs have great latitude in deciding which bills will receive hearings and which bills will be marked up for subcommittee and full committee votes. Chairs have greater authority to allocate staff, hold hearings, and launch investigations. Ranking minority members on committees and subcommittees also control more institutional assets than most members. Although all legislators face the problem that the jurisdictions of their committees cannot match their interests perfectly, policy entrepreneurs need the institutional assets afforded committee and subcommittee chairs if they are to play the jurisdiction game successfully. Flexibility in assigning committee staff, the ability to call hearings and markups, and other mechanisms for agenda control are all highly valued by policy entrepreneurs.

With an increase in the number of subcommittees in the House (the number doubled from 1955 to 1974, for example), more and more majority party members have been able to get a hold on the institutional assets that come with being a subcommittee or committee chair. In 1955, less than a third of the Democrats in the House chaired a committee, subcommittee, or select committee. That number topped 50 percent by the early 1970s. When the Republicans controlled the Senate in the mid-early 1980s, only two Republicans were denied the chance to chair a panel. In 1992 all but six of the 56 Democrats in the Senate could be called "chair."[53] Several recent developments in the House of Representatives have undermined the independent authority of subcommittee chairs. The number of House panels (including standing committees, subcommittees and special committees) has been slashed, from 146 in 1994 to 110 in 1996. Committee staffs and budgets have been cut as well. Proxy voting (through which chairs could manipulate committee votes) was eliminated in January 1995. Term limits of six years now apply to committee chairs, and as a final blow to the committee system, task forces are being more widely used now than at anytime since 1816.

In all likelihood, these developments will not have much impact on how turf wars are fought. None of the incentives motivating policy entrepreneurs has changed. The formal and informal processes by which turf wars are launched and resolved remain. In terms of resources, the present committee system resembles the House structure in the 1950s and 1960s, when there were recurrent turf wars. As we will see, the overall level of assets a committee can invest in a turf war is less important than the relative position of one committee against another. With fewer committee resources, policy entrepreneurs may want to become more aggressive about protecting turf and projecting power into politically beneficial areas. With task forces, too, policy entrepreneurs may venture into jurisdictionally ambiguous issues in order to help their standing committees claim expertise in future turf battles.

The recent decline in the number of subcommittees has few historical precedents (save for 1946, which is discussed in Chapter 3). This decline, however, should have no appreciable impact on the ways in which turf wars are launched or the ways in which they are adjudicated. Members will still be attracted to committees because of their turf, and jurisdictions will never perfectly match member interests. So legislators will still either have to move onto other better-matching committees (and risk losing within-committee seniority) or they'll have to stay on a committee and contemplate launching turf wars.

Committee and subcommittee chairs, of course, cannot act unilaterally. In order to expand a committee's jurisdiction, they seek the support of like-minded legislators on the committee. Because of self-selection onto committees based on jurisdictions, like-minded legislators are usually not difficult to find.

STEP TWO: PARLIAMENTARIANS REFER JURISDICTIONALLY AMBIGUOUS BILLS

The House parliamentarian figures prominently in the theory of jurisdictional evolution. Parliamentarians are nonelected House employees who serve, ostensibly, at the pleasure of the Speaker. In practice, though, parliamentarians are expected to stay for their entire working lives. They remain while Speakers come and go and when the partisan control of the House switches from one party to the other. It is not a partisan appointment—at least in the House. The evolution of the House parliamentarian's position from that of a political hack playing to the Speaker's whims into an "institutional guardian" is discussed in detail in Chapter 4. The relative neutrality of the parliamentarian in turf wars will surprise many observers, as it surprised me. "In the U.S. Congress, as in most legislatures across the world," writes Krehbiel, "the task of creating and maintaining well-designed legislatures (or any other political entity, for that matter) is not delegated to a single, neutral, collective-welfare maximizing agent."[54] With respect to jurisdictional arbitration, however, this is precisely what appears to have happened. Importantly, though, the parliamentarian does not stand outside of or above the political process. Rather, the parliamentarian is constrained by the need for approval from the whole legislature—not just the Speaker's faction or the majority party.

The House parliamentarian, along with deputy and assistant parliamentarians, handles all bill referrals, and the overwhelming majority of these are routine. On precedent-setting bill referrals (those establishing common law jurisdictions), the parliamentarian uses a decision rule called "the weight of the bill" by which jurisdictionally ambiguous bills go to the committee with "closest" jurisdiction. Of course, just how close a committee's jurisdiction is can be a political question, and policy entrepreneurs try to influence perceptions of jurisdictional proximity by using several strategies, such as holding hearings on a bill before it is even introduced. The use of such strategies, and the anticipated reactions of the parliamentarian, are why people involved in the process call it a "game."

DISTRIBUTIVE AND INFORMATIONAL PERSPECTIVES ON THE "WEIGHT OF THE BILL"

The "weight of the bill" decision rule used by the parliamentarian means that bills on jurisdictionally ambiguous issues (all else equal) go to the committee that already has the "closest" jurisdiction. Why would the parliamentarian use this particular decision rule? The parliamentarian is (at least in the letter of the House Rules Manual) an agent of the Speaker, so why not give the new issue to whichever committee the Speaker happens to favor on that day? As in the Japanese Diet, the Speaker could appoint a special panel to refer jurisdictionally ambiguous bills. In Austria, the *Obmannerkonferenz* (a panel consisting of the president, two deputies, and various committee chairmen) refers jurisdictionally ambiguous bills. The Russian Duma employs a similar panel, under the control of party leaders. So too in Nicaragua. In India, Israel, Canada, and Ireland, bill referrals can be overturned by floor majorities—giving the majority coalition an opportunity to shape borders. And in the Netherlands, bills are referred by the Presidium, a panel that includes the chamber president and vice-presidents.[55] Clearly, there are any number of decision rules other than jurisdictional proximity that the House parliamentarian could conceivably use. Why do they use the weight of the bill? Perhaps turning to a current debate among political scientists might help to answer that question.

In "The Industrial Organization of Congress," Barry Weingast and William Marshall ask "why legislatures, like firms, are not organized as markets."[56] Their answer is that free markets undermine the ability of firms (committees) to collude (logroll). Logrolls create an inherently unstable market for votes.[57] The problem then becomes how to organize a legislature to maximize the distributive benefits available to legislators *without* relying solely on logrolls. "Instead of trading votes," claim Weingast and Marshall, "legislators in the committee system institutionalize an exchange of influence over the relevant rights [to change the status quo]. Instead of bidding for votes, legislators bid for seats on committees associated with rights to policy areas valuable for their reelection."[58] As a consequence of self-selection and policy specialization, committees are composed of "preference outliers," which creates subsets of the legislature that do not represent the preferences of the whole body.

What might committee borders look like in a legislature designed to ease the provision of distributive benefits? Jurisdictions would include common trading partners because "trades among committee members are more likely to succeed than those across committees."[59]

A senior lobbyist for a major interest group in Washington explained it this way:

> Just look at the Agriculture Committee, for example. You have a tobacco subcommittee; you have a dairy subcommittee; you have a cotton subcommittee . . . A dairy congressman doesn't give a damn about tobacco, and a tobacco congressman doesn't give a damn about cows, but they scratch each other's back and get a bill out that they both can live with.[60]

That is the essence of institutionalizing logrolls; to the extent possible, keep coalitions within committees, thereby minimizing the chance that trading partners will renege. Weingast and Marshall claim that "drawing the jurisdictional boundaries between committees is an important strategic variable that affects the pattern of coalitions . . . so that the optimal pattern of jurisdictions must in part reflect the expected pattern of trades."[61]

If jurisdictions are devices to facilitate "gains from trade," we would expect jurisdictional *changes* to enhance the ability of legislators to distribute electorally significant benefits to their districts while spreading the costs nationally. Using logic similar to Weingast and Marshall, Morris Fiorina speculates that

> the periodic pressures to reorganize committee systems so as to provide the committees with jurisdictions approximately equal in importance reflects the effort to protect the veil of ignorance—universalism and reciprocity agreements are easier to maintain under such conditions than when some committees know they deal in cheaper substance and therefore stand a better than even chance of entering minimal winning coalitions.[62]

From this perspective, we would expect jurisdictional changes to be "leveling," favoring a committee system that carves out distributive turf roughly equally. As will become clear in Chapter 3, this is precisely what *does not* happen. The tendency of policy entrepreneurs to arise on only a subset of the committees, and the decision rules used by the parliamentarian explicitly advantage some committees and disadvantage others.

Is there a role, then, for distributive politics in turf wars? Certainly. Motivations to provide distributive benefits are an important reason why policy entrepreneurs try to change the jurisdictions of committees in the first place (stage one of the two-stage theory). Furthermore, there are distributive politics elements in information theories. Committee systems, argues Krehbiel, are the tools of legislatures for processing heavy workloads, and a rationally designed committee system takes advantage of members' interests and their expertise while creating committees that are as similar to the floor as possible. An informationally efficient legislature exploits variations in membership expertise to create committees that give the full legislature good "signals" about how to vote on the wide range of issues that the legislature confronts. Writes Krehbiel, "An organizational design that fosters informative committees is an institutional means to policy ends via the reduction of uncertainty."[63]

It is also in the interest of the legislature to create committees that will produce policies in line with what a fully informed legislature would have created in the absence of a committee. While the distributive theorists emphasize "gains from trade" as an impetus to committee development, information theorists highlight the role of specialization. Jurisdictions, then, presumably reflect the array of policy areas for which a legislature previously needed specialization. Specialization arises when processing demands from "broader and increasingly complex policy environments." Though Krehbiel implies that jurisdictions may change in response to the emergence of new social problems, for the sake of clarity in his modeling he assumes that jurisdictions are static, writing, "From session to session . . . they can plausibly be regarded as exogenous."[64] Nevertheless, an informational efficiency argument about jurisdictional change might be made.

When a jurisdictionally ambiguous bill is introduced, the level of information about how potential policies relate to outcomes is especially low. A rational legislature that is informationally efficient would refer the bill to the committee possessing the greatest wealth of related expertise. New issues should go to those committees that can become low cost specialists. This is simply another way of saying that the bill would be assigned to the committee that already has the "closest" jurisdiction.

From interviews with staffers, lobbyists, and the parliamentarians, there are strong and consistent signs that the House parliamentarians have informational efficiency (though they do not use that phrase) in mind when referring jurisdictionally ambiguous legislation. I asked current and former parliamentarians why they use the "weight of the bill" criterion instead of some other decision rule. Their answer was "jurisdictional proximity," which of course is simply another way of saying the "weight of the bill." When I pressed, they thought my question was a silly one because the answer is so obvious. There came a quick and unanimous reply. Jurisdictional proximity, they said, is the guiding rule because "that's where the experts are . . . Of course," they try to match bills up with skills "because *that is their job.*"

Committee members and staff develop a valuable knowledge base within their jurisdictions, and the parliamentarian says this is taken into account when establishing referral precedents. In fact, the previous trail of referral precedents, so critical in establishing common law turf, testifies to a committee's expertise. This can be our final hypothesis, to be tested along with the others in upcoming chapters: *common law jurisdictions are allocated in ways that reward committees with expertise on closely related issues.* If this proves true, then we should not be so quick to label turf wars and fragmentation as evils of distributive politics. The nature of congressional committee jurisdictions is not so dastardly as that.

TWO

The Nature of Committee Jurisdictions

At one level, a committee's borders seem remarkably stable. Broadly defined, farm bills have been sent to the Senate Agriculture Committee since its inception in 1825. Broadly defined, foreign affairs bills have gone to the House International Relations Committee since 1822. How can we reconcile the fact that committees maintain long-standing control over some issues with our expectations that there are political rewards for waging—and winning—turf wars? Despite appearances, jurisdictions are never broadly defined. Politics is in the details. General descriptions—"health," "transportation," "agriculture"—matter much less than the trail of specific and often narrow bills sent to committees by parliamentarians (in the U.S. Congress) and chief clerks (in state legislatures).

At extremes, a committee system's borders might be either entirely fluid or completely rigid. Constantly shuffling jurisdictions undermines the effectiveness of committee systems; conversely, legislatures with static boundaries cannot adapt when new issues arise. "The life of the law has not been logic," wrote Oliver Wendell Holmes, Jr., "it has been experience."[1] It is the same with jurisdictions. Committee boundaries need to be flexible enough to adapt when new issues arise.

Jurisdictions are, at once, both rigid *and* flexible. There are two dominant sources of jurisdictional legitimacy: statutory law (based on written rules) and common law (based on precedent-setting bill referrals). Statutory jurisdictions are fixed (at least in the short run), but committee systems are flexible through common law turf. As we see in this chapter, turf wars are usually fought over common law—not statutory jurisdictions.

This chapter accomplishes three things. First, the distinction between statutory and common law jurisdictions is more carefully drawn. Second, the notion of a "policy entrepreneur" is introduced, focusing on John Dingell (D-MI). Third, a history of the House Commerce Committee highlights the turf wars it has won and lost.

Sources of Jurisdictional Legitimacy

Recall from the first chapter how one committee staff director describes turf. "Jurisdiction boils down to whether you'll have a seat at the table when important decisions are being made. If you're not at the table, you're a nobody." There are two main ways to get a seat at the table. The first—and best-known—way is to be on a committee that has turf hard coded into the House or Senate written rules. In practice, the rules of a preceding Congress are used by subsequent sessions with minor and infrequent changes.

Beyond rules and precedents, formal memoranda of understanding and (occasionally) informal understandings between committees can confer jurisdiction. Following the rise of task forces in 1995, one can expect that some task force members will try to claim turf on behalf of their standing committees. These additional routes are rarely used, and they are discussed in Chapter 5. Turf changes in Congress are driven by the relationship between common law and statutory jurisdictions.

STATUTORY JURISDICTIONS

Detailed jurisdictions first appeared in the House and Senate rules following the 1946 Legislative Reorganization Act, which became a federal statute (60 Stat. 812). Subsequent changes in statutory jurisdictions (1974 and 1995 in the House, for example) have been made through resolutions. Jurisdictions of House committees are spelled out in Rule X. Rules have to be ratified by a majority of the House or Senate, so there is a natural parallel between statutory jurisdictions and the more familiar legal term "statutory law." In statutory law, judges endeavor to uncover and follow legislative intent, which is presumed to be expressed when a majority can be mustered to pass a bill.

As the folklore maintains, statutory jurisdictions are jealously guarded. Committees reiterate them at the beginning of printed hearings; committee calendars are typically structured to emphasize that work is being done in all of their statutory areas; annual activity reports—required by law—list the numbers of bills and hearings by a committee's statutory jurisdiction, and some committees print occasional summaries of laws within their borders. All of these efforts trumpet jurisdictional property rights laid out in the written rules.

Long before the 1946 Legislative Reorganization Act, statutory jurisdictions were notoriously imprecise. Old House Rule 87 described the duty of the Committee on Military Affairs as the "consideration [of] all subjects relating to the military establishment and public defence." On the same day that Military Affairs was created, March 13, 1822, a similar Committee on Naval Affairs was born. This committee was "to take into consideration all matters which concern the naval establishment."[2] Jurisdictional ambiguities were inevitable. The *written* rules gave no guidance as to which committee oversaw coordination between the army and the navy.

The old House rules were overhauled and renumbered in 1880, but committee borders did not become more precise. For some panels, just the opposite happened when duties were described as part of the bill referral process. The rules on bill referrals began by saying that "all proposed legislation shall be referred to the committee in the preceding rule, as follows, namely, subjects relating to . . . ," and then the rules reported turf. The statutory jurisdiction of the House Commerce Committee throughout the first half of the twentieth century was one word, "commerce."[3] For the Agriculture Committee, the statutory jurisdiction was "agriculture and forestry." The Judiciary Committee's statutory jurisdiction was "judicial proceedings, [and] civil and criminal law."[4]

With broad, imprecise, and overlapping territories, committee boundaries were like gerrymandered electoral districts, carved out for political power brokers. Especially before the rise of the House parliamentarian as an arbiter early in this century, jurisdictions were contorted to reflect shifting political coalitions. Committee borders were not *entirely* up for grabs, however. Heed was usually paid to referral precedents, giving jurisdictions an element of stability. In the House, though, these referral precedents could be overturned by a floor majority (until 1890) or by the Speaker (from 1890 through 1910). So while jurisdictions were often stable, there was the real threat that they could be taken away because the House and Senate rules left open so much room for interpretation and for political manipulation.

The clearest cases of jurisdictional change would seem to be when new committees emerge, when old committees disappear, and when committee names change—as when the House Committee on Education and Labor became the Economic and Educational Opportunities Committee in January 1995. Figure 2.1 shows the eighteen standing committees that today make up the jurisdiction of the House Judiciary Committee.[5] Congress has occasionally formed standing committees to address topical issues, like the committees on Freedmen's Affairs

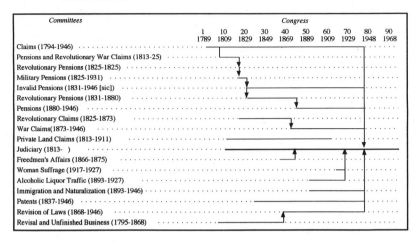

Figure 2.1 Consolidation of Committees into House Judiciary Committee, 1794–1996 (Source: *Guide to Records of the U.S. House of Representatives at the National Archives: 1789–1989* [Washington, DC: National Archives, 1989], 73, 201)

(founded in 1866), Alcoholic Liquor Traffic (1893), and Woman Suffrage (1917). The general structure of the Judiciary Committee, however, appears to have changed little since 1946. One should not jump to the conclusion, though, that the Judiciary Committee's *jurisdiction* is unchanged.

According to reformers, the 1946 Legislative Reorganization Act (detailed in Chapter 3) was supposed to get rid of jurisdictional fluidity once and for all. "The jurisdictions of the reformed committees," boasted reformer George Galloway, "will be clearly defined in the rules."[6] Today, most House and Senate committees have ten to twenty specific things listed in their boundaries. "Child labor" in the House, for example, is under the control of Economic and Educational Opportunities because it is included among the fourteen issues granted the committee in House Rule X, clause 1. Table 2.1 shows the statutory jurisdiction of the Senate Committee on Finance, as of 1996.

If one counts up the number of issues listed for each House committee in the mid-1990s, one finds 19 for the Agriculture Committee, four for Appropriations, 17 for International Relations, and nine for Ways and Means. If our minds are fixed only on statutory jurisdictions, we might guess—wrongly—that the Ways and Means turf is about half the size of the Agriculture Committee's territory. Statutory jurisdictions

Table 2.1 Statutory Jurisdiction of the Senate Finance Committee, 1996

1	Bonded debt of the U.S., except as provided in the 1974 Congressional Budget Act
2	Customs, collection districts, and ports of entry and delivery
3	Deposit of public moneys
4	General revenue sharing
5	Health programs under the Social Security Act, or financed by a specific tax or trust fund
6	National social security
7	Reciprocal trade agreements
8	Revenue measures generally, except as provided by the 1974 Congressional Budget Act
9	Revenue measures relating to the insular possessions
10	Tariffs and import quotas, and matters related thereto
11	Transportation of dutiable goods

are easy to quantify, and they rarely change. Eric Schickler and Andrew Rich have tracked down all instances of statutory jurisdiction changes from 1919 through 1994. They found 27, most of them minor.[7] Furthermore, only a handful of those jurisdictional changes pitted one party against the other. Little partisan heat was generated. Rather, *common law* jurisdictions, which at their boundaries are always up for grabs, are where one finds eyewitnesses to Washington's turf wars.

COMMON LAW JURISDICTIONS

The second way to get a "seat at the table when important decisions are being made" is to be on a committee that has been granted common law jurisdiction. Even when jurisdictionally ambiguous bills are introduced, they still have to be referred to one committee within 24 hours. These referrals establish binding precedents for all future bills on the same subjects, thereby resolving jurisdictional ambiguities. For example, in addition to child labor laws, House Economic and Educational Opportunities (as opposed to the Judiciary Committee) has long claimed a set of juvenile delinquency bills, but that property right is not actually written down in the rules.[8]

One committee print describes the process succinctly: "Committee jurisdictions expand and contract over time for several reasons . . . Subject areas not of concern to the Congress at the time jurisdictions were enacted into law or became part of the *Rules* come before Congress, are referred to committee, and thereby add to the jurisdiction of committees."[9] Precedents are paramount, and turf wars usually revolve around establishing binding bill referrals—long before House and Senate rules are rewritten in those occasional fits of reform. "Precedents," wrote former House Parliamentarian Lewis Deschler, "may be viewed as the 'common law,' so to speak, of the House, with much the same force and binding effect."[10]

Just how often jurisdictions change is an empirical question that we take up later in this chapter. Interview evidence consistently points to changing jurisdictions. When the House parliamentarian learned some observers think of turf as what is written down in the rules, implying that jurisdictions are largely static, he replied,

> I can see why, from a political scientist's standpoint, there would be some confusion. But we simply have to use past referral decisions to guide what we do. You just never know what new things are going to come up.
>
> *Question: Then through referral precedents, jurisdictions can change. Do you think they have changed much in your time here?*
>
> Oh heavens yes, they're much different than when I came to Congress. Yes there are changes. There are always changes. Look at the battle over OCS [outercontinental shelf]. Look at the jurisdiction over national parks and the Interior Committee. Look at what constitutes a fee and what is a tax. There are too many like these to name.[11]

The comparison between statutory and common law jurisdictions parallels the distinction lawyers and judges make between statutory and case law. Edward Levi writes that "the basic pattern of legal reasoning is reasoning by example," and this also applies to committee property rights.[12] Jurisdictions build from something a committee is already doing, leading to a long chain of referral decisions linking widely disparate issues.

In courts, the common law grows by analogies that are strategically supplied by people with political interests.[13] Legal decisions, like bill referral decisions, can be based either on statutes or on a trail of past cases covering the legal question at hand. Seeking comfort in the courts, one does not care whether a judge bases standing on cases or statutes. One only cares if one's case is justiciable. It is the same for committees.

From the point of view of legislators, there is little difference between statutory and common law jurisdictions because they have the same impact on what issues a committee can and cannot address. This is not to say that committee members are indifferent between having a property right defined as a statutory or common law jurisdiction. Statutory grants are better because they reflect the embrace of the floor majority when House and Senate rules are affirmed every two years. Proclamations of statutory jurisdictions are public and indisputable.

Common law jurisdictions, while binding for future bills on the same subject, are easier for other committees to undermine in turf wars covering closely related subjects.

Precedent-setting referral decisions are made by the House and Senate parliamentarians routinely (in several senses of the word routinely). They use a predictable and nonpartisan set of decision rules for handing out turf (discussed in Chapter 4), and players in the jurisdiction game have come to count on these decision rules when drafting legislation.[14] The resolution of jurisdictional ambiguities is also commonplace. From 1935 through 1963, an average of eighteen new common law expansions were recorded every year in Clarence Cannon's *Procedure in the House of Representatives,* and that underestimates the true number because many were only recorded in the *Congressional Record.*[15]

An example of how jurisdictions were recorded early in this century is shown in table 2.2. The table summarizes referral precedents recorded in the 1920 edition of Cannon's Procedure.

Referral precedents usually cover discrete bills—not large issue areas. Committee borders expand bill by bill, not general issue by general issue. No single committee, for example, has ever had full jurisdiction over rivers. In 1840, the House Commerce Committee received a bill conferring jurisdiction over the maintenance of inland waterways as they pertain to interstate commerce. This was made part of the committee's *statutory* jurisdiction 106 years later in 1946. In 1846, the Public Works Committee gained common law jurisdiction over man-made canals. *Man*-made canals were not considered rivers and therefore were jurisdictionally ambiguous. The Agriculture Committee has had

Table 2.2 Common Law Jurisdiction, Sample from the 1920 Edition of Cannon's *Procedure*

Bill Referral Precedents Covering	House Committee
Debris, mining debris	Mines and mining
Dead, deceased soldiers by War Department	Military Affairs
Dead, deceased soldiers by French Republic	Foreign Affairs
Debate, reporters of	Accounts
Debt, bonded debt of United States	Ways and Means
Declaration of war	Foreign Affairs
Decorations from foreign countries	Foreign Affairs
Defense, public defense	Military Affairs
Defense, appropriations for coastal defense	Appropriations
Deficiencies, appropriations for	Appropriations
Delivery and entry ports	Ways and Means

jurisdiction over watershed sites since 1864, and by 1935, the Merchant Marine and Fisheries Committee (now abandoned, with its turf split among three committees) gained common law jurisdiction over much of the remainder of water transportation.

Man-made canals and God-made canals were overseen by different committees for over a century—a perfectly typical example of how a "new" issue can lead to jurisdictional fragmentation. Fragmentation did not go away when the House started depending on the parliamentarian to adjudicate turf wars early this century. The logic leading to fragmentation is compelling, at least to policy entrepreneurs. Imagine a jurisdictionally ambiguous space between two committees, such as the one shown in figure 2.2 below. A bill might be introduced at any point along the continuum between the committees. The closer a bill is to a committee's current turf, the more likely it is that the committee will win a referral, thereby moving the jurisdiction out to the point in the policy space at which the bill was introduced. Conversely, the farther away a bill is from a committee's jurisdiction, the more likely it is that *another* committee will gain the territory. Figure 2.2 is not intended to be a formal statement about policy dimensions, though it correctly captures the way that policy entrepreneurs talk about the gray areas between committees. The farther from a committee's boundary a bill is introduced, the more likely that bill will be referred to a competing committee, destroying hopes of getting the turf in the future.

Policy entrepreneurs play an expected value game, and in interviews

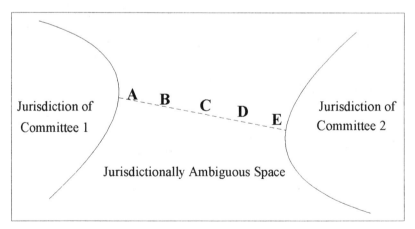

Figure 2.2 The Common Law Logic of Jurisdictional Fragmentation

they use this language explicitly. A member on Committee 1 in figure 2.2 knows that the probability of landing a bill introduced at point A is higher than one introduced at the midpoint, C. To maximize the probability of getting a referral, bills are often introduced that only slightly expand a committee's jurisdiction into ambiguous policy spaces. If a committee makes too large of a move at once, it risks having the bill referred to another committee, and in the words of one staff director, when you've lost with the parliamentarian, "you've lost forever." That is an important fear. If Committee 1 introduces a bill at B and it is referred to Committee 2 instead, Committee 2's borders expand to B, and Committee 1 may never again compete for turf at C, D, or E. Accordingly, Committee 1 is likely to take A first, and then advance on B. Likewise, Committee 2 first takes E, followed by D. Few panels want to take too large of a bite out of most new issues and risk losing a critical bill referral to a rival committee. Instead, several committees may eat away at the edges of a jurisdictionally ambiguous issue by trying to define things in ways most clearly relevant to what they are already doing. Fragmentation is inevitable.

Fragmentation is also nothing new in Congress.[16] Picture America 100 years ago. Even before the 1898 Alaska gold rush, several committees were rushing to stake claims to policies in this new territory. The Agriculture Committee had long since established referral precedents over the protection of *farm* animals, but entrepreneurs on Merchant Marine and Fisheries successfully argued that jurisdiction over nonfarm animals in Alaska rightly belonged to their committee. Then in the 1880s the Ways and Means Committee claimed jurisdiction over furbearing animals in Alaska that could be sold to produce revenue. Not to be outdone, the Commerce Committee claimed jurisdiction over the interstate transportation of dead game animals, including those from Alaska, in 1900.[17] At the height of the Alaska gold rush, then, four House committees were trying to get in on the action via living, dead, farm, and nonfarm animals. No single committee had jurisdiction over Alaska.

The distinction between statutory and common law turf helps us understand how, when, and why turf wars are launched. It takes policy entrepreneurs on committees to actually prosecute turf wars, however, and we need to be careful when we talk about personalities in politics.[18] Journalistic accounts of turf wars tend to emphasize personal vendettas and gigantic egos, but personalities, per se, are not why turf wars are launched or won. Policy entrepreneurs (some of whom have quite dry personalities) spark turf wars by launching skirmishes into jurisdictionally ambiguous turf.

Policy Entrepreneurs

Dozens of people tell versions of the same story. John Dingell, former chair of the House Commerce Committee, is said to have passed a picture of the world taken from space. Gesturing toward the blue planet, he boasted, "Now there, that is *my* jurisdiction."[19]

John Dingell was a classic policy entrepreneur, described by the *Congressional Quarterly* as "a recognized master of territorial expansion."[20] Two reporters quipped that under Dingell the Commerce Committee claimed "jurisdiction over anything that moves, burns or is sold."[21] In the late 1980s, one *National Journal* cover featured John Dingell posing over a chessboard. That magazine's lead article, "Plotting Every Move," was a study in how policy entrepreneurs win turf wars. Said Dingell, "Timing, patience, instinct all count."[22] More substantive legislation passes through the Commerce Committee either as a single bill or as part of a multiple referral than passes through any other House committee, and during Dingell's tenure, more and more legislators tried to transfer onto his committee.[23] One Commerce Committee member, reflecting on territorial aggressiveness, allowed that "Dingell [didn't] want his committee to have the whole world, just all the areas surrounding its jurisdiction."[24] Of course, the larger the jurisdiction, the more territory there is nearby.[25]

Appearing on the ABC News program *Nightline* in January 1992, Representative Dingell talked about Japan's reluctance to open its markets to U.S. products. "If the President of the United States isn't going to do something," said the chair of the Commerce Committee, "then by God or by shoehorn, John Dingell will!" The "shoehorn" in this case was made possible by the Commerce Committee's jurisdiction over trade, which it shares with the Ways and Means Committee. Commerce's trade jurisdiction was reasserted recently—in the early 1980s.[26] A decade after staking the claim, Commerce now has the power to make good on promises to restrict Japanese access to U.S. markets.

Jurisdictionally ambiguous bills arise within issue areas that are not yet clearly defined *and* within issue areas that are undergoing redefinitions. When the House Ways and Means Committee exercised primary jurisdiction over trade, it was under the heading of "reciprocal trade agreements." Dingell's approach was to add another dimension—trade "fairness"—to the debate. Only then could he stake a claim to the ambiguous turf.[27] Ambiguities arise, therefore, not merely over entirely new issues (like acid rain) but also over how settled topics are redefined in the light of new events.[28]

Though John Dingell is, for the moment at least, the House member most closely associated with turf wars, new Republican chairs have picked up right where the Democrats left off. Policy entrepreneurs throughout the Capitol play the "jurisdiction game" with varying success. Rick Boucher (D-VA) chaired the House Science Subcommittee from 1991 through 1994, and he credits John Dingell with teaching him how to play the jurisdiction game. "Mr. Boucher says he has 'learned well' from Mr. Dingell, whom he calls 'the master of this art' of creatively expanding power by publicizing problems and then solving them."[29]

Representative Boucher, like other policy entrepreneurs, sees turf as malleable—especially when expanding into "new" areas such as those made possible by scientific breakthroughs. "The power of a congressional subcommittee," argues Boucher, "is limited only by the creativity of its staff, chairman, and members."[30] Some fear that such students of turf wars might use the committee system for personal aggrandizement and political whims. Most journalistic discussions about jurisdictions and turf battles are of this quality, emphasizing personality and "power motives" instead of examining policy aims or the broader role of committees in the legislative process.

This is not a book about personalities, though they do make turf wars more interesting to watch. Jurisdictions are institutional facts that policy entrepreneurs try to change, but their likelihood of changing the institution depends on much more than the force of their personalities. In fact, Representative Dingell's immediate predecessors as chair of the Commerce Committee, Harley Staggers (D-WV) and Oren Harris (D-AK), were not widely considered to be aggressive powers in the House.[31] Some thought Oren Harris a bland and slow-talking country boy from El Dorado, Arkansas. Maybe so, but as will be seen in the next chapter, the rate of jurisdictional expansion under his tenure was just as great as it was on John Dingell's watch.[32] Now under the chairmanship of Thomas Bliley (R-NC), Commerce's jurisdictional expansion will likely continue apace, much to the frustration of reformist Republicans and other committee chairs.

How is it that legislators with such differing personalities as Oren Harris, John Dingell, Patrick Moynihan, and Ted Kennedy·can all be considered "entrepreneurs?" The political scientists Paul Teske and Mark Schneider, writing about innovations in city governments, offer useful insights. "Entrepreneurs engage in the act of 'creative discovery'—they try to take advantage of newly discovered or newly created opportunities to push forward ideas and policies."[33] Entrepreneurs are, in short, "strategic individuals who attempt to sell their ideas in the best ways possible."[34] These notions of creative discovery and strategic gamesmanship are attractive, and they are more helpful than Carol Weissert's familiar notion of entrepreneurship as "expertise and persistence."[35] Most legislators are experts on some subjects, and many are persistent, but few are real entrepreneurs pushing issues that have long evaded the political agenda.

Scholarship on political entrepreneurs is often biographical, emphasizing the roles of chance and personalities.[36] This makes it difficult to generalize about the circumstances—and institutions—likely to give rise to entrepreneurial behavior.[37] Generalizable theories about entrepreneurs focusing on individuals in an institutional context are rare, but encouraging work has been done recently. Using an extensive survey of city managers, for example, Teske and Schneider speculate about conditions under which political entrepreneurs are likely to arise. The emergence of entrepreneurial mayors is demonstrably related to competitive mayoral elections and the frequency of mayoral elections. Apparently the tendency to offer policy innovations has an electoral connection.[38]

Entrepreneurs are motivated by policy, in some cases, elections in others. Former representative James Florio (D-NJ) was a subcommittee chair in the mid-1980s, and his statement is typical of many I encountered during not-for-attribution interviews:

> "We're expanding our jurisdiction. We've got authority over the FTC [Federal Trade Commission], and that gets you to anti-trust and regulation. We've begun to deal with some trade issues. There was a headline the other day, 'Florio on Trade.' The legislative credentials and the jurisdiction give you a forum on almost everything. From the forum you affect public opinion, and from that you get clout."[39]

Clout is something George Miller (D-CA) sought for the House Natural Resources Committee when he took over as chair in 1991.[40] Miller pledged to defend aggressively his committee's jurisdiction, something the previous chair, Morris Udall (D-AZ), failed to do during an extended illness. Miller wanted to pursue an environmentalists' agenda through energy conservation measures, but while the Natural Resources Committee had "a lot to say about energy *production* issues," it had "virtually no jurisdiction over energy *conservation*."[41]

Chairman Miller needed a turf war strategy to stake a claim on energy issues, and he opted to propose sweeping limitations on hydroelectric power development on public lands. Though *public lands* have long been in Natural Resources' jurisdiction, *hydroelectric damns* on public lands have been jurisdictionally ambiguous. More to the point, they *were* jurisdictionally ambiguous. Using the types of strategies discussed in this book, Chairman Miller's committee staked a solid claim to a growing list of energy conservation issues.[42] Entrepreneurs exploit jurisdictional ambiguities.

In Chapter 6, we will explore more closely just what kinds of legislators are likely to become policy entrepreneurs, and why. The important point to remember now is that legislators work within an institutional context, and even the most territorially aggressive entrepreneurs need a firm foundation from which to launch turf wars. In the mid-1990s, even after Republicans tried clipping its wings in 1995, the House Commerce Committee maintains Congress's most expansive territory. How did this happen, and what can the Commerce Committee teach us about turf wars? We look at Commerce to give the conventional wisdom (the hypothesis that jurisdictions are static) its toughest test. If we fail to find common law adaptations here, we should not expect to find them anywhere.

Jurisdiction of the House Commerce Committee

Originally named the Committee on Commerce and Manufacturers and dating from 1795, Commerce is one of the House's oldest committees. Its broad mandate was to "take into consideration all such petitions and matters of things touching the commerce and manufacturers of the United States."[43] The committee's jurisdiction was split in two in 1819, creating the Committee on Manufacturers (which was eliminated in 1911) and the Committee on Commerce. Commerce was renamed Interstate and Foreign Commerce in 1892, became Energy and Commerce in 1981, and was shortened to Commerce once again in 1995.[44]

THE STATUTORY JURISDICTION
OF HOUSE COMMERCE

House Commerce's statutory jurisdiction is reported in table 2.3. The issues are listed in the order they appeared in the rules. Much of the committee's statutory jurisdiction dates to the 1946 Reorganization Act. Beyond "interstate and foreign commerce generally," the committee was given property rights over civil aeronautics, communications, securities and exchanges, and public health, among other things. Some apparent gains and losses happened in 1974, 1980, and 1995.

Commerce's jurisdiction is exceptionally broad, partly because the committee's fortunes have been tied to the commerce clause in the U.S. Constitution, and that clause has been a base from which federal

Table 2.3 Statutory Jurisdiction of the House Commerce Committee

Jurisdiction	Year Gained	Year Lost
1 Interstate and foreign commerce generally	1946	
2 Regulation of interstate and foreign communications	1946	
3 Interstate oil compacts, and petroleum and natural gas, except on public lands (wording changed to "interstate energy compacts" in 1980)	1946	
4 Securities and exchanges	1946	
5 Regulation of interstate transmission of power, except the installation of connections between government water power projects (subsumed under no. 20, below, in 1980)	1946	
6 Public health and quarantine	1946	
7 Railroad labor and railroad retirement and unemployment, except revenue measures relating thereto	1946	1995
8 Inland waterways	1946	1995
9 Regulation of interstate and foreign transportation except transportation by water not subject to the jurisdiction of the Interstate Commerce Commission	1946	1974
10 Civil aeronautics	1946	1974
11 Weather Bureau	1946	1974
12 Bureau of Standards, standardization of weights and measures, and the metric system	1946	1954
13 Consumer affairs and consumer protection	1974	
14 Travel and tourism	1974	
15 Health and health facilities, except health care supported by payroll deductions	1974	
16 Biomedical research and development	1974	
17 National energy policy generally	1980	
18 Measures relating to the exploration, production, storage, supply, marketing, pricing, and regulation of energy resources, including all fossil fuels, solar energy, and other unconventional or renewable energy resources	1980	
19 Measures relating to the conservation of energy resources	1980	
20 Measures relating to (a) the generation and marketing of power (except by federally chartered or federal regional power marketing authorities), (b) the reliability and interstate transmission of, and ratemaking for, all power, and (c) the siting of generation facilities, except the installation of interconnections between government water-power projects	1980	
21 Measures relating to general management of the Department of Energy and the management of	1980	

continued

Table 2.3 *continued*

Jurisdiction	Year Gained	Year Lost
all functions of the Federal Energy Regulatory Commission		
22 Measures relating to energy information generally. (Deemed superfluous in 1995. Still handled by the committee.)	1980	—
23 Measures relating to the commercial application of energy technology	1980	1995
24 Regulation of the domestic nuclear energy industry, including regulation of research and development reactors and nuclear regulatory research	1995	
25 Nuclear and other energy, and non-military nuclear energy and research development, including the disposal of nuclear waste	1995	

powers have expanded since the Great Depression. As the new Republican majority seeks to send power back to the states in the mid-1990s, the Commerce Committee seems a natural target.

In order to assess the relative importance and size of statutory as opposed to common law jurisdictions, we need a way to measure both. There are various methods to consider. Steve Smith and Christopher Deering have measured the size of a committee's turf by counting up the number of issues listed in the rules.[45] As we have seen, that approach only captures statutory jurisdictions. A second approach might exploit committee calendars, but indexing schemes vary widely from committee to committee and from year to year. A third method, counting the number of entries in the books of precedents, is better, but Cannon's *Procedure* has not been published since 1963, and even if it were published regularly, not all referral precedents are recorded in such lists.[46]

This chapter introduces a method based on committee hearings.[47] The Congressional Information Service maintains a computerized listing of all published hearings. For Commerce Committee records, I extracted the number of days the committee held hearings, the number of pages of hearing documents printed, and the number of bills associated with each hearing. After reading one- to two-page descriptions, each subject raised in a hearing was coded. Covering 1947 through 1994, 2,847 hearings were examined, and 226 distinct topics were identified. This allows us to construct a time series of the rise and fall of issues in the Commerce Committee.

With public hearing records, one can gauge how frequently a committee works in various parts of its jurisdiction. In the early 1950s, one of the Commerce Committee's 12 statutory areas was "Bureau of Standards, standardization of weights and measures, and the metric system." But this should not count as 1/12th of the committee's jurisdiction. From 1947 through 1958 the committee held no hearings on the subject.[48] During the same 11 years, 14 hearings were held in another statutory area, "railroad labor and railroad retirement and unemployment," and 33 hearings were held on the "regulation of interstate and foreign communications," including well-publicized investigations into television game show scandals. What we need is a measure of committee turf that is sensitive to the issues of the day, and the content analysis used below gives us this flexibility.

I measure a committee's "hearing activity" by the total number of pages of hearings for more than 200 subjects. With this approach we find, for example, that 23.44 percent of the Commerce Committee's hearing activity in 1949 and 1950 was on air transportation. Since the measure we use here depends on committee activity, we have to be especially careful to watch for the strategic uses of committee *inactivity*. Bills occasionally are sent to the committee that the House wants moved but fail even to get a hearing—most recently on banking deregulation in the early 1990s. It is far more common, however, that bills tagged "dead on arrival" at the Commerce Committee have no wide constituency pushing for them. When the committee stopped holding regular hearings on airline issues by the late 1960s, it was not because the members became suddenly hostile to flying. Rather, the committee moved onto other more politically rewarding issues (like consumer protection), all the while allowing the Public Works Committee to encroach on its air space. This is in contrast to the general tendency for committees jealously to guard their boundaries. Commerce let air transportation slip away because the members lost interest in the cause. The processes by which fallow turf can be appropriated by other committees is discussed in the next chapter, but it is important to note that neglected issues are lost through the acquiescence of the committees of jurisdiction.

Beyond identifying issues, each of the 226 topics was categorized as either based on the committee's statutory jurisdiction or based on bill referral precedents. Here it was important to be conservative and err on the side of overestimating the percentage of hearings growing out of turf written down in Rule X. For example, in 1947, the following hearings were all identified as justifiable based on the committee's statutory turf: "Agreements between Carriers" (interstate trucking), "Alaska

Airports" (civil aeronautics), "Amendments to the Natural Gas Act" (interstate pipelines), and "Iodized Salt" (public health). Also in 1947, the committee was referred a bill and held hearings on food adulteration inspections. By referral precedents, such bills had long been handled by the committee, but it does not fall in the committee's jurisdiction as written in the House rules.[49] Similarly, the committee authorized the creation of the National Science Foundation, which may have its merits but is not even remotely mentioned in the 1947 *House Rules Manual.* The National Science Foundation was coded as part of the committee's common law jurisdiction.

Figure 2.3 shows the percentage of the Commerce Committee's hearing activity on issues in the committee's statutory jurisdiction. The figure is based on 746 hearing documents from 1947 through 1974. This number only includes hearings on referred bills, and a three-year moving average is reported.[50] Oversight hearings in which no bills were referred are excluded from the dataset because it is the referrals (not simply the hearings) that establish binding precedents. As explained in Chapter 5, however, oversight hearings are sometimes used to lay the groundwork for precedent-setting bill referrals.[51] The data span the period between the 1946 and 1974 reform acts, when House Rule X was changed. Hearing activity is measured by the percent of the printed pages in hearings that were devoted to each topic.

Several things stand out in figure 2.3. First, immediately after the 1946 Legislative Reorganization Act, more than 90 percent of the com-

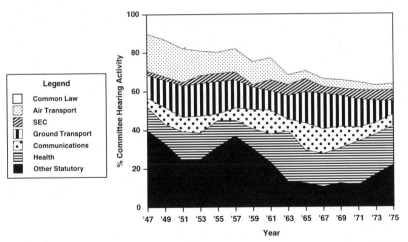

Figure 2.3 Commerce Committee Activity in its Statutory Jurisdiction, 1947–1974

mittee's hearing activity was on issues in the committee's statutory jurisdiction. The rules of this period were remarkably accurate descriptions of what the committee was actually doing. For the most part, the 1946 reformers apparently accomplished what they set out to do, but in the decades that followed, their jurisdictional specifications slowly collapsed in the face of new issues and gradual adjustments.

Second, by 1974, the year before new jurisdictional wordings were incorporated into the rules, more than a third of the Commerce Committee's activities were on issues not in the statutory jurisdiction of the committee. If we extended the time line, we would see that less than a third of the committee's activities in 1994 were granted to them in the rules in 1947. The remaining two-thirds of the committee's hearings have been on issues that were either given the committee through the 1974 and 1980 rules changes or were taken by the committee through bill referral precedents. Further, the committee's common law turf more than tripled from 1946 to 1974, as the committee's turf expanded to include (among other things) certain patent infringements, daylight savings time, automobile insurance, and solid waste disposal.

Third, attention shifts yearly from issue to issue. In the late 1940s, the committee handled dozens of bills and held numerous hearings on civil aviation. About 20 percent of the committee's efforts were devoted to problems like the building of airports and the safety of jet engines. By the mid-1960s, only 5 percent of the committee's agenda was taken up by aviation. Attention shifted to other issues, like the safety of automobiles and deceptive advertising, and staff resources were consciously taken away from aviation.

The committee's statutory jurisdiction over the commerce clause in the U.S. Constitution proved a convenient staging area for turf wars.[52] One committee member boasted:

> We're the only committee that I know of that has a specific constitutional responsibility. It's spelled out. And in a sense we can interpret that as everything involved in commerce. And if the Saint Louis elevators can be in interstate commerce, as the Supreme Court said they were in the 1930s, I don't see why just about anything isn't in our jurisdiction. That was the history of the [19]40s, the implementation of the Commerce Clause. And basically that helps us.[53]

The codified grant of "interstate and foreign commerce generally" in the House rules justified hearings on such diverse topics as the transportation of flammable fabrics (March 4, 1947), interstate sales of switchblade knives (April 17, 1958), and interstate obscene phone calls (January 30, 1968). It is clear that these issues arise out of the committee's statutory jurisdiction, but the committee has also launched into areas that seem remote to the grant of power outlined by the rules.

COMMON LAW JURISDICTION
OF HOUSE COMMERCE

Common law jurisdictions grow when an argument can be made that a new issue is closely related to something that a committee is already doing. One referral precedent is used to justify making another referral precedent, and so on. As a result, the nature of committee jurisdictions is that their expansion is dependent on the path that previous bill referrals have taken. Like the view of evolution in Stephen Jay Gould's *Wonderful Life,* committee jurisdictions would emerge differently if we re-ran the clock of history.[54] Just one changed bill referral a generation ago could have made for a dramatically different constellation of jurisdictions today.[55]

The path-dependent nature of jurisdictional change is evident in how Commerce acquired health policy in the 1800s. Congress in the 1790s was preoccupied with foreign trade, primarily the "protection of American international and domestic trade markets and shipping rights," which put the Committee on Commerce and Manufacturers in the middle of the fray.[56] The Ways and Means Committee (formed in 1795) received tariff bills relating to customs houses, and the Commerce Committee handled navigation safety.[57] The first public measure ever sent to Commerce was "a bill authorizing the erection of a lighthouse on Baker's Island, Massachusetts."[58] Soon the Commerce Committee was authorizing the building of piers and requiring the use of proper life-saving devices on ships. Its first foray into health policy was in the 4th Congress (1796–97) when it worked on a bill permitting ships to be quarantined for health reasons. The law was designed to control the spread of diseases, and from this base, the committee slowly expanded its territory into other areas of health policy.

In 1798 Congress, through the Commerce Committee, created the Marine Hospital Service to oversee quarantines of immigrants at entry ports on the Atlantic seaboard and to care for sick sailors in the merchant marine.[59] The hospital service opened several facilities along rivers away from the Atlantic seaboard after 1837, and these became centers for research into communicable diseases.[60] Infusions of federal money into medical research followed the cholera epidemics of the 1850s and the yellow fever epidemics of the 1870s. This kind of service was far removed from the Commerce Committee's initial jurisdiction over navigation safety, and the Hospital Service was eventually reorganized as the Public Health Service.[61]

A second part of the tenuous path from safe navigation to health policy grew out of the dangers of steamboat travel. Beginning in the 1830s and continuing through the end of the century, steam-powered merchant ships ran a booming business. In the 1850s, steamboats on just three rivers—the Ohio, Missouri, and Mississippi—carried more cargo than all of the steamboats in England combined. Boiler explosions were common, especially during the 1850s. From 1848 through 1852, 1,155 lives were lost in boiler explosions just on the western rivers.[62] There was public outcry at the loss of life, and Congress responded by ordering the Marine Hospital Service to locate hospitals along heavily traveled rivers where boiler explosions and other maritime disasters were likely. The hospitals were controlled by federal as opposed to state authorities because the rivers were used in interstate commerce.

When the cholera and yellow fever epidemics hit the Great Plains, the marine hospitals were the federal government's closest facilities. Soon the Commerce Committee, whose members were initially more likely to have backgrounds in business than medicine, were overseeing the nation's health. With the Marine Hospital Service as a base, the Commerce Committee gained "broad jurisdiction over bills relating to the subject of health generally."[63] By the close of the nineteenth century, the committee's grasp of health jurisdiction was firm and unchallenged. The path of common law jurisdictional expansion went from navigation safety to quarantines and from boiler explosions to marine hospitals to health policy more generally.

It was clever to link quarantine bills and navigation safety to exploding boilers and marine hospitals, but the strategy of drawing analogies between issues that a committee wants and issues that it already controls is typical. From 1947 through 1994, the Commerce Committee received bills on 137 issues that expanded the committee's jurisdiction. That is an average of three precedent-setting bill referrals every year. Many of those expansions were minor. (For example, the committee used its jurisdiction over travel and tourism in 1983 to solidify its claim to a bill related to international sporting events.)[64] The committee, however, also took major steps into new territory. From its jurisdiction over interstate and foreign transportation, the committee gained jurisdiction over automobile safety in 1956.[65] Commerce was then well positioned to respond to the regulatory challenges posed by Ralph Nader in the mid-1960s.

Of the 137 issues over which the Commerce Committee established a referral precedent from 1947 through 1994, 114 (or 83.2 percent) were issues raised in conjunction with a bill over which the committee had already established jurisdiction. Again, jurisdictional change is path dependent. Turf wars are usually launched from a firm base, for if they are not, the parliamentarian is more likely to hand a committee a defeat.

Another example shows how the path-dependent nature of jurisdictional expansion leads in unexpected directions. In 1958, the committee picked up a Public Health Service proposal, in the form of HR 9368, to set health standards for unburned hydrocarbon emissions from automobiles.[66] The first Air Pollution Control Act was a partial result of such efforts. In 1965, the committee used amendments to the Clean Air Act to extend its jurisdiction over automobile emissions by requiring new pollution control devices on some cars.[67] Ten years later Commerce encouraged innovations in automobile design to gain fuel efficiency.[68] In 1980, the committee went a step beyond air pollution and fuel efficiency by promoting a NASA-led federally funded research and development program to help the auto industry design automobiles of the future.[69] The proposal was defeated, but the committee held hearings, thereby strengthening its jurisdictional claim (possibly at the expense of the Science Committee).

Figure 2.3 gave indirect evidence that the Commerce Committee's common law turf expanded between the 1946 and 1974 reforms. Take a closer look at figure 2.4, which is based on a content analysis of 1,635

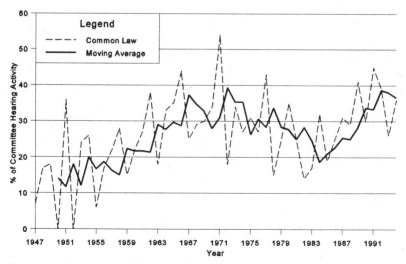

Figure 2.4 Growth of Commerce Committee's Common Law Jurisdiction, 1947–1994

hearing documents published by the Commerce Committee from 1947 through 1994. Only hearings on referred bills (52 percent of all hearings during the period) are reported. The reason this part of the analysis is based solely on hearings weighing *reported bills* is that other hearings do not in themselves confer jurisdiction. A committee can hold hearings on just about anything its members choose, and entrepreneurs are increasingly likely to use such public forums to enhance their expertise and credibility. The House parliamentarians report that this public posturing has no impact on how they refer jurisdictionally ambiguous bills, but the flurry of hearings seems unabated.

From 1947 to 1974, the Commerce Committee's agenda gradually included more and more common law issues. Much of the increase was from consumer protection problems like the testing of food additives (1957), product labeling laws (1958), seat belt regulations (1962), the safety of children's toys (1969), and deceptive advertising (1971).

There are two trend lines in figure 2.4: the percentage of common law hearing activity and a three-year moving average. The moving average indicates gradual upward change, but there are also wide swings from year to year as the committee launches into new areas. In 1958, for example, Commerce worked on a medical education bill (which could have gone to Education and Labor) and on air pollution legislation. The next year its common law activity dropped by half as it turned its attention to the Securities and Exchange Commission and to railroad unemployment, both in its statutory jurisdiction. Still, an upward trend is unmistakable between 1947 and 1974. Use of the committee's common law agenda peaked at 54 percent in 1971 with extensive hearings on air pollution control, solid waste recycling, cigarette labeling, and automobile safety, none of which was yet in the committee's statutory jurisdiction.

Through the late 1960s and early 1970s, the amount of committee activity on common law issues averaged about 35 percent. As one would expect, this dropped following the 1974 jurisdiction reforms. Between the 1974 and 1980 House reforms, the percentage of the committee's hearing activity spent on common law issues averaged about 30 percent with no general trend up or down.

The committee's common law activity would have dropped even more were it not for the energy crisis. John Dingell—then a subcommittee chair—launched into energy issues just as committee attention to consumer protection (codified in the rules in 1974) faded. During the late 1970s, nearly all of the committee's common law activities were on energy-related issues such as synthetic liquid fuels, energy conservation, solar energy, and a national energy strategy. None of these issues was in the jurisdiction of any other committee during this period, so the committee staked a claim and then worked to protect it.

The 1980 reforms locked the Commerce Committee's energy jurisdiction into the House rules, and the committee's common law agenda fell from 35 to 15 percent in two years. The gradual, incremental process of common law expansion began anew, as the committee has successfully staked claims to jurisdiction over the insurance industry, international trade, and some securities- related banking activities.

The rate of jurisdictional expansion under former Chairman John Dingell (D-MI) in the 1980s was almost identical to the rate of expansion under Oren Harris (D-AK), who chaired the committee from 1957 through 1965. That result might surprise people who think that Dingell's aggressive personality has led to the committee's recent successes. But there is more to winning turf wars than having certain character traits. Put John Dingell in charge of the Committee on International Relations and he would still be a policy entrepreneur, but he would not have as many successes as he has had on Commerce because the merchant marine's jurisdiction is not as broad.

Two lessons seem clear from our look at the Commerce Committee's jurisdiction. First, jurisdictions are malleable through common law referral precedents. Second, the trend toward common law issues appears incremental, as committees gradually move away from some issues and embrace others. With clever bill drafting and incremental moves into new territories, the nature of congressional committee jurisdictions is lively indeed. Jurisdictional fragmentation is a direct result of so many policy entrepreneurs trying to stake out claims to pieces of larger issues like the environment and national health care. Devoid of common law turf and the politics of bill referrals, no static notions about Congress can account for the ongoing turf wars among committees.

THREE

What Happens When Jurisdictions Are Reformed?

When Republicans took control of the House following the November 1994 elections, a package of internal reforms was high on the agenda. On January 4, 1995, the new majority ushered in a set of rules that (among other things) abolished three committees, cut the number of committee staff by a third, eliminated proxy voting in committees, modified the process by which single bills could be sent to more than one committee, and established term limits for committee chairs. It was, by all accounts, a sweeping and historic moment, ranking alongside the 1946 Legislative Reorganization Act.[1] For all the ink that has been spilled spelling out why major change is (virtually) impossible in Congress,[2] the events of early 1995 seem especially sobering.

Committee jurisdictions, however, escaped with only modest changes. By the summer of 1995, the House Republican's chief reformer, David Dreier of California, announced the appointment of a task force to tackle jurisdictions anew.[3] Representative Lee Hamilton (D-IN), who also has a strong history of supporting reform, agrees with Dreier that "jurisdictional reform is the No. 1 priority."[4] Besides the committed reformers, however, members of the House leadership are overwhelmingly skeptical that substantial changes in turf will be made anytime soon. Said a close associate of Speaker Gingrich,

> "It's just too hard. Why would we want to do it and bloody the party in the process? . . . Sure, the committee system is fragmented. Sure, some committees hog most of the good issues . . . Real reform? Short of a massacre, it's just not going to happen."[5]

Political insiders likely said the same kinds of things about the jurisdictional reforms of 1974 and 1980, but the tone today is surprisingly pessimistic. As we saw in Chapter 2, jurisdictions do in fact evolve. That was true before Speaker Gingrich, and it remains true. How could it be that the most dramatic institutional reforms in a generation, adopted in 1995 with the help from eager first-termers, failed substantially to change jurisdictions?

Two years earlier, the House and Senate formed a special "Joint Committee on the Organization of Congress," which held hearings and honed most of the reform ideas enacted once the Republicans were in power. For many witnesses appearing before the Joint Committee, committee boundaries (and the jealousies they inspired) received the most attention.[6] Explained Drier, "I felt very strongly that rather than having an omnipotent committee or two or three close-to-omnipotent committees, we needed to have greater diversity and more opportunity for Members to participate."[7] The Joint Committee's recommendations never made it to the House and Senate for a vote, but Dreier's proposals became the blueprints for wholesale changes following the Republicans' November 1994 election victory. When the dust settled, "Senior House Republicans, taking over committees for the first time in their lives, balked at wholesale changes."[8] The new chairs "successfully resisted a plan considered by the leadership to radically restructure committee jurisdictions."[9]

What happened to committee jurisdictions during the sporadic bursts of reform since World War II gives us insights into how legislatures change. This chapter reviews four periods of jurisdictional reform: 1946, 1974, 1980, and 1995. The lessons we draw will give little encouragement to the likes of David Dreier and Lee Hamilton, because committee members of both parties close ranks around their panels when their borders are threatened. Furthermore, many highly touted "reforms" have amounted to little more than the writing of common law jurisdictions into the House and Senate rules manuals. Certainly, some jurisdictional changes occasioned during the reforms *have been* significant. The House Commerce Committee lost primary jurisdiction over railroads and nonnuclear energy research and development in 1995. The Merchant Marine and Fisheries Committee, among others, disappeared entirely. Reformers can take some comfort in such victories. I do not want to leave the impression that all jurisdictional reforms are an empty show. Still, as we will see, the overwhelming tendency is for institutional reforms to codify common law claims to turf that build up between the sporadic reforms.

"Reform" seems to imply a plan, a thoughtful way to get from how things are to how things ought to be. Congressional reforms are marked by commissions, special committees, and hoopla. The 1946 Legislative Reorganization Act (LRA) was widely supported in and reported by the news media, and attention focused on congressional reform a generation later through the 1974 Bolling Committee. Likewise the 1995 reforms were front page news and were incorporated into the Republican Contract with America. In all these cases, efficiency experts were called upon to help Congress run more "efficiently" and "effectively."[10]

Perhaps congressional reforms are purposeful and collectively ratified breaks from the past.[11] One interpretation of jurisdictional reforms is that they are occasional but highly significant tools for changing the institution. Call that the "rational problem solving model" in which proposals are carefully planned and collectively ratified. Congressional reform is not necessarily synonymous with change, however, and although reform plans are sometimes passed by the whole House or Senate, institutional change is usually piecemeal and far removed from full floor decisions. Some observers—Representative Dreier's plaudits about the 1995 reforms notwithstanding—have long argued that the rational problem-solving model is unrealistic. "However attractive such an orderly reformation might be, its preconditions—consensus on goals and precise calculations of means-ends relationships—are rarely realizable in real-world situations."[12] Former Oklahoma Senator Mike Monroney has said that "congressional reform is a mosaic of many building blocks rather than a single, spectacular alteration,"[13] and the consummate congressional insider, former Speaker Thomas Reed (R-ME), described reform situations as times when "an indefinable something is to be done, in a way nobody knows how, at a time nobody knows when, that will accomplish nobody knows what."[14]

The truth about what congressional reforms accomplish likely lies someplace between Speaker Reed's characterization and the rational problem-solving model. When legislatures vote on reform proposals, the reforms are indeed well planned and highly publicized events, but what do they really change? Some reforms, like those following the revolt against Speaker Cannon in 1910, are clear and significant breaks from the past, and it is now in fashion to call recent Congresses "post-reform," as if the mid-1970s qualitatively changed the institution. Newt Gingrich's attack on proxy voting in committees has had a dramatic effect on committee attendance and member workloads. What of the landmark 1946 Legislative Reorganization Act, the 1974 Bolling Committee jurisdiction reforms, the 1980 changes in energy jurisdictions, or the modest 1995 changes in jurisdictions? If these are to be our models for how the internal structures of Congress are reformed, what lessons can they teach us?

I will argue that formal rule changes (like the writing of statutory jurisdictions) often *follow* institutional changes (such as common law adaptations in committee turf). If we want to understand change, we should focus not just on "reforms" but on the incremental day-to-day changes in the unwritten rules. Reforms can, indeed, be consequential, and I do not want to argue that they should be ignored. By focusing only on sporadic reforms, however, students of Congress might miss the subtle politics of incrementalism. Former representative Richard Bolling (D-MO) understood the limitations of formal rule changes, calling them "the product of modification, change, and codification."[15] Codification comes last.

1946 LEGISLATIVE REORGANIZATION ACT

World War II Congresses were widely ridiculed for alleged inefficiency, myopia, and (most of all) obstruction of President Roosevelt's war efforts.[16] Congress, designed for a horse-and-buggy age, was said to be unprepared for the blitzkrieg of politics in the 1940s and beyond. Wrote one columnist, "The ignorance and provincialism of Congress render it incapable of meeting the needs of modern government."[17] The popular President Franklin Roosevelt had the upper hand in legislative battles, resorting to veiled threats if Congress failed to pass his bills by set deadlines.[18]

In early 1941, a committee of the American Political Science Association launched a study of congressional mechanisms "seeking to stimulate congressional interest in self-improvement and public interest in legislative reform."[19] Both the Committee on Congress report titled *The Reorganization of Congress,* and *Strengthening the Congress* by the National Planning Association emphasized the need to restructure committee jurisdictions and powers so that Congress could be a more potent check on the executive branch. These reports helped bring about the formation of the Joint Committee on the Organization of Congress in 1945, which was cochaired by Wisconsin Senator Robert La Follette, Jr., and Oklahoma Representative Mike Monroney. Perhaps the most important impact of the APSA committee's report was that it helped launch George Galloway, the report's author, into the position of staff director of Congress's special joint committee on reform.

Galloway, La Follette, and Monroney were the primary architects of the 1946 LRA. Leading their list of objectives were streamlining committee structures, eliminating the use of select committees, and clarifying committee jurisdictions.[20] The reformers were also political operators, and they knew they would have to confront committee chairs who were content with their perks and powers under the status quo. The perks of being a chair were especially valuable; among other things, chairs enjoyed additional staff and an extra office. During the 78th Congress (1943–44), four chairs held onto these resources even though *no* bills were referred to their committees.[21] Further, the reformers had to mollify the House and Senate rules committees, which specifically precluded the Joint Committee from making recommendations that would overturn any of the House or Senate rules.

Given these constraints, the results of the 1946 LRA are impressive. The act reduced the number of standing committees from 33 to 15 in the Senate and from 48 to 19 in the House. Fifty-eight percent of the committees disappeared overnight. For the first time in the history of Congress, committee jurisdictions were carefully delineated in the House and Senate rules.[22] On the face of it, these seem like remarkable achievements. Galloway set the tone for most subsequent commentaries on the act, calling it "the outstanding development in the organization and operation of Congress during the past fifty years."[23] Then again, Galloway had a vested interest in writing a favorable history.

The 1946 LRA passed with the help of committee chairs. Since over half of them were guaranteed to lose their positions, one wonders why committee chairs supported the reforms. The answer is that chairs of inactive committees were assured they would benefit from the increase in staffs even though they would lose their committee staffs, and less senior chairs were promised seats on more prestigious panels.[24] Politically pragmatic deals like these, not a keen eye for the most "efficient" committee structure, drove the consolidation of committees.

To streamline a committee system with 48 committees in the House, reformers began by aiming for committees with 25–27 members each. They wanted to limit almost every member to one committee assignment. The number of postreform committees was simply derived by dividing the number of representatives (435) by the desired size of committees (25) and rounding up, yielding 19.

Starting with 48 committees, there were 1,128 possible pairwise combinations that could have been used to create 19 committees, and the apparent decision rule employed in selecting among all the possible pairwise combinations was to emphasize preform patterns of shared committee memberships, because that is what was politically expedient. It was expedient because committees that shared large numbers of members were, in a sense, already working together, and the prereform committees could be made into postreform subcommittees on a single panel.

The conjecture that prereform intercommittee memberships were central to the postreform structure is tested in table 3.1, where possible pairwise combinations of committees are ranked by the sum of joint memberships. (Two committees each sharing 25 percent of their members would score 50 percent.) Nine committees[25] with nine or fewer members are excluded because their small size would skew the percentages and because eight were combined into the House Administration Committee. This leaves 39 committees, or 741 possible pairwise combinations of prereform panels. For these 39 committees, 44 pairwise combinations were actually used. Of all the possible ways of shoehorning the committees together, 10 of the 15 committees with the highest shared memberships ended up together. That rate is much higher than one would expect by chance ($p = .000454 \times 10^{-6}$).

For a committee system in which most legislators served on only one panel, the results in table 3.1 are striking. Intercommittee memberships drive the results. Sixty percent of the members of the Public Lands Committee also served on the Committee on Irrigation and

Table 3.1 Intercommittee Memberships of House Committees Consolidated by the 1946 Legislative Reorganization Act

Possible Pairwise Combinations	Sum of Joint Membership (%)[a]	Post-Reform Committee
1 Public Lands ↔ Irrigation	117	Interior
2 Mining ↔ Indian Affairs	76	Interior
3 Public Lands ↔ Mining	72	Interior
4 Public Lands ↔ Indian Affairs	70	Interior
5 Public Buildings ↔ Pensions	66	X
6 Irrigation ↔ Insular Affairs	65	Interior
7 Irrigation ↔ Indian Affairs	62	Interior
8 Civil Service ↔ Claims	59	X
9 Flood Control ↔ Roads	58	Public Works
10 Public Buildings ↔ Patents	58	X
11 Claims ↔ Revision of Laws	56	Judiciary
12 Expenditures ↔ Accounts	55	X
13 Irrigation ↔ Mining	53	Interior
14 Civil Service ↔ Census	52	Post Office
15 Rivers ↔ Territories	52	X

[a]This column reports the sum of two percentages: (1) the percentage of Committee A that is also in Committee B, and (2) the percentage of Committee B that is also in Committee A. These two percentages are rarely the same because committee size varies.

Reclamation, and 39 percent of the Public Lands Committee served on Mines and Mining. Likewise 37 percent of the Mines and Mining members served on Indian Affairs, and 30 percent of the Indian Affairs members were on Irrigation. It is no surprise that these committees were bundled together. The postreform committees embraced membership patters found before the reforms, thereby reinforcing coalitions rather than forging new ones.

Committee jurisdictions were not significantly changed by the 1946 LRA. They were *codified,* but they were not significantly changed. Of the 19 postreform committees, 10 were spared being consolidated with other committees, and they were jurisdictionally identical in every way to their prereform counterparts. The remaining nine committees embraced established patterns of jurisdictional coordination. In almost every case, the specific descriptive words used to list committee jurisdictions, though new to the written rules after 1946, were taken *verbatim* from earlier books of precedents compiled by Asher Hinds and Clarence Cannon.

For example, two generations before the 1946 act, the House parliamentarian described the Banking Committee's jurisdiction as (among other things) "public credit, issues of notes and taxation and redemption thereof," "propositions to maintain the parity of the money," and "the issue of silver certificates as currency."[26] It is no wonder, then, that the "new" statutory jurisdiction of the Banking Committee after 1946 included almost identical language. "Money and credit, including the issuance of notes and redemption thereof; gold and silver, including the coinage thereof." That pattern is repeated for every House and Senate committee. This evidence is consistent with George Robinson's observation that "much of the [1946] Act which has been publicized as being completely new is merely a compilation in written form of what the committees had been doing for a long time."[27]

1974 Jurisdictional Reforms

There were plenty of unexpected consequences of the 1946 reforms. By reducing the number of committees, the power of subcommittee chairmanships was increased just when Southern legislators were ascending to the chairs of powerful committees.[28] In the House, the number of subcommittees grew by nearly 50 percent from 1945 to 1975. The explosion of subcommittees in the Senate was even more pronounced, growing 250 percent within 10 years.[29]

By 1965, a new joint committee on congressional reform began extensive studies and hearings aimed at reorganizing the committee system and its jurisdictions. The 1965 reform efforts failed, largely because there was little pressure from outside of Congress to make even cosmetic changes.[30] However, there was some interest, especially among junior members, in realigning committee jurisdictions. Interviews with 118 House members in 1963 and 1964 found 57 percent calling for reformulated committee jurisdictions, though only 14 percent of the members thought that the reforms they had in mind were likely to happen.[31] This pessimism seemed warranted six years later when all attempts at updating the rules on jurisdictions were deleted from the 1970 Legislative Reorganization Act before it passed the House.

Committee reform was on the agenda once again in 1974 in the House of Representatives with the Bolling Committee, the express purpose of which was "a wholesale realignment of jurisdictions and a limitation of one major committee per member."[32] Bolling Committee proposals faced stiff opposition from committee chairs, and almost all of the reform suggestions were defeated in the House Democratic caucus.[33] A second committee, chaired by Washington Democrat Julia Butler Hansen, was established by the Democratic caucus to offer scaled-down alternatives to the Bolling Committee recommendations. The eventual House resolution (no. 988, 93d Congress) primarily reflected the more modest Hansen Committee recommendations and passed the House on October 8, 1974. Although the compromise fell far short of what most reformers wanted, changes were made in the statutory jurisdictions, including:

> Transportation. Most transportation issues were transferred to the Public Works Committee, renamed the Committee on Public Works and Transportation. This included aviation and surface transportation (from Interstate and Foreign Commerce) and mass transit (from the Committee on Banking and Currency).
>
> Health. Interstate and Foreign Commerce was given jurisdiction over "health and health facilities, except health care supported by payroll deductions" (which went to the Ways and Means Committee).
>
> Banking. The Banking and Currency Committee, renamed Banking, Currency and Housing, was given jurisdiction over federal monetary policy, urban development, and international finance, among other issues. The Foreign Affairs committee lost jurisdiction over international monetary organizations.

Like the reforms in 1946, these and other jurisdictional realignments *appear* to have been significant reforms shifting issues from committee to committee and adding otherwise overlooked subjects to committee agendas. The reforms changed the Commerce Committee's statutory jurisdiction by adding four issues and deleting three. The committee gained "consumer affairs and consumer protection," "travel and tourism," "health and health facilities," and "biomedical research and development." Lost to other committees was their jurisdiction over the Weather Bureau, civil aeronautics, and almost all transportation issues except railroads.

Looking just at the *Rules Manual* (recall figure 2.2), Commerce's acquisition of consumer protection issues seems to be an important (though delayed) institutional response to the calls for consumer protection legislation throughout the late 1960s. In fact, though, the Commerce Committee helped define what we mean by "consumer protection" by its actions in the 1960s.[34] Even before consumer protection began to be thought of as a certain cluster of issues, the Commerce Committee won turf wars over health and safety problems. Paired with its statutory jurisdiction covering aviation, the committee regulated food inspections of agricultural products shipped by air in 1954. In 1957, the committee held hearings on seven related bills to "prohibit the use of new chemical food additives without adequate pretesting for safety."[35] The committee began to stake out jurisdiction on the deceptive labeling of automobile stickers a year later.[36] Hearings on the regulation of cigarette advertising were held in 1965, followed by investigations into the safety of children's toys and radiation from household electric devices.[37] Through the active efforts of John Moss (D-CA), the committee received a series of product labeling bills, and by the time "consumer protection" gained its modern meaning, the Commerce Committee had already established a precedential track record on consumer issues. Consumer protection unquestionably became part of House Commerce's turf years before the 1974 reforms. When the Consumer Product Safety Act was introduced in Congress in 1971, the bill was naturally, and without objection, referred to the Commerce Committee—four years before Congress added consumer protection to Commerce's statutory jurisdiction.

On health care issues, the 1974 reforms both solidified the committee's existing jurisdiction over "public health and quarantine" and gave the Commerce new powers that are not traced to previous bill referrals. The "Bolling/Hansen reforms shifted to commerce jurisdiction over those health titles of the Social Security Act not financed by payroll deductions, including Title 5 (Maternal and Child Health), Title 19 (Medicaid), and portions of Title 18 (Part B of Medicare)."[38] In this instance, and at the expense of the Ways and Means Committee, jurisdictional change was nonincremental. Leading up to the 1974 reforms, however, Commerce moved into health issues that were not necessarily implied by the 1946 reforms. The committee was working on a national health insurance program by 1949. By 1957, committee staffers were investigating the quality of instruction at dental schools, an issue that could have been legitimately claimed by the Committee on Education and Labor.[39] The humane treatment of animals used in medical research was the subject of two bills referred to the committee in 1962.[40] And as drug abuse became more acute, the committee claimed new and politically relevant turf by drawing parallels between drug abuse and public health problems.[41] This eventually led to the committee's oversight of several Drug Enforcement Agency programs, a function that might seem more naturally to be Judiciary Committee business.

Travel and tourism issues were codified in the House rules in 1974, but the Commerce Committee reported a bill establishing the U.S. Travel Bureau as early as 1948.[42] The committee also established the Office of International Travel and Tourism in 1960 to encourage foreign tourism in the United States. The Travel Bureau was established within the Department of the Interior, but it was subject to Commerce Committee oversight (not Interior Committee oversight) because of referral precedents. When the Interior Committee received a bill on the Arctic Winter Games in 1972, Chair Wayne Aspinall (D-CO) asked that the issue be rereferred to the Commerce Committee because it involved tourism.

Finally, bills related to biomedical research and development had been referred to both the Commerce and the Science committees, but Commerce was working actively on the issue at the time that the jurisdictional reforms were being contemplated. During September 1974 alone, the Commerce Committee held hearings on eleven bills dealing with biomedical research and development.

In three of the four areas (consumer protection, tourism, and biomedical research) over which the Commerce Committee gained statutory jurisdiction in 1974, common law jurisdictions had already been established. Jurisdiction over health-related issues in the Social Security Act were indeed nonincremental, but they flowed naturally from the committee's long-standing claim to health more generally. For the most part, the Hansen Committee took the path of least resistance, embracing the status quo in the name of reform. However, the Commerce Committee also lost three areas of jurisdiction in 1974. If statutory jurisdictions largely ratify common law jurisdictions, then we would expect to find that Commerce's activity on the issues that were lost, primarily transportation related, diminished significantly from 1947 to 1974.

By 1974 the nation's transportation system went through remarkable changes following World War II. The highway system, sold by President Dwight Eisenhower as a defense program but handled in the House by the Public Works Committee, brought cities closer together and enabled suburban bedroom communities to develop. Mass transit problems followed. The preeminence of rail for passenger and cargo services was challenged, and by the early 1970s railroad companies along the eastern seaboard were filing for bankruptcy. For all practical purposes, Commerce limited its transportation jurisdiction to aviation and rail—leaving almost everything else up for grabs.

Since jurisdictions are usually characterized as well defended, why would the Commerce Committee let others encroach on their transportation turf? Two former staff directors of the committee give the same answers. First, they blame a lack of expertise and interest among committee members. Second, they note that the committee was engaged in turf wars over consumer protection and energy, and it did not have the resources to prosecute three turf wars at once.

In the Commerce Committee's absence, others joined the fray, most notably the Public Works Committee. A scramble for bill referrals throughout the 1950s and 1960s created a fragmented and confusing transportation subsystem. Mass transit, for example, somehow wound up in the Banking Committee. Apparently the logic was that monetary policy directly affects housing, housing affects urban areas, and mass transit serves urban areas—hence, the Banking Committee was entrusted with mass transit. To complicate matters, two other committees held sway over related programs: Public Works controlled mass-transit funds pried loose from the highway trust fund; Commerce handled rail transit as well as transportation research and development.[43]

Transportation is characterized by close relationships between committees and interest groups. Groups interested in transportation policies tend to be particularly insulated from other issue areas, however, which fosters committee-centered myopia.[44] Policy communities forming around transportation are highly fragmented, "with the result that the left hand sometimes does something that profoundly affects the right hand, without anyone ever seeing the implications."[45] A jurisdictional reorganization would seem to have been in order in 1974, and the Commerce Committee willingly relinquished its jurisdictional claim to aviation. It held on, however, to all of its railroad jurisdiction. Commerce Chair Harley Staggers, a Democrat from eastern West Virginia, steadfastly refused to give up rail issues. His district was coal country, and the rails were its main arteries.[46] (Commerce eventually relinquished its railroad turf in 1995.) Nonetheless, in 1974, the committee gave up jurisdiction over aviation and ICC regulations concerning trucks and buses.

It is not entirely clear why Commerce handed away most of its transportation turf in 1974. For the most part, it seems, members lost interest, and they were willing to give the jurisdiction away to promote the appearance of reform. Around the mid-1950s, Commerce Committee members simply stopped paying much attention to many transportation issues. In reading transcripts from that decade, one sees attendance at transportation hearings dramatically lower than for other issues. And as committee staffers were removed from transportation issues, the number of hearings dropped as well. Right after the 1946 Act, about a quarter of the committee's attention went to transportation (primarily aviation). The committee oversaw the development of a national system of airports, and it held investigations into accidents. Consuming a quarter of the committee's time in hearings, committee staffers in the 80th and 81st Congresses devoted a great deal of attention to transportation. By 1974, committee activity on transportation dropped below 5 percent. Of that 5 percent, all of the activity was on the routine business of overseeing and maintaining long-established airports. The Commerce Committee was no longer sponsoring new transportation projects. Removing "transportation policy" from the committee's statutory jurisdiction was no great loss because they had let the turf lay fallow for years.

While Commerce largely ignored transportation issues throughout the 1960s and early 1970s, Public Works was increasingly active, in part because it oversaw the Highway Trust Fund and could pay for new programs out of its own committee. In a novel attempt at justifying taking over some of Commerce's aviation turf in the 1960s, Public Works members argued that their committee should oversee airport runways. After all, Public Works already maintained the nation's highway system, and runways are little more than highways for airplanes. The argument worked. When the 1974 reforms were codified, many of the jurisdictional changes in transportation that had been underway since the end of World War II were simply written into the rules.

1980 Energy Jurisdiction Reforms

By now one can guess what happened in 1980 when the House passed a reform proposal originally intended to focus energy issues in one committee. Like the others, this round of statutory changes largely updated the rules and locked in common law turf that had been taken during the 1970s. The jurisdictional tangle on energy issues seemed especially acute in the late 1970s as the country faced its second energy crisis in the decade.[47] One report decried the consequences of common law jurisdictional expansions, noting:

> The present operational structure in Congress for energy jurisdiction is fragmented among numerous committees. It is now as much a product of legislation initiated by a particular committee or assigned to it by the Parliamentarian as it is the result of carefully circumscribed rules and procedures.[48]

The fragmentation of energy issues among panels was no accident. It came from policy entrepreneurs playing the jurisdiction game, and John Dingell proved a master strategist. Witness the following exchange from an interview with one of Dingell's former staff directors:

> *Staff Director:* One thing few people realize is that we never had jurisdiction over energy. Never. Because nobody had jurisdiction over energy. Until 1970, energy costs were so small that they didn't enter into most people's budgets. Think about it. I guess the first energy legislation, um.

> *Author:* You could have made a claim that you had the Federal Power Act. You had a couple of small things.

> *S.D.:* Right. But we never did anything with them. We had the Federal Power Act only because we had the FTC. The Federal Power Act actually didn't come out of our committee. We amended it . . .

> *Author:* These ideas—Energy, Trade, Insurance—where are they coming from? Are they coming from a member who said . . .

> *S.D.:* The power stuff came from Dingell. It was his idea. You gotta remember that [the] Energy and Power [subcommittee] was set up at the time of the first energy crunch. And because we had the Natural Gas Policy Act—I believe we handled that in the 1930s—and because gas is clearly in interstate commerce, we just expanded it to all forms of energy. Dingell then created that jurisdiction out of whole cloth.

It was that fabric of referral precedents that the 1980 reforms threatened. After several years of what Eric Uslaner calls "jungle warfare over jurisdictions," two reform proposals, one by the House Select Committee on committees and another last-minute substitute by the Select Committee's Chair Jerry Patterson (D-CA), were aimed at creating a new Energy Committee and taking all energy issues away from Commerce, Interior, and Public Works.

John Dingell, on the verge of becoming the Commerce Committee's chair, led the other committee chairs in a floor fight against the Select Committee proposal, which would have stripped Dingell's Energy and

Power Subcommittee of much of its jurisdiction and given it to a new and separate energy committee. An alternative proposal was offered, solidifying Commerce as the panel with principal jurisdiction over national energy policy. Dingell won; the real battle over energy jurisdiction, however, did not happen between Dingell and the 1980 Select Committee. Rather, Commerce gained important parts of the energy turf during the mid to late 1970s. From his newly created Subcommittee on Energy and Power,[49] John Dingell managed during the late 1970s to gain jurisdiction over a wide variety of jurisdictionally ambiguous energy issues, like conservation and a "national" energy policy. Though the Commerce Committee had done little to expand its energy jurisdiction before 1974, that was certainly not true of other committees. The mid-1970s witnessed a large-scale energy turf war among a half-dozen House committees.

Figure 3.1 shows the Commerce Committee's hearing activity on energy issues that were granted to the committee in the 1980 reforms. In the year before the reforms, more than 18 percent of the committee's efforts were on energy issues not yet formally granted to them in the rules. From the time John Dingell's Subcommittee on Energy and Power was created in 1975, the committee sought to establish binding referral precedents over otherwise unclaimed energy turf.[50]

With a subcommittee in place, hearings on proposed oil import taxes were held, followed quickly by investigations into synthetic liquid fuels, solar energy, and energy from helium. Soon John Dingell's subcommittee began publishing a biennial compilation of energy related acts within its jurisdiction. Dingell also hosted widely publicized

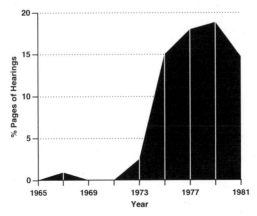

Figure 3.1 Commerce Activity on Energy Issues That Were Granted Jurisdiction in the 1980 Reforms

hearings outlining a national energy strategy, hearings that were so extensive they filled eight large volumes. In 1977 Commerce reported a bill creating the Department of Energy, the future oversight of which firmly established the Commerce Committee as a major player in all energy legislation. Dingell's success, however, by no means settled the issue. Other committees spent the mid-1970s carving out their little pieces of energy turf, though every other committee's accomplishments were swamped by the accomplishments at Commerce. The 1980 reforms actually wrote into the rules a complex pattern of fragmentation, as substantial energy prerogatives remained with other panels. As with the earlier reforms, the Commerce Committee's common law jurisdiction expanded before its statutory jurisdiction was recast. Eric Uslaner aptly called the 1980 jurisdictional changes "Deja Vu" reforms, "a reinforcing of the status quo in the name of reform."[51]

1995 REFORMS

Promising to do more than reinforce the status quo in the name of reform, Newt Gingrich and the Republicans took control of the House following the November 1994 elections. Indeed, Republicans had been chafing under the old status quo for 40 years, and their frustration spilled out in hearings before the 1993 Joint Committee on the Organization of Congress. The Joint Committee was charged with conducting a comprehensive study of House rules and procedures, and extensive hearings were held.[52] Jurisdictional reforms were pushed by minority party members (chief among them David Drier of California) partly because they highlighted the Democratic leadership's reluctance to touch turf issues. As Evans and Oleszek explain, "[R]aising committee jurisdictions as a reform issue allowed House Republicans to publicly criticize the Democratic leadership for impeding reform, with little risk to the prerogatives of Republican committee leaders."[53] The Joint Committee's recommendations were considered by the Rules Committee in 1994, but its package failed to make it to the House or Senate floor.

By the early 1990s, jurisdictions seemed ripe for reform. A handful of committees did most of the work on most of the bills, with Commerce and Ways and Means leading the way. "Rather than having two or three omnipotent committees," argued Dreier, "I think that we should have 10 or 11 very important committees."[54] Fully 40 percent of the House's legislative business went through the Commerce Committee, much of that multiply referred with other panels. Multiple referrals encouraged committees to be especially protective of their turf, which accentuated already-worsening fragmentation. In 1994 there were 266 committees and subcommittees between the House and Senate combined. There were 107 of those panels which claimed some jurisdiction over the Pentagon; 90 claimed jurisdiction over the Environmental Protection Agency, and 52 claimed some authority over programs dealing with families and children.[55] Such examples of alleged Democratic mismanagement hit a responsive chord among Republican voters.

While Representative Dreier failed to find a friendly audience with the Democratic leadership, he turned his attention to Newt Gingrich's emerging "Contract with America." Dreier proposed making jurisdictional reforms part of the rules changes promised for the first day of the next Congress, but Gingrich balked. One Republican staffer recalled, "From the beginning, Newt didn't want to do jurisdictions and I think he was right . . . He wanted unanimous Republican support for everything on the opening day reforms and a dirty fight within the transition would mess that up."[56] However, after the surprising November elections, Dreier persisted, proposing that the transition team consider four specific jurisdictional proposals. A November 16 meeting "produced an explosion of jurisdictional infighting within the Republican conference." This persisted until a compromise plan was announced on December 2, 1994.[57]

Representative Dreier's November blueprint and the December compromise are summarized in table 3.2. The original proposal would have abolished five committees, among them Post Office and Civil Service, Small Business, Standards of Official Conduct, Merchant Marine and Fisheries, and Veterans Affairs. As we saw in the 1946 reorganization act, abolishing committees does little to change jurisdictions if the committees simply become subcommittees of other panels. Beyond slashing committees, however, Dreier pushed substantial turf realignments. The Agriculture Committee would lose its hold over food stamps; Ways and Means would say farewell to Welfare and Medicare. Economic and Educational Opportunities (formerly Education and Labor) would gain tremendous authority, including housing subsidies, Aid to Families with Dependent Children, and drug abuse programs. The Resources Committee would also gain, becoming the lead panel on all environmental issues. The biggest loser, by far, was Dingell's old Energy and Commerce Committee, which stood to see its powers stripped of all energy and environmental policies as well as railroads and securities regulations.

From mid to late November, committee members of both parties closed ranks against Dreier's proposal. Some chairs had been waiting patiently for their turn at the gavel for two decades, and they invested

Table 3.2 Jurisdictional Changes in the 1995 House Rules

Committee	Original Reform Proposal	Reform That Passed
Agriculture	− Nutrition and Food Stamps	+ Food Inspections (from Commerce)
Banking and Financial Services	− Housing Subsidies + Securities Regulations + Small Business Committee	+ Primary Jurisdiction over Securities Sold by Banks (from Commerce)
Commerce	+ Medicare − Securities Regulations − Railroads and Railway Labor − All Energy Policies − All Environmental Policies	+ Sole Telecommunications Turf (at Judiciary's expense) − Securities Sold by Banks − Food Inspections − Railroad and Railway Labor − Nonnuclear Energy R&D − Trans-Alaska Pipeline − Inland Waterways
Economic and Educational Opportunities	+ Nutrition and Food Stamps + Housing Subsidies + Welfare + Drug Abuse and Rehabilitation	No Turf Change
Government Reform and Oversight	+ P.O. and Civil Service Committee + D.C. Committee	+ P.O. and Civil Service Committee + D.C. Committee
House Oversight	+ Standards of Official Conduct Committee − Campaign Finance Oversight	Administrative Duties Reduced
National Security	+ Merchant Marine	+ Merchant Marine (from old committee)
Resources	+ Primary Environment Turf + Fisheries and Wildlife − Some Energy Issues	+ Fisheries and Wildlife (from Merchant Marine) + Endangered Species (from Merchant Marine) + Trans-Atlantic Pipeline (from Commerce)
Science	+ Energy	+ Nonnuclear Energy R&D (from Commerce)
Small Business	Abolished	No Turf Change
Standards of Official Conduct	Abolished	No Turf Change

continued

Table 3.2 *continued*

Committee	Original Reform Proposal	Reform That Passed
Transportation and Infrastructure	+ Coast Guard + Railroads and Railway Labor − Water Pollution	+ Coast Guard (from Merchant Marine) + Railroads and Railway Labor (from Commerce) + Inland Waterways (from Commerce)
Ways and Means	− Welfare − Medicare	No Turf Change

years studying the issues in their committee's purview. Committee loyalties outweighed devotion to the abstract notion of reform. Thomas Bliley (R-VA), the presumptive chair of House Commerce, was especially energetic in protecting his committee even though Gingrich personally asked him to relinquish some turf.[58] As Schickler and Rich argue, "[T]he reason that partisan coalitions have put through few major revisions in committee jurisdictions may well be that membership on committees creates a source of cross-cutting cleavages that is generally viewed as a legitimate basis for opposing party leaders." Time and again, party proposals to change jurisdictions have been defeated, and Dreier's original plan soon followed course. Roger Davidson explains,

> Those who expect to lose power are invariably more vocal than those who stand to gain. Domains of the powerhouse committees are still hard to breach. Even members who had yet to wield a gavel resisted surrendering their hoped-for patrimony. Carving up powerhouse committees like Energy and Commerce or Ways and Means seemed an urgent priority when they were chaired by the likes of Democrats John Dingell (Mich.) or Dan Rostenkowski (Ill.); but when the chairs were Republicans Thomas Bliley (Va.) and Bill Archer (Texas), the script quickly changed. In the end, little damage was done to the former committee, and none at all to the latter.[59]

When the Republican transition team settled on their final proposal, reformers put a good face on the results. "We have come up with a bold and dynamic reform proposal, the greatest in half a century," said Dreier. "It will go a long way towards addressing the concerns of the American people and making this institution more accountable and deliberative."[60] The jurisdictional coup that received the most attention was the alleged undoing of House Commerce. Gone from its domain were food inspections (to Agriculture), railroads, railway labor,

and inland waterways (to Transportation and Infrastructure), the
Trans-Alaska Pipeline (to Resources),[61] nonnuclear energy research
and development (to Science), and primary jurisdiction over securities
sold by banks (to Banking and Financial Services). Dreier proudly announced that, although he hoped to axe a third of Commerce's jurisdiction, Republicans succeeded in cutting the committee's turf by at least
a fifth. "On balance," said Dreier, "20 percent of the jurisdiction that
the Commerce Committee had has been shifted to other areas. I think that
in itself is monumental."[62] Soon this figure, 20 percent, was recounted
in story after story as evidence of a dramatic change on Capitol Hill.[63]
With the Commerce Committee's turf diminished, Representative
Dreier bubbled (prematurely), "[T]urf battles have come to an end."[64]

Of course, turf battles did not come to an end, which is why Dreier
began conceiving yet another reform panel by the summer of 1995.
Statements to the contrary were just for public consumption, as was the
widely reported 20 percent jurisdiction loss by the Commerce Committee. Publicly, Thomas Bliley seems happy to perpetuate the 20 percent
myth, apparently hoping that the myth will help protect his committee
from the next round of reforms. Privately, Commerce Committee
staffers are very pleased with how little turf their panel actually lost in
1995. If we measure a committee's activity by looking at public hearings, the Commerce Committee lost slightly less than 5 percent of its
turf, not 20 percent. Figure 3.2 shows committee activities broken
down by issues lost in the reforms.

Railroads comprised the largest swath of territory yielded by Com-

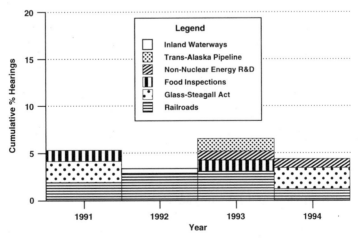

Figure 3.2 Commerce Committee Activity on Issues Lost in 1995 Reform

merce, but the committee was relatively quick to yield it, even though Chairman Bliley had a large CRX terminal in his Virginia district. The Transportation Committee had been coveting railroads for years, and except for magnetically levitated trains (discussed in Chapter 6), Commerce had done very little with the issue. Rather, Commerce Committee members loathed the almost annual railway labor disputes. One member called railway labor "a major headache" that "transportation can enjoy."[65] It is worth remembering that Commerce held onto railroads in 1974 because of strong lobbying by Chairman Harley Staggers whose West Virginia district depended on rails to export coal. There was no similar constituent for rail on Commerce by the early 1990s.

Energy was another matter entirely. With its own subcommittee and an extensive staff built around the issue, Dreier's proposal to strip Commerce of energy set off alarms in the entire energy community. The Science Committee had been engaged in turf wars over "industrial competitiveness," and some of those battles involved energy research and development, but even in Chairman Robert Walker's (R-PA) wildest dreams, he did not imagine getting all of the jurisdiction that Dreier offered. Science did not have an established track record of expertise on energy issues (unlike the record Transportation had on railroads), and by the end of November, Dreier's proposal was scaled down to include nonnuclear energy research and development. As we saw in figure 3.2, less than 1 percent of Commerce's activities have been on energy research and development in the 1990s. Former Energy and Power Subcommittee Chairman Phil Sharp (D-IN) called the reorganization plans "insignificant,"[66] though in a show of reform the committee's name was shortened from "Energy and Commerce" to simply "Commerce."

The theory detailed in Chapter 1 focuses on common law changes in turf, and I argue that the House parliamentarian adjudicated jurisdictional disputes in ways that enhance the informational efficiency of the committee system. Can the same be said when the whole house arbitrates jurisdictional disputes, as it did when the 1995 reforms were ratified? Here the evidence is mixed, though one finds clear markings of distributive politics. Take, as examples, food inspections and the Trans-Alaska Pipeline.

Food inspections, in Commerce's common law domain for nearly a century, were claimed by the Agriculture Committee. Although Commerce had established expertise in consumer protection, one could argue that Agriculture Committee members might be better versed in the intricacies of agricultural inspections. Then again, Agriculture Committee members would likely have the most to gain from relaxed inspections—creating a clear distributive incentive to raid the Commerce Committee's turf. In January 1995, the average Agriculture Committee member came from a district that was 40.1 percent rural. Among Republicans, the average Commerce member's district was 29.6 percent rural, a substantively and statistically significant difference of means ($p = 0.047$). In all likelihood, the 1995 reforms strengthened the distributive benefits that Agriculture Committee members can provide their members.

Likewise, the Commerce Committee's loss of control over the Trans-Alaska Pipeline can be attributed to distributive pressures. In this case, Don Young, an Alaska Republican and chairman of the Resources Committee, heavily lobbied David Dreier's reform group to give him the pipeline. It wasn't that the Resources Committee had substantial expertise handling pipeline issues. Chairman Young wanted the turf as part of a broader plan to relax environmental regulations restricting oil exploration and export. The original Dreier proposal slated the Resources Committee to receive all of Commerce's environmental jurisdiction. It is instructive that the only portion yielded was one Chairman Young found useful politically.

The critical distinction to consider between the 1995 reforms and more gradual common law changes is that the players are different. Committee chairs and floor majorities decide statutory changes—and they can be enticed by the allure of distributive politics. Not so with the parliamentarians.

While members of the Commerce Committee were publicly lamenting a "twenty percent" loss in turf, Jack Fields, chairman of Commerce's Telecommunications and Finance Subcommittee was quietly rejoicing. Before 1995, Commerce shared telecommunications bills with other panels, most often the Judiciary Committee. With the demise of multiple referrals, however, Commerce gained status as the lead committee on all telecommunications issues, thereby enhancing the committee's ability to tackle telephone deregulation in the 104th Congress.[67]

On paper at least, the most important jurisdictional loss suffered by Commerce in 1995 was in its authority over what securities banks can sell. This has been regulated under the Glass-Steagall Act, with shared jurisdiction between Commerce and Banking. Dreier's original proposal would have stripped Commerce of all securities oversight, including being a watchdog for the Securities and Exchanges Commission. The final compromise made Banking the lead committee on Glass-Steagall, but Commerce has been promised a sequential referral, so it is not out of the game entirely.[68] The Commerce Committee had been a dungeon, of sorts, for banking reform bills ("'Every time banking bills were referred to Commerce, they died courtesy of John Dingell,' a lobbyist said"),[69] and this points to a shortcoming with the way we have measured committee activities in this chapter. A committee's power comes not just from what it chooses to do in hearings but in what it does not to do. Committee *inactivity,* when it is strategically aimed, can have as many policy consequences as committee *activity.* It is too early to tell just how much Commerce's grip on banking reform has been relaxed. Of this we can be certain, though: if Chairman Bliley pursues jurisdictionally ambiguous issues related to the U.S. banking system, his committee remains well positioned to chip away at the issue. The 1995 reforms did not settle this once and for all. Jurisdictional reforms rarely do, as long as committee entrepreneurs can conceive of ways to link established turf to ambiguous issues.

Reform is not synonymous with change. Our focus should not be on the temporary floor majorities mustered to pass public proposals. Rather, jurisdictional change happens through bill referrals, and our attention should be on policy entrepreneurs and the parliamentarians. With clever bill drafting and incremental moves into new territories, the nature of congressional committee jurisdictions is lively indeed. Jurisdictional fragmentation is a direct result of so many committees trying to stake out claims to pieces of larger issues—like the environment and health care. Devoid of common law jurisdictions and the politics of bill referrals, no static notions about Congress can account for the ongoing turf wars being waged—today—on Capitol Hill.

I do not know how common it is for political institutions to go through procedural reforms only to codify incremental and longstanding changes. It happens in the U.S. Congress, and I suspect it happens in every majority rule institution. Because it takes a majority to update the written rules of most political bodies, the easiest thing to agree on is to embrace the status quo, even though the status quo is itself not stable. *It does not take an act of Congress to change the status quo.* That happens every time written rules are reinterpreted, every time behavior is modified, and every time a precedent is set. We need to pay more attention to how and why these things are done.

FOUR

Parliamentarians as Institutional Guardians

When William Brown stepped down as the House of Representative's head parliamentarian in September 1994, he was only the second person to hold that post since 1928. Over 67 years, 13 Speakers, and several changes in party control, the House employed just two chief parliamentarians. On the Senate side, generations of stability in the parliamentarian's office were disrupted in the early 1980s because some rulings were seen favoring one party over the other. It was a lesson not lost on anyone, especially in the House. A parliamentarian's legitimacy comes from placing the interests of the Congress above the interests of a party.

The parliamentarians have figured prominently in previous chapters because they have been imbued with something akin to guardianship over rules and precedents. This chapter focuses more directly on the causes and consequences of this guardianship. Why, for example, would legislatures delegate some politically important decisions to unelected clerks? As we have seen, policy entrepreneurs try shaping jurisdictions to advance their interests. Constituent demands, ideologies, and personal backgrounds motivate them, but the interests motivating parliamentarians are fundamentally different. Although the parliamentarians do not use this language, they act as if they are constrained not by the Speaker or the majority party but by the sense of the House's median voter. Parliamentarians have acquired rights whose exercise minimizes the damage policy entrepreneurs would otherwise inflict on the committee system. Further, jurisdictional contests tend to be decided in ways that enhance the informational efficiency of the committee system.

An idealized committee system is a collective good; everyone benefits from the division of labor, expertise, and deference that comprise legislatures. Like all idealized collective goods, committee systems are difficult to maintain because legislators quickly find it in their interests to exploit the situation to their own benefit, at the expense of others. In theory, at least, committee systems almost inevitably fall far short of their ideal form. It is a classic collective goods problem.

Students of Congress have tried to solve this problem in two ways. The first is by specifying a set of institutional devices (such as autonomous committees with fixed jurisdictions) that help protect the system from devolving into "chaos."[1] The literature in this tradition has provided valuable insights into how a legislature's rules and committees—when they are in equilibrium—keep chaos at bay. The choices of institutional rules themselves, however, also devolve into a collective action problem that needs to be solved.[2]

The second approach endows a subset of elected officials (like the House Speaker and minority leader) with motives to look out for the Congress's collective interests.[3] Legislative leaders then use threats and incentives to entice back benchers not to pursue personal interests at the expense of everyone else. There is one significant weakness in this approach, however. The motivation to defect is linked to electoral incentives; since leaders are themselves elected, they must certainly fall prey to selfish pressures to pursue their individual interests as well. Who looks out for Congress as a whole?

Legislatures are not alone in facing collective action dilemmas, yet many organizations find ways to solve them. Individuals are increasingly likely to solve collective action dilemmas if they confront the same problems repeatedly.[4] Over time, one should not be surprised to see people within organizations developing ways of coping with collective action problems. Such solutions need not rely on altruistic individuals. Rather, they may grow out of a sometimes selfish search for collective benefits.[5] I argue that in the House of Representatives (and in many state legislatures) the search for an institutional guardian led to the parliamentarians' office. Evidence is drawn from the history of how bills have been referred to committees. In short, parliamentarians adjudicate border disputes because members cannot trust themselves to do it alone. The House parliamentarians transcend elections, helping to maintain institutional integrity.

This chapter has two sections. First, the House parliamentarians are described as neutral arbiters of jurisdictional disputes. Although these guardians are agents of the Speaker, who is an agent of the majority party, the Speaker abides by advice from the parliamentarians when turf wars arise. Second, a history of the bill referral process is discussed in the context of the theory I sketched in Chapter 1. The parliamentarians have been central to jurisdictional disputes since (roughly) 1910. The House used various other arbiters before that, but none could protect the collective goods aspects of the committee system. Until 1889, floor majorities arbitrated jurisdictional disputes, but leaving the decisions up to the whole House lead to chaos and deadlock. House Speakers controlled jurisdictions from 1890 through 1910. This strengthened the Speakers, but the whole House was less likely to pass the bills that came out of the highly partisan committees. Today, although the House rules say that the Speaker refers bills, the Speaker's referrals are overwhelmingly guided (and usually written) by the parliamentarian. Following the revolt against Cannon in 1910 (and the brief "King Caucus" period of the early 1910s), jurisdictional arbitration was largely taken out of partisan hands and given to the parliamentarian, who uses nonpartisan decision rules that reward jurisdictionally proximate committees.

The Parliamentarians

The House parliamentarians are long-serving employees, trained in the country's top law schools, and unelected either by voters or by legislators. The parliamentarian sits at the right hand of the Speaker when the House is in session, in full view of the C-SPAN cameras yet virtually invisible to most Americans. Charles Johnson explains that the parliamentarians

> must be attorneys licensed by a state or district of the United States; experience is the only other qualification. Parliamentarians must be nonpartisan, even though appointed by the Speaker, because they serve him in his administrative capacity as presiding officer, not as party leader. They give impartial advice to all Members and staff on the rules and procedures of the House of Representatives, and are involved in virtually every stage of the legislative process, primarily by advising the Speaker and assuming the authority he delegates to them . . . The Speaker must be completely nonpartisan when determining committee jurisdiction and ruling on points of order. He relies on the advice of the parliamentarian, who must always be perceived as nonpartisan.[6]

Though parliamentarians ostensibly serve "at the pleasure of the Speaker,"[7] Lewis Deschler, House parliamentarian from 1928 through 1974, worked for nine Speakers, both Democrats and Republicans. The current structure of the office finds one head parliamentarian (Charles Johnson who took over when William Brown retired), two deputy parliamentarians, and two assistant parliamentarians. When sitting together in a room, the parliamentarians look like several generations of a family. There is the grandfather figure, long steeped in the ways of the House. There is the middle-aged uncle, preparing to take over the family business when the old man passes on. And there are the younger members of the clan, both male and female, taking notes and eagerly learning the family trade.

In the House, William Brown worked with Lew Deschler for 16 years before becoming the head parliamentarian in 1974, a position he held for two decades. Deschler's "master plan"[8] was to cultivate future parliamentarians through years of apprenticeship, inculcating them with respect for the institution and its rules.

Political scientists do not know much about the parliamentarians, and it seems odd for us to imagine that there could be essentially impartial guardians at the heart of a political institution. In her studies of the House leadership, Barbara Sinclair briefly discusses the parliamentarians, taking the position that they are under the Speaker's control. "The parliamentarians," writes Sinclair, "owe their first duty to the Speaker; their job is to help him accomplish his aims within the rules. Since the House rules are immensely complicated, the Speaker's access to the parliamentarians' expertise becomes itself an important resource."[9] (In fact, every legislator has access to the parliamentarian's expertise.) Sinclair implies that the parliamentarians slant interpretations of the rules for political purposes.

This description (and Professor Sinclair is certainly not alone among political scientists)[10] does not square with reports from staffers, lobbyists, and legislators. Pure measures of impartiality are difficult to come by, but there is an overwhelming bipartisan consensus that the parliamentarians abide by nonpartisan decision rules. One staff director of a prominent committee told me that "the parliamentarian has a constituency of one." Expecting a comparison with the president's chief of staff, I anticipated the answer. "The Speaker?" I asked. "No," he replied, "the parliamentarian's constituency is the House."

That statement sounds like hyperbole—and maybe it is. Sometimes the parliamentarians can be useful shields for the Speaker to stay out of bitter battles that jurisdictional power plays elicit. A former assistant parliamentarian described it this way: "Think about people like Dingell and Rostenkowski. When they're fighting over jurisdiction, they're standing toe-to-toe pissing on each other. Frankly, the speaker doesn't want to be in the middle of that."

"We are technicians, not politicians," reports an assistant parliamentarian. "We take pride in our office being out of the partisan fight . . . [and] if we're ever seen as partisan, particularly by the minority party,

our place here [in the House] would disappear." Another parliamentarian consistently used the language I have adopted in this chapter. "We
are guardians. Absolutely, we think of ourselves as guardians." Narrowly cast, they record and guard legislative rules and precedents. It is
in that sense that they think of themselves as stewards of a public trust.
In a broader sense, however, the parliamentarians guard the institutional integrity of the legislature itself.

The House is not alone. Every state legislature has a group of long-
serving assistants overseeing rules and precedents, though jurisdictional disputes—at the state level—are more often directly handled by
the Speakers.[11] While we know little about the national parliamentarians, we know even less about state legislative clerks. They deserve a
closer look. In Minnesota, for example, Edward Burdick has been a
fixture in the state House since 1941, and he has served as chief clerk
(the equivalent of the head parliamentarian) for more than 30 years.
Steadfastly nonpartisan, Burdick has worked for Democrats and Republicans. Everyone in the Minnesota clerk's office is elected by the
whole House, not by the majority party caucus.[12] Similarly, in Texas,
Bob Johnson served as parliamentarian of the state House from 1963
to 1980 and as parliamentarian of the Texas Senate from 1991 until his
death in 1995. Even among members of the minority party, Johnson
was hailed as "always honest, straightforward, and as helpful to the
forces for reform as to those in control."[13] Burdick and Johnson are not
rare creatures in American legislatures. Not at all; most state legislatures have people like them, widely considered "above partisan
politics." There is even a national organization, the Association of Legislative Clerks and Secretaries, that hosts conferences on parliamentary procedure and nonpartisanship. Such is the legacy of "institutional
guardians" that political scientists are just beginning to explore. As in
Minnesota, many state parliamentarians are elected by the whole legislature, making the floor's median voter—not a single party's faction—
critical.

In background interviews for this book, Democrats and Republicans alike called the House parliamentarian "the image of Congress"
and "the embodiment of the House." Again, it may be that such statements are little more than rhetorical flourish, and there were occasional members who complained about the parliamentarians. The
handful of criticisms were just as likely to come from Democrats as Republicans, and slightly more likely from women who see the guardians
as "typical old boys." If there is any received wisdom about them
among political scientists, it tends to be of the sort that Professor Sinclair reveals. Perhaps parliamentarians (and their counterparts in state

legislatures) are indeed instruments of the Speaker and the majority party. Certainly the parliamentarians are in close communication with the Speaker about points of order and other important elements of floor business. They also make first drafts of Rules Committee rules, which often keep the minority party from offering floor amendments. Still, the overwhelming sense among legislators and staffers is that the parliamentarians "play it straight."

Assume, for a moment, that the House parliamentarian's job *is* partisan. Interpreting points of order and adjudicating turf wars to benefit the Speaker, the minority party would seethe with frustration. They would inveigh against partisan rulings, plotting to overthrow the parliamentarian upon becoming the majority party. Something similar has happened in the U.S. Senate with every change in partisan control since 1980.[14] That is the scenario that might have played out in the House in January 1995, but it did not happen. Charles Johnson ascended to the head parliamentarian's office the previous September, after being an understudy for nearly 30 years—all under Democratic speakerships.

Newt Gingrich and his Republican transition team, headed by Jim Nussle (R-IA), promised wholesale staff changes. The nonpartisan House administrator was sent packing, as were the clerk of the house, the sergeant at arms, the doorkeeper, the head of the food service, the house postmaster, and employees in more than a dozen smaller posts. Even the little known and strictly nonpartisan House historian, Raymond Smock, was replaced with Gingrich friend and nonhistorian Christina Jeffrey.[15] If there was ever a time to sack a partisan parliamentarian, it came and went in early 1995. For a while, Gingrich toyed with giving the job to William R. Pitts, Jr., a well-respected aide to outgoing minority leader Robert Michel (R-IL). As *Roll Call* reported, "[T]he downside to naming Pitts is that Democrats might interpret the move as an attempt to politicize a nonpartisan slot."[16] Pitts took a private lobbying position instead, and Gingrich reaffirmed his faith in Charles Johnson. That move, notes *CQ Weekly Report*, "maintains a tradition of nonpartisanship in the post."[17]

When Democrat John Nance Garner (Texas) took over as Speaker from Republican Nicholas Longworth (Ohio) in 1931, partisans called for Lew Deschler's head. Deschler, a Republican, had been appointed by Republicans, but "his knowledge of the House's complex procedural rules was so extensive and his loyalty so unquestioned that he was kept on as parliamentarian by succeeding Speakers until his retirement in 1975." Sam Rayburn (D-TX) became Speaker sixteen years later, and "Garner's first advice was to retain Deschler and keep him by his side at all times. . . . It was perhaps the best advice Rayburn ever got from the old warrior."[18]

The parliamentarians shun the spotlight, sometimes even declining to be photographed for newspaper and magazine articles about Congress.[19] In interviews for this book, the House parliamentarians emphasized the hands-off nature taken by Speakers. "On jurisdictions," said one parliamentarian, "all the speakers have given our office absolute discretion to decide referrals. All the speakers believe that the referral process should not be politicized."[20] In William Brown's letter announcing his retirement, he reflected on the staff of parliamentarians he was leaving behind: "Each is dedicated to the proposition that the rules of this great institution should be applied and enforced without political considerations."[21] However, we would *expect* the parliamentarians to say that. Impartiality is the basis of their legitimacy.

In interviews with majority and minority party committee staffers and with lobbyists playing the jurisdiction game, the impartiality of the parliamentarians was routinely cited as fact, not fiction. One minority staffer on the Rules Committee who regularly interacts with the parliamentarians said that "sometimes you get a little hint that they're being reined in by the speaker, but *not on bill referrals.* They're straight about that." A former assistant parliamentarian who was hired by the Democratic leadership to "try to mix together policies and procedures" also said that the parliamentarians are surprisingly protected from partisan bickering and from majority party control. There are limits, though. "Even the parliamentarians," he said, "have to be careful, frankly, that they don't piss off the leadership too much by giving advice that's totally contrary to where the leadership wants to go. There is some politics mixed in, but they would never admit it. But if you want to know, does anyone tell the parliamentarians what to do or how to refer bills? Absolutely not. No."[22]

The parliamentarians are rarely mentioned by name on the House floor, but Robert Michel (R-IL), then the minority leader, and Speaker Foley rose to honor William Brown when he retired in 1994. Said Foley, "[I]f I had any tendency to veer from [fairness and objectivity], I would find resistance—very strong resistance—from the Parliamentarians of the House, who are committed in an almost religious sense to ensuring that the rules are absolutely impartially observed here."[23] Similarly, on the occasion of Lewis Deschler's thirty-fifth year as parliamentarian in 1963, House Speaker John McCormack (D-MA) praised Deschler for his "nonpartisan impartiality," and Hale Boggs, the majority whip from Louisiana, added that "no one ever questions his impartiality . . . no one ever questions the fairness or objectivity of Lew Deschler."[24] Then again, McCormack and Boggs were majority party leaders and may have had a stake in perpetuating this image of the impartial parliamentarian. A tougher test is to see what the minority party has said about the parliamentarians.

Charles Halleck, the Republican minority leader in 1963, summarized the collective action problem we addressed in Chapter 1 and also noted the parliamentarians' role as an institutional guardian:

> Obviously, without [the rules], we never would get anything done around here. Sometimes I think it is a miracle that we accomplish what we do even with the rules to keep us in line with proper procedure. Certainly one of the reasons is because we have a parliamentarian who, throughout his career, has shown a capacity for *a completely fair application* of those rules . . . I say without equivocation that never have I known Lew Deschler's advice, his judgment or his decisions to be influenced by any partisan considerations whatsoever.[25]

It stands to reason that the parliamentarian's office would not receive such praise from the minority party if the parliamentarian were simply a partisan tool for the Speaker. Joseph Martin, who served as Speaker when the Republicans briefly controlled the House in the early 1950s, also held up the parliamentarian's office as an example of the House "rising above itself" in the form of an institutional guardian who "loves this House" and is "a stalwart defender of its privileges, its rules and its dignity."[26]

The House parliamentarians—and their state counterparts—did not emerge as jurisdictional arbiters by accident. As discussed in Chapter 1, the parliamentarians' primary decision rule, the "weight of the bill," rewards jurisdictionally proximate committees because "that's where the experts are." Committees that have a background in an area related to a jurisdictionally ambiguous one are rewarded. Committees with heterogeneous jurisdictions attract heterogeneous memberships. And the more diverse a committee's membership, the more likely it is that a policy entrepreneur will try pushing the committee in yet another direction. In the next section, we review the history of the bill referral process to give us some insight into why the referrals were put in the hands of the parliamentarians and why they use the "weight of the bill" as a decision rule.

A History of Bill Referrals

Though referrals structure so much of what happens in the House—including hearings, markups, and floor action—they are something of a mystery. "Referral," writes Charles Tiefer, "is one of the most 'iceberg'-like aspects of congressional procedure: massive in importance, it lies almost entirely below the surface."[27] Only a member of the House can introduce a bill, which is done by placing it in a mahogany box called the "hopper" at the front of the chamber.[28] The subject matter of a bill may fall in the jurisdiction of one or more committees, and upon introduction all bills must be referred to one or more committees within a day.[29] Very rarely, the Speaker may be asked to explain why he referred a bill a certain way, but the parliamentarian's reasoning is usually well understood through preintroduction discussions.[30]

If a member thinks that a bill was referred incorrectly, an objection may be raised on any day after the reading of the *Journal.* In practice, however, it takes the unanimous consent of the House to change the Speaker's referral. Motions authorized by committees objecting to referrals are in order following the approval of the *Journal,* and these motions are not debatable. Even an erroneous referral, if uncorrected by unanimous consent and by agreement of the committees involved, is considered a precedent and confers jurisdiction if a report is made later.[31]

The Speaker certainly does get appraised of contentious jurisdictional disputes, and committee chairs will not hesitate to raise turf issues directly with the Speaker. And, of course—technically—the Speaker refers all bills. In practice, the Speaker relies almost exclusively on the parliamentarian for advice about referral precedents, and all routine bill referrals are decided by the parliamentarians, in the Speaker's name. In interviews I conducted with members and aides, not one person could recall a single instance when a House Speaker referred a bill to a committee against the advice of the parliamentarians or in violation of the House rules. There is—technically— nothing stopping the Speaker from ignoring the parliamentarians when referring jurisdictionally ambiguous bills. Speakers, however, have been remarkably faithful to the referral traditions established in the mid-1910s.

Threats to the integrity of the committee system are seen throughout the history of bill referral. An overview of the development of the referral process is shown in table 4.1.

When jurisdictions were open to debate by the House floor (through 1889), long and bitter debates over referrals were common, virtually deadlocking the House sometimes for days. In effect, the policy preferences surrounding bills were being debated through referral motions. One important rationale for having committees in the first place— increasing the opportunities to legislate—was undermined by the

Table 4.1 Overview of the History of Bill Referrals

	Committee System Typified by	Arbiter of Jurisdictional Disputes	Effect on the Committee System
1789–1815	Ad hoc committees	Speaker and floor coordinate	Floor paralysis as workload increases
1816–1889	Rapid growth in number of standing and se-lect committees	Floor majority rou-tinely overturns initial referral deci-sions by Speaker	Floor paralysis over referrals. Jurisdictional fragmentation even over "set-tled" issues
1890–1910	Stable number of committees. Speaker domi-nance	Speaker makes final call on jurisdic-tionally ambiguous bills and rewards allies	Jurisdictional frag-mentation over "new" issues. Committee reports attacked as biased
1911–1974	Strong committee fiefdoms. Chairs by seniority	Speaker relies on parliamentarian's advice as an institu-tional guardian	"Weight of Bill" decision rule enhancees-informational ef-ficiency. More fragmentation
1975–present	Subcommittee power. Increased-attention to jurisdictions	Parliamentarian. Speaker strength-ened by time limits on sequential referrals	Intercommittee coordination increases. Fragmentation-continues

open floor debates over referrals. During the next phase of strong Speaker discretion over referrals, members often complained that the Speakers were "playing politics" with referrals. Committee outputs were less likely to be seen as the product of subsets of policy experts. Legislators complained bitterly that the Rules Committee—chaired by the Speaker—refused to allow rules to "fix" the mistakes made in committees. Partisan biases fostered by the Rules Committee was one of the elements in the 1910 revolt against Speaker Cannon. This revolt is pivotal in the institutionalization of the parliamentarian as an insti-tutional guardian. As Deschler explained, the "reference of bills to committees was standardized" after the revolt against Cannon; while "today the office of the [parliamentarian] is judicial in character," and the parliamentarian's decisions "are judicial and mediatory rather than polemic and partisan."[32] There was a period of "King Caucus" associated with Speaker James B. (Champ) Clark (D-MO) from 1911 through 1918, but this proved a transition toward the professionalization of the parliamentarian's office rather than a partisan capture of it.

What follows reads, at times, like a Whig history of the referral process in which things inevitably get better and better. I should caution readers against coming away with that conclusion. There was nothing inevitable about the way that Congress eventually handled bill referrals, and although the parliamentarians have been ensconced as arbiters for most of this century, their reign is by no means guaranteed. The history I offer is not a teleological march of progress, and I do not believe that institutions inevitably solve collective goods dilemmas. Solutions are contingent, not inevitable.

1789–1815: INSTITUTIONALIZATION OF COMMITTEES

During its earliest sessions in the 1790s, standing committees were rarely used in the House. Many members doubted that a selective subset of the parent chamber could faithfully represent the interests of the whole House, and they were loath to give standing committees much autonomy.[33] Instead, bills were routinely drafted and debated in the Committee of the Whole. The Committee of the Whole is another name for the full body of the House when the House operates under a special set of parliamentary rules. The Committee of the Whole is open to all members and conducts its business in the House chamber, not in special committee rooms. Committees of the Whole were mainstays of colonial state legislatures, and their use in Congress seemed a natural extension.

Operating in the Committee of the Whole, bill referrals were simple in one respect; there was no confusion over which members and which committees could work on a bill. It was open to everyone. In another respect, referrals were maddeningly difficult; only one bill could be debated on the floor at a time, and tremendous logjams resulted from the members' reluctance to create committees and from their enthusiasm for long-winded debates. The persons who controlled access to the House floor controlled bill referrals.

Throughout the first Congress, how and when to schedule the consideration of a mounting number of proposals was often coordinated by Alexander Hamilton, President Washington's treasury secretary. Accordingly, the referral of bills to the floor was strongly influenced by the needs of President Washington's executive departments. Hamilton was a Federalist, and Federalists in Congress went along with what seems to us to be a usurpation of congressional power, believing that the heads of executive departments were "themselves a cabinet similar in some respects to the English cabinet."[34] Indeed, several Anti-Federalists complained loudly that the early Congresses had been "converted into a Committeeship of sanction, that never withholds its assent."[35]

Hamilton's influence over Congress continued until late 1794 when Anti-Federalists, led by Thomas Jefferson, wrestled control. Without a routinized way to consider various bills, the 3d Congress drifted into deadlock. The critical task of raising revenue went nowhere, and the Committee of the Whole was "completely at sea."[36] Ad hoc special committees, which lived only long enough to draft a bill and report it back to the House, became the usual way out of bottlenecks in the Committee of the Whole. In 1793–1794 alone, 305 ad hoc committees were established—all essentially controlled by the House floor.[37]

While the Federalists used the Committee of the Whole to ratify executive bills, and therefore did not need standing committees, Jefferson's supporters used the Committee of the Whole because they "abhorred the notion of a small group of legislators disproportionately influential at the prelegislative stage."[38] Jefferson's supporters were more likely to use ad hoc committees, but only after the general principles of legislation were hammered out in the Committee of the Whole. They saw anything less to be distinctly nonmajoritarian.[39]

During the early 1800s, special committees were used more and more, and they gained some autonomy from the floor when shaping bills. In an odd twist, it is more accurate to say that bills were not referred to committees but that special committees were created and were then referred to bills. To the extent that the Committee of the Whole merely ratified what these committees reported, ad hoc committee members had a disproportionate, if fleeting, influence over a jurisdiction. In this situation, the Speaker, who appointed people to ad hoc committees, could structure the "referral" so that it would face a friendly or a hostile audience.

Under Jefferson's supervision, this referral system helped the House produce a steady stream of legislation until the machinery ground to a halt in 1809. Factional fighting in the Committee of the Whole during the 10th and 11th Congresses (much of it over the chartering of a national bank) was so intense that some members dropped their objections to the use of standing and permanent select committees. The hand of the Speaker, in the person of Henry Clay, steadied the Congress. Clay wiped away the practice of first referring bills to the Committee of the Whole, and he encouraged the formation of standing committees. Clay "wrought basic and permanent changes in the role of the Speaker. Once he assumed the office in 1811 he transformed it from a weak and rather apolitical position into the focal point of leadership within the House."[40] The impact on the committee system was lasting. "By 1816 the House had accustomed itself to the extensive use of standing committees."[41] Usually beginning as select committees, the number of standing committees more than doubled from 1811 through 1820. Issues that had been treated almost exclusively on the House floor found homes in semiautonomous bodies with exclusive jurisdictions.

1816–1889: FLOOR MAJORITY CONTROL OF JURISDICTIONS

Where the Speaker once referred ad hoc committees to bills, by the 1820s most bills were referred to standing committees. The Speaker's discretion over which audience would judge a bill was somewhat diminished, though he still had almost complete latitude choosing committee memberships. Throughout the mid-1800s, referrals were hotly debated on the House floor. "The rules which established the jurisdiction of the standing committees did not make reference to them mandatory," and arguments for routinized referrals "rested largely on informal factors [including] the new norms of specialization and deference" to standing committees.[42] During this period, floor majorities could vote on any referral motion, so jurisdictionally ambiguous issues went to the committees that could muster enough political support on the floor.

We should distinguish here between two categories of bills that were used throughout the 1800s. There were public bills that sought to change public policy, and private bills.[43] Private bills were usually petitions on behalf of a constituent for increases in disability pensions or land grants in the territories (functions that would today be taken up by a federal bureaucracy). Private bills amounted to nearly 85 percent of all bills passed by Congress for several sessions following the Civil War.[44] The distinction is important because the rules about bill introduction and reference were different for both. Since private bills could not change public policy with respect to an issue area, there were few battles over their reference. These matters were almost always referred by the House clerk (in the name of the Speaker), paving the way for an expansion of the clerk's referral duties in the next century.[45] Members' interests were much more likely to be evoked by the substance of *public* bills.

We also need to be clear about who was introducing bills in the mid-1800s. Today, bills are introduced by placing a copy in the hopper, and the names of the members who sponsor the bills are included upon introduction. This method did not become standard practice until the late 1800s.[46] In the mid-1800s bills were usually drafted in committee rooms and introduced in the name of the committee. They would then naturally be referred to the committee in whose name the bill was introduced. Public bills were not placed in a hopper stealthily; they were introduced by announcing the title and subject of the bill to the whole House in open session. If an individual (as opposed to a committee) wanted to introduce a public bill, special permission, known as a "motion for leave" had to be granted.[47] Public bills were considered "inchoate laws"—not merely drafts of laws—so when they were introduced by a committee, for referral to that committee, House members treated debate over the referral motion like debate over the substance of the "law" itself.

Throughout most of the 1800s, jurisdictions were up for open debate, and turf wars were fought right out on the House floor. Since committee boundaries were subject to the will of a floor majority, Lauros McConachie noted in the late 1800s that "there was much dispute and consumption of time as to where a resolution, bill, or petition should go."[48] One can scarcely read *The Congressional Globe* from the mid-1800s without encountering time-consuming debates over bill referrals. Every public bill that was introduced by a committee, or by a member, and every policy message from the president or an executive agency needed a formal motion on the floor of the House to be referred to a committee. Although most of these referrals were routine (as they are today), entrepreneurs were quick to launch turf wars when they thought they might win.

A typical example of floor control is the debate surrounding the referral of President Franklin Pierce's State of the Union speech in early 1854. The main issue areas in the speech were divided into twelve resolutions specifying which committee had jurisdiction. To the House Foreign Affairs Committee went, among other things, "the claim of the subjects of Spain for losses in the case of the schooner Amistad, [and] making the boundary between the United States and the British possessions in the northwest."[49]

Even in the midst of a seemingly routine referral, entrepreneurs might expand their turf if they could assemble a floor majority. Thomas Bayly of Virginia, the chair of Foreign Affairs, tried to expand the referral of President Pierce's speech to include regulation of the "guano trade" for his committee. "Guano" is sea bird manure that was imported from islands off Peru and used as a fertilizer. The guano trade was taxed by a tariff, which normally would put the issue in the jurisdiction of the Ways and Means Committee. With floor majorities controlling turf, Chairman Bayly saw an opportunity. George Houston of

Alabama, the Ways and Means chairman, objected wildly to amending the referral motion, and guano remained in his committee. Still, one can see why jurisdiction over the money raised by taxing bird manure made the issue attractive to the Foreign Affairs Committee and, one assumes, to other committees as well.[50] Votes on motions to refer bills occurred routinely in the House, and they afforded many opportunities for policy entrepreneurs to act strategically. One observer approvingly wrote that a member introducing a bill "has the advantage, if the committee to which it is sent does not report, of presenting it again for reference to some other committee."[51]

In the two decades before the Civil War, the question of slavery so vexed Congress that debate on the floor often dragged into paralysis. Tempers occasionally flared, and some members even carried weapons into the chamber to brandish during heated and extended arguments. More often, though, debates on the floor were "boring" and "inconsequential,"[52] in part because the federal government had yet to eclipse the states and counties for legislative predominance.[53] The period after the Civil War was marked by several weak presidents and shifting control of Congress between the Democrats and Republicans. The minority party used the rules to delay action on most of the majority party's programs. A typical maneuver was the "disappearing quorum," in which the minority party would sit silently in the chamber during roll call votes. By refusing to vote, they were not recorded as present in the chamber, making it difficult for the House to reach a quorum.[54] It took a virtually unanimous presence from the majority party to raise a quorum, something made more difficult by frequent illnesses, out-of-town trips, and slim numerical control of the House to begin with.

The minority party exercised its procedural powers to obstruct the majority party in part because they fully expected to be back in the majority shortly. But finding themselves in the majority, members who once obstructed now had to put up with disappearing quorums themselves, and very little got done. "The majority party could and did have its pocket picked, not by some valiant, righteous minority of high conscience but simply by a few members, exercising obstructing tactics permitted by the cumbersome and outdated rules."[55] Congress, in short, was not working as the members and as the public thought it should work. There was a chorus of complaints. " 'Slowly Doing Nothing,' *The Washington Post* said. 'Legislative Lunacy,' growled *The New York Herald.* In the fall of 1889, Representative Henry Cabot Lodge of Massachusetts wrote: '[T]he American House of Representatives today is a complete travesty upon representative government, upon popular government, and upon government by the majority.' "[56]

During the tenure of John G. Carlisle, a Kentucky Democrat who served as Speaker from 1883 through 1889, the Speaker's office was increasingly used to advance his party's platform. Carlisle helped set the stage for an era of strong Speakers, and in 1887 he promoted a package of rules changes that limited the amount of time the House spent debating bill referrals. These rules changes of the 50th Congress allowed the Speaker to refer bills without any motion being approved by a majority. Motions to appeal the initial decisions of the Speaker were in order "on any day immediately after the reading of the Journal"; so in the 50th Congress the floor majority still had the final say over jurisdictions, and the legislative day was not so consumed by routine referral motions. Carlisle attempted, with some success, to stir the House into legislative action (primarily on his lower tariff pledge) after many years of inaction on a host of national problems.[57]

1890–1910: Speaker Control of Jurisdictions

In the election of 1888, Republicans won both houses of Congress as well as the presidency. It was the first time in 14 years that the Republicans controlled both branches, but this "control" was very slight. They held the House "by a bare seven-vote majority, 166 to 159; they controlled the Senate by a two-vote margin; and President Harrison had claimed the White House while trailing Cleveland by eighty thousand popular votes."[58] Thomas Brackett Reed (R-ME) was elected Speaker, and he resolved to overhaul the rules or resign as Speaker.[59] A storm brewed over the adoption of a new set of House rules for the 51st Congress as Reed confronted a disappearing quorum on January 19, 1890. For three days he sat in the Speaker's chair ruling Democratic dilatory motions out of order. Eventually, all members present in the chamber were counted as part of a quorum, and "Reed's Rules" passed. The collective good—a Congress that actually got things done—was advanced. Ronald Peters notes:

> Working under the new rules, but with the slimmest of majorities, the Fifty-first House under Speaker Reed's leadership was the most productive since the Civil War. It passed a total of 611 public bills, the largest number in history to that date. Included were several major bills including the Oklahoma Territories Act, the Sherman Anti-Trust Act, the McKinley Tariff, and the Sherman Silver Purchase Act.[60]

The Reed Rules marked an important change in the way bills were referred. While routine referrals were handled (in the Speaker's name) by the "clerk at the speaker's table," all complicated turf wars were referred by the Speaker. Almost over night, the final say on bill referrals was passed from floor majorities to the crafty Maine Republican. Complete discretion was left to Reed, who was bound by the rules to do little more than report the disposition of the bill in the *Journal* on the following day.[61] In March 1890, Reed caused an uproar on the House floor when he refused to follow a handful of referral precedents, saying that he would be setting all the precedents from then on. Reed's use of the precedents was highly selective—and strategic. As he said during the January 1890 debate over the rules, "If we have broken the precedents of a hundred years, we have set the precedents of another hundred years nobler than the last."[62] The Speaker's referrals could not be changed without unanimous consent, and the ability to make motions to rerefer was severely limited.

Referral precedents were wiped clean to rid the House of what Reed decried as "jurisdictional overlaps." What Reed did, though, was create jurisdictional overlaps of his own when referring ambiguous bills. To Reed, eliminating jurisdictional fragmentation was not nearly as important as who held the authority to create the fragmentation in the first place. Reed's control over bill referrals built on Carlisle's more modest rules change in 1887. "The new system makes errors in commitment less common," wrote Mary Parker Follett, "and tends to save much time. But the new system also increases the power of the Speaker . . . The line of jurisdiction between certain committees cannot be so distinctly marked that difference of opinion shall never appear."[63]

Reed ushered in a period of strong Speakers and centralized leadership. When the Democrats regained control of the House in the fall of 1890, Charles F. Crisp, Speaker for the 52d and 53d Congresses, abolished most of Reed's Rules, but later saw the wisdom of them (thanks to then Minority Leader Reed's newfound enthusiasm for obstructionism) and reinstated them in 1893. So pleased was Crisp with his new referral powers that he expanded them further in the 53d Congress after ruling that motions to rerefer bills were not debatable.[64]

Under Reed and Crisp, there was no one person yet given the title "parliamentarian," and many of the duties that the parliamentarian later took over were handled by the "clerk at the speaker's table." The clerk routed routine bill referrals and consulted with the Speaker about any jurisdictional ambiguities. Though Deschler would later be hailed by some members as "the embodiment of the House of Representatives," certainly nobody would have said that about Crisp's clerk. Crisp's clerk was no impartial and nonpartisan arbiter responsive to the floor's median voter. Crisp's clerk was his son, Charles R. Crisp, and he was there to do his father's bidding.

Thomas Bracket Reed took back the Speaker's chair for the 54th and 55th Congresses, followed by fellow Republican David Henderson from Iowa for the 56th and 57th Congresses. With Republican control firmly established, Joseph Cannon from Illinois was elevated to the Speaker's chair in 1903. He served there until 1911, a year after an internal revolt stripped him of much of his power.

Asher Hinds was the "clerk at the speaker's table" from the beginning of Reed's second tour to the revolt against Cannon, and he was the first clerk systematically to record a large number of precedents for later publication. Earlier annotated copies of the House rules had been published, but they tended to be sketchy, thin, and based more on the precedents of England's House of Commons than on the U.S. Congress.[65] Hinds's comprehensive collection of precedents—published in 1907 and 1908—recorded referral precedents that are followed to this day. As noted in Chapter 3, many of the issues that became part of a committee's statutory jurisdiction in the 1946 Legislative Reorganization Act were lifted verbatim from *Hinds Precedents* and the follow-up volumes of *Cannon's Procedure*. The precedents were treated by the Speakers of this period to be much more binding than precedents had been treated before 1890. Because the floor majority was severely restricted in its ability to rerefer jurisdictionally ambiguous bills, the Speaker's rulings were even more important, since referral precedents essentially conferred lasting turf.

The 1910 revolt against Speaker Cannon was made possible by an alliance between insurgent Republicans and Democrats.[66] Cannon, like all Speakers since Reed, chaired the powerful five-member House Rules Committee.[67] Under Cannon, the Rules Committee fashioned highly restrictive rules protecting the policies of the more conservative wing of the Republican party. The Speaker, through the Rules Committee, also controlled committee assignments, and Cannon used this to punish members who did not help advance his policies. Controlling both committee assignments and bill referrals, the Speaker wielded great potential power. Sensing threats to his chair, Cannon used the rules to get as much leverage as possible. For example, he stripped some members of their coveted committee slots after they voted against the Payne-Aldrich Tariff in 1909. The rules—whether interpreted by Asher Hinds or the Speaker himself—were seen as partisan tools for a wing of the Republican party. Calls for reform were widespread not only in Congress but in every major newspaper and periodical in the country. "The debate over Cannonism," writes Peters about the House rules, "may be viewed as having hinged on the question of whether it was the function of [the] rules to ensure reasonable conditions of impartiality in the House or to guarantee the speaker's power to control its business."[68]

Cannon lost the fight over the size and chairmanship of the Rules Committee in 1910, though he held onto the speakership until the end of 1911 when the Republicans lost control of the House. For future turf wars, two important trends began with Cannon's defeat.[69] First, the "clerk at the speaker's table"—renamed the "parliamentarian" in 1927—gained greater control over bill referrals. One member said they needed the parliamentarian to "protect us from our own worst tendencies." Second, power in the House shifted from a centralized Speaker to committee chairs.[70] With legislative authority spread out after 1910 in what Ronald Peters calls a series of feudal fiefdoms, policy entrepreneurs on committees gained institutional assets with which to launch territorial expansions. This coincided with the expansion of the role of the federal government during the New Deal era. With more and more jurisdictionally ambiguous issues on the congressional agenda, the parliamentarian's referral decisions were especially critical.

1911–1974: PARLIAMENTARIANS AND THE "WEIGHT OF THE BILL"

The transformation of the "clerk at the speaker's table" into an impartial parliamentarian did not happen overnight. The clerk during part of Champ Clark's tenure (he was Speaker from 1911 through 1919) was none other than *his* son, Bennett C. Clark.[71] Though the *Congressional Directory* lists Bennett Clark as the clerk at the Speaker's table, most of his parliamentary duties were actually performed by his friend from Missouri's Ninth District, a young Clarence Cannon (no relation to Joseph Cannon). Clarence Cannon, though beholden to the Speaker for his position, held closely to the precedents recorded by Hinds, and he was viewed by Republicans and Democrats as impartial. Through Clarence Cannon, and coming on the heels of the 1910 revolt, the office of the parliamentarian was completely remade. Representative Charles Halleck, an Indiana Republican, said of Cannon, "It can be rightly said that by his wisdom and his fairness he gave the office of the Parliamentarian in this body a truly nonpartisan, professional status."[72]

If a person named Clarence Cannon had not come along during the brief "King Caucus" period, perhaps someone else would have served the same role. This sketch overlooks the reign of "King Caucus" under the Democrats from 1911 to 1915 during which party government continued to function through the majority leader, Oscar Underwood, acting through the caucus, which often dictated which committees should and should not report and how members should vote on the floor.[73] Reacting to Underwood as well as to former Speaker Cannon, House members very consciously tried to depoliticize the parliamentarian's functions. During the 1910s, legislators easily recalled that majority control over referrals (until 1889) undermined the committee system and tied up the floor. Speaker control over referrals (until 1910) made turf a political chit to be handed out to friends, further diminishing the willingness of the floor to accede to the actions of the committees. The emergence of a neutral arbiter in jurisdictional disputes was no accident. It was a solution.

The publication of *Hinds Precedents* played an important role in legitimating the parliamentarian's rulings because it made the increasingly important precedents available to all members. Clarence Cannon was a Democrat, but when the Republicans took control of the 66th Congress in 1919, Speaker Frederick Gillett retained Cannon, who remained until he ran for Champ Clark's Missouri seat in 1922. As parliamentarian, Cannon followed Hinds's practice of comprehensively updating and publishing precedents. His collection of precedents appeared in 1920 and was updated periodically until 1963.[74] With Cannon's departure in 1922, his aide, Lehr Fess, took over and continued to enhance the office's reputation as that of an impartial arbiter. Lehr's title was still officially the "clerk at the speaker's table," but informally he had been called the "parliamentarian" for years by the time the official title was changed in 1927, a year before Lewis Deschler took the job.

With the rise of the parliamentarian as an institutional guardian, the office took on the important function of helping to educate new members about the ways of the House. The parliamentarian sits next to the Speaker's rostrum so that he can be heard by whomever is presiding. It makes for an Edgar Bergen–Charlie McCarthy routine. "Once I was in the Chair," recounts former California Democrat Tom Rees, "and I didn't know what to say. From my right I heard a still small voice whispering in my ear, 'For what purpose does the gentleman from Montana rise?' And this happens all the time."[75] Many new members from both sides of the aisle make their way to the parliamentarian's office to introduce themselves and to get quick lessons on parliamentary procedure. Deschler took some of his greatest pride, though, in protecting the House rules from being reinterpreted by floor majorities. "From the beginning of the 70th Congress, in 1927," wrote Deschler upon his retirement, "there have been only eight appeals from decision of the Speaker, and in seven of these eight cases the decision of the Speaker was sustained."[76]

The weight of the bill decision rule has been articulated by Deschler, though it was clearly in use before his tenure. Weight of the bill, to reiterate, means that the parliamentarian refers jurisdictionally ambiguous bills (thus granting turf) to committees with the "closest" jurisdiction. The term is similar, not surprisingly, to the "weight of the evidence," on which courts are supposed to decide civil cases. The parliamentarians want to maintain an image of themselves as judge-like, but exactly how jurisdictionally proximate a bill is becomes something that can be swayed by clever drafting and good referral precedents cited by policy entrepreneurs.

There are two exceptions to the weight of the bill. First, if any portion of a bill includes a provision that will change a rule of the House, even if it is a very small part of the bill, the Rules Committee gets the bill. Second, any bill that includes a tax—or something that looks like a tax—is referred to the Ways and Means Committee. With multiple referrals after 1975, Ways and Means gets only the parts of bills that include taxes, but before 1975 the tax committee was singly referred legislation that might more reasonably have gone other places. A former parliamentarian said that even if "there's one itty bitty tax provision, Ways and Means'll get a referral." Because of this exception to the "weight of the bill," Ways and Means established common law jurisdiction over the Airport Trust Fund, the Highway Trust Fund, and Social Security. Amendments to the Social Security Act have also been referred to Ways and Means, further extending its jurisdiction into disability insurance, Medicaid, Medicare, Aid for Families with Dependent Children, and Unemployment Compensation.[77] Such programs have given the tax committee an impressive jurisdictional endowment from which to move into new issue areas. To the extent that this Ways and Means exception rule was undermined by multiple referrals (after 1975), a rules change in 1983 explicitly said that all bills carrying a tax provision have to be referred to the tax committee.[78]

One of the parliamentarians is always on the House floor, and when a bill is placed in the hopper the parliamentarian on the floor takes a quick look at it and might make a small note about the likely referral. Almost all jurisdictionally ambiguous bills would have been run by the parliamentarian's office several times before being introduced, just to get an indication of how the bill might need to be changed for a desired referral. Staffers on two committees said there is a strategy to introducing bills: watch C-SPAN to see which of the parliamentarians is on the floor because some are more likely to be "strict constructionists" on the rules. Former and current parliamentarians say this bit of superstitious learning is nonsense. Eventually, all of the parliamentarians look over all of the bills before referring them anywhere.[79] It makes no difference who picks them out of the hopper.

At the close of the day the parliamentarians gather to make referrals, and the overwhelming number are routine. But on jurisdictionally ambiguous bills, there may be some disagreement among the parliamentarians as to which committee should get a bill or, more likely since 1975, whether a bill should be jointly referred. In the end, though, the head parliamentarian is responsible for all the referrals. One deputy parliamentarian said of Charlie Johnson's predecessor, "He may get conflicting views from his staff, [but] Bill Brown makes the final call because he is *the* Parliamentarian."

Throughout this century, policy entrepreneurs have used the strategies outlined in Chapter 5, many tailored to influencing the parliamentarians' impression of the jurisdictional proximity of their bills, to stake claims to new issues. "The committee system is a pragmatic instrument," said Speaker Carl Albert in 1973, but that does not mean the referral process was yielding universal acclaim.[80] Recall from Chapter 3 that removing jurisdictional fragmentation was a rallying cry for the reformers pushing the 1946 Legislative Reorganization Act. That act did indeed reduce some jurisdictional fragmentation, often by reinforcing preexisting patterns of intercommittee cooperation. Only nonexclusive committees were consolidated, however, and fragmentation involving the exclusive committees (Ways and Means and International Relations, for example) were unaffected by the 1946 act. Without the possibility of multiply referring bills that overlap jurisdictions, referral precedents created a quilt of committees covering issues like trade, energy, environmental protection, and health.

By the early 1960s, there were once again calls in Congress to reform the committee system to reduce jurisdictional overlaps, but a Joint Committee on the Organization of Congress, created in 1965, failed to gain majority support to change jurisdictions.[81] Through clever bill drafting, and with the weight of the bill on their side, policy entrepreneurs carved out territory that, one would think, should have gone to other committees instead. By the early 1970s, bill referral precedents undercut the House Agriculture Committee's jurisdiction on a wide variety of issues. Banking and Currency claimed jurisdiction over cattlehide exports, international wheat agreements, and rural housing. The Commerce Committee had organic food farms and cruelty to animals. Judiciary wrote the Family Farm Act. Merchant Marine and Fisheries had jurisdiction over endangered species. Public Works reported bills on rural water pollution, and Ways and Means oversaw legislation promoting rural job development.[82] Every House committee could recount jurisdictional overlaps at least as extensive as these.

The irony here is that the decision rules employed by the parliamentarians helped produce such a fragmented committee system. The parliamentarian emerged as a solution to the problems witnessed during the mid-1800s and during the era of strong partisan Speakers. The fragmented committee system, though, at times undermined the House's ability to present a unified voice on some social problems. "House committees should be organized," wrote the House Select Committee on Committees in 1973, "to give coherent consideration to a number of pressing problems whose handling has been fragmented."[83] Jurisdictional overlaps were one of the main motivations behind the 1974 reform efforts.

Jurisdictional reform provisions that came out of the 1974 House Select Committee on Committees were gutted before the Hansen plan was substituted for the Bolling proposal. Richard Bolling, who later chaired the Rules Committee, was the driving force behind the Select Committee. Bolling proposed to make the Rules Committee the final arbiter of turf wars, allowing for any committee chair to "request the Rules Committee to review any referral of a bill to which his or her committee might have jurisdictional claims." These requests could be made within five days of the initial referral, and the Rules committee "would undertake a review of the bill referral in question and make a ruling on the appeal."[84] According to a long time top aide to Bolling, he was as much after the power such a provision would give the Rules Committee as he was after making jurisdictions more "rational." This jurisdictional appeals process was not accepted by the House, but a provision allowing the Speaker to multiply refer bills was. Bolling's former aide said he was especially proud of "sneaking the multiple referrals" rules change by the House. Multiple referrals were never the focus of much discussion in the Democratic caucus, and they were adopted without careful attention to the possible consequences.[85] Bolling, however, anticipated that multiple referrals would reduce the tendency to fragment jurisdictions by allowing the parliamentarian to modify the "weight of the bill" rule, and he thought that sequential referrals would strengthen the Speaker's hand, something Bolling had long desired. Bolling was right on both counts.

1975–Present: REFERRAL STRATEGIES AND FRAGMENTATION

The ability of the Speaker to refer a bill to more than one committee dates to January 3, 1975, when the Bolling-Hansen reforms became effective, and the 1995 reforms severely limited most types of multiple referrals. During this 20-year period, three types of multiple referrals were allowed under Rule X(5)(c): joint, split, and sequential.[86] The percentage of bills that are multiply referred in the House tripled from 1975 through 1994. Part of this is due to the decrease in the total number of bills per Congress following changes in the number of cosponsors permitted on each bill,[87] but it is clear nonetheless that multiple referrals were used with greater frequency. The possibility of requesting sequential referrals heightened the attention committee leaders pay to the jurisdictional implications of bills initially referred to other committees.

Among the three types of multiple referrals, *joint referrals* were the most common, comprising more than 94 percent of all multiple referrals in the 99th Congress.[88] With a joint referral, all titles of a bill were simultaneously sent to two or more committees upon introduction. An example is the 1991 banking reform bill, which ultimately failed on the floor. Referred jointly to the House Banking and the House Energy and Commerce committees, the bill was used by the Commerce Committee to carve out turf regulating the extent to which banks enter securities markets—a contentious and highly visible issue. Most joint referrals, however, were neither contentious nor highly visible. They became routine. In the 101st Congress (1989–1990), for example, multiply referred bills included S.J. Res. 237, providing for the commemoration of the 100th anniversary of Dwight Eisenhower's birth. Three committees got that bill. Two more received H.J. Res. 546 designating May 13, 1990, as "Infant Mortality Awareness Day." So while multiple referrals have indeed increased opportunities for cooperation among committees, joint referrals do not always elicit mad jurisdictional scrambles. Also in the 101st Congress, however, the Americans with Disabilities Act was referred to four committees, and problems of coordination threatened to scuttle the bill.

Jointly referred bills may at first appear to throw open the gates to jurisdictional raids because all titles of a bill are sent to several committees. Indeed, Collie and Cooper argue that "in opting for multiple referrals, legislators . . . increased the uncertainties associated with committees' autonomy over legislation. They have, in short, surrendered autonomy for access."[89] In practice, though, committees have most assuredly *not* surrendered autonomy. Even under joint referrals, jurisdictional boundaries are assiduously guarded. Though not specified in the written rules, the practice under joint referrals is that committees are strictly limited to working only on issues within their established domain. To do anything else welcomes challenges at the

Rules Committee and on the floor, something most committees are eager to avoid. Jointly referred bills reinforce, rather than tear down, jurisdictional walls. Committees under multiple referrals may share a broad bill, but they do not share broad jurisdictions. Fine lines are drawn among issues, and they are carefully monitored by committee "border cops."

During the 98th Congress, 7.2 percent of all jointly referred measures were ultimately passed on the House floor. This compares to a "success" rate of nearly 17 percent for all singly referred measures during the same period.[90] Oleszek, Davidson, and Kephart speculate that jointly referred bills were less likely to succeed because "by their very nature, bills that are sent to two or more committees are complex and multifaceted. As a general proposition, this raises the possibility of conflict and controversy."[91] This is certainly true for some measures, such as recent banking reform bills, but one of the parliamentarians suggests another reason: "A great many jointly referred bills are dead on arrival anyway, so there's no harm in giving everyone a piece of the action." The point is that many of these bills would have seen no "action" regardless of the type of referral.

Split referrals can be thought of as a special type of joint referral, and they are by far the least common. During the 99th Congress, less than 0.5 percent of all multiple referrals were split, and they have been used even less since then.[92] When a bill is split for referral, titles or sections of the bill are sent to different committees, and all committees receive their sections of the bill at the same time. To accomplish this, the parliamentarians carefully select which committees have jurisdiction over different sections, and they divide accordingly. The referral of President Carter's national energy bill is an example, for "Section 701 of the bill was sent to the Government Operations Committee and Sections 721 through 746 were referred to the Public Works Committee."[93] Split referrals were originally conceived to keep committees from raiding jurisdictions during a joint referral, but as discussed above, such raids are limited because committees have adopted the practice of respecting committee boundaries—at least when bills are jointly referred. Bills that would have been split for a referral several years ago are now sent out as a joint referral, thereby sparing the parliamentarians the tedium of parceling out sections of bills.

The third type of multiple referral, a *sequential referral,* is qualitatively different from joint and split referrals, and it offers the clearest opportunities for committees to play the "jurisdiction game." A modified form of this referral survived January 1995, and we can expect entrepreneurs to find new ways to use sequential referrals to protect their turf. A sequential assignment is the rereferral of a bill after at least one committee has already reported it. Assume, for example, that the House Commerce Committee reported a bill that included a provision regulating the type of information that suppliers to the nuclear weapons industry must provide the government about international customers. From the view of the Commerce Committee, this is in their jurisdiction, which includes "measures regulating the commercial application of energy technology." The International Relations Committee, however, oversees "export controls, including nonproliferation of nuclear technology and hardware," and one could well imagine that the chair of the International Relations Committee would ask the parliamentarians to give International Relations a chance to work on the bill before sending it to the floor.

Though very few bills are eventually sequentially referred, the parliamentarians report that most of the singly referred bills are "potentially sequential." One parliamentarian explained,

> Of all bills introduced, the far greater percentage of bills are potentially sequential, not concurrent, because we have been able to discern a committee of primary jurisdiction and there are fragments of other jurisdictions in the bill.
>
> *Question: Can you think of an issue in your time here that almost made you throw up your hands because you weren't sure which committee should be the lead committee?*
>
> Well, I can think of a lot of such situations. I guess since the multiple referral process has evolved, especially in the last few years . . . It is more accepted today, and it helps us avoid, oh, interminable meetings with members and staff. . . There are just so many examples of times when we referred a bill to one committee only to find out the next day that we should have multiply referred it. In those cases, the committees usually work something out themselves either through suggesting language in the vehicle or by getting clearance for an amendment on the floor. We sometimes turn those into sequential referrals too.

Requests for sequential referrals are usually made by committee chairs in writing to the Speaker, and they are then handed over to the parliamentarian. Sequential referrals are "also made informally (telephone calls, for example, by chairmen, individual members, and committee staff aides)."[94] Since 1977, the Speaker has been able to set time limits on the second committee in a sequential referral, thereby letting the Speaker discharge a bill on short notice. "Although they are only a tiny portion of all multiple referrals," notes Roger Davidson, "sequential referrals are almost always applied to important leadership packages."[95]

Sequential referrals dramatically increased the amount of communication between committees. One staff director said that he is on the phone "almost daily" monitoring what other committees are doing that might give rise to a sequential referral. The committee reports of some large bills now contain letters from other committee chairs reflecting jurisdictional agreements, and the Ways and Means Committee now includes a section in its written calendar that records other committees' bills over which it has asserted jurisdiction. Subcommittees in different committees are more likely than ever before to hold joint hearings and to coordinate witnesses. Still, sequential referrals are not without detractors. The Speaker's hand has been strengthened considerably by being able to discharge bills from committees through time limits on the referrals. And some members complain that the possibility of asking for sequential referrals has heightened jurisdictional tensions.

Never one to miss a chance to strengthen the Speaker's hand even more, Newt Gingrich and the Republicans introduced a modified sequential referral, called an "initial additional" referral. Write Evans and Oleszek, "Republicans wanted to reduce the internecine turf fights that often erupted between competing chairmen during the Democratic majority. Under the new House rules, the Speaker must designate a primary committee of jurisdiction upon initial reference of a measure, but he also has significant flexibility in determining whether, when, and how long additional panels will receive legislation."[96] By designating a primary committee, one panel is held accountable, though additional committees may be called on to help craft legislation already in their territory. These additional referrals are subject to time limits imposed by the Speaker, effectively allowing one person to discharge the committee. Time will tell what impact this has on turf wars, but the new referral procedures unquestionably give the Speaker more power.

FIVE

Essential Strategies for Staking Claims

n turf wars, policy entrepreneurs compete against each other using strategies that anticipate how the parliamentarian adjudicates turf disputes. The four most common strategies include amending public laws that are already in their committee's jurisdiction, citing referral precedents on similar legislation, investing in gaining committee expertise (usually by holding investigatory hearings), and petitioning for sequential bill referrals. Subcommittees are sometimes used to help solidify claims, and they provide care and feeding to emerging policy experts. House task forces—largely controlled by the Speaker and crossing jurisdictional boundaries—came to prominence in 1995, thereby opening another avenue for policy entrepreneurs to stake claims. Because only standing committees (not task forces) can actually report bills, members of standing committees jockey to get on task forces to demonstrate their expertise and boost the odds of having precedent-setting bills sent to their standing committees. This chapter reviews the basic strategies, and it closes with a look at the birth and death of subcommittees waging turf wars.

Amend Public Laws

Amendments may be made to a public law if those amendments are, in the opinion of the parliamentarian, germane to the public law. When a jurisdictionally ambiguous bill is written as an amendment, that bill is referred to the committee with jurisdiction over the public law being amended. As long as the amendment is germane, then there is no uncertainty about where it will be referred—and hence there is no uncertainty about which committee will expand its jurisdiction to include the topics touched on in the amendment. Among policy entrepreneurs, the amendment strategy is, by far, the preferred way to expand turf. Of 137 issues over which the Commerce Committee established a referral precedent from 1947 through 1994, 114 (or 83.2 percent) were issues raised in conjunction with a bill over which the committee had already established jurisdiction. This figure, 83.2 percent, includes times when the new issue was linked to any issue in the committee's jurisdiction—not just times when the committee debated amending a public law.

The coupling of a new issue with existing public laws naturally colors the way that the issue will be handled. From the point of view of pressure groups searching for favorable venues in which their legislative interests might be considered, committee shopping is like the "judge shopping" that prosecutors and defense attorneys do. Perhaps the most important part of committee shopping is finding old public laws in favorable committees that can be amended. This happens routinely in Washington, and, says one Speaker's aide, "I'm sure there are people making way too much money consulting on this kind of thing." There are several lobbyists in Washington specializing in committee shopping for groups trying to influence the jurisdictions of committees.

Washington's jurisdiction consultants have found a niche because referral decisions can have important consequences for their clients. Recall the "pesticides residue" issue from Chapter 1. In 1972, President Nixon proposed legislation to control pesticides. As originally written, the Federal Environmental Pesticide Control Act of 1972 would have amended the Toxic Control and Substances Act, which was (and is) in the jurisdiction of the House Commerce Committee.[1] Pesticide manufacturers thought that the Commerce Committee would be hostile to their interests, and they much preferred that the bill be referred to the friendlier House Agriculture Committee instead. House Agriculture Chair W. R. Poage (D-TX) was also "very concerned about putting this industry in the hands of the Commerce Committee rather than in the hands of the USDA and Agriculture Committee." Poage sent committee staffers to the White House with a plan to change the bill that would be amended from Commerce's Toxic Control and Substances Act to the long-dormant Federal Insecticide, Fungicide and Rodenticide Act of 1947, or FIFRA. FIFRA, not coincidentally, was in the Agriculture Committee's jurisdiction. The White House agreed to the plan, and one staffer recalls,

> I took out a pencil, crossed out the Toxic Substances and Control Act and wrote in FIFRA . . . This was all very very important. It could have gone to the Commerce Committee, and history, for better or worse, has

been molded by that little decision. Ever since, all those pesticide bills go to Agriculture, and the whole "enviro crowd" has had to deal with us. And that was just because of a couple lines, and I did the drafting. I can remember it clearly. I just changed that line.

When using amendments to expand jurisdictions, policy entrepreneurs are careful to select public laws that can be interpreted as broadly as possible. One committee staff director explains that "you don't want to make a precedent on too small a base. You want to get on a base that's a new base." How "far" away from the committee's current jurisdiction policy entrepreneurs are willing to amend public laws depends to a large extent on the likelihood that other committees might be able to stake a plausible claim to some of the issues in the amendment. This was especially true from 1975 through 1994, with the chance that the parliamentarian might multiply refer a bill—even a bill amending a public law—to two or more committees.

Cite Referral Precedents

Because common law jurisdictions build upon referral decisions, policy entrepreneurs arguing for a favorable bill referral maintain careful notes on past committee activities. During an interview, one committee staff director pointed to nine large three-ring binders. The binders are divided into policy areas, and each page chronicles committee activities that can be cited in negotiations with other committees and in arguments before the parliamentarian. When I asked to spend some time alone with the binders, he jokingly agreed, as long as I realized that he "would then have to kill" me afterward. That staff director feared another committee finding out about how his committee might link referral precedents covering the "new" area of "global competitiveness."

It is hard to overstate the importance of precedents in most legislatures. Lewis Deschler wrote, "The precedents may be viewed as the 'common law,' so to speak, of the House." Precedents are the bedrock of parliamentary law, and "parliamentary law has come to be recognized as *law,* in the sense that it is binding on the assembly and its members."[2] In citing referral precedents, then, policy entrepreneurs present the parliamentarian with their own interpretations of the laws of the House.[3] This fits naturally with the legal training of the parliamentarians and staffers, as lawyering remains the modal occupation on Capitol Hill.

Policy entrepreneurs fashion interpretations of referral precedents that are designed to improve their changes of a favorable referral, so their interpretations cannot be considered entirely neutral. Some committees are more skilled than others at crafting precedent-based arguments. A few staffers on the House Judiciary Committee, for example, worry that they have worn out the parliamentarian's patience by peppering his office with letters trying to claim jurisdiction over issues far removed from the committee's base. (The parliamentarian called this worry "silly," but judiciary staffers are not taking any chances.) Other committees, notably Commerce, approach the parliamentarian's office with formal written letters only sparingly, choosing instead to maintain regular contact with the parliamentarians while bills are being drafted. Still other committees rely on outside consultants, such as lobbyists and the Congressional Research Service, to research referral precedents and make suggestions. One Commerce Committee staffer said committees depending on others for advice about referral precedents "are run by a bunch of idiots."

While drafting bills that might be jurisdictionally ambiguous, committee members and staffers routinely contact the parliamentarian's office to discuss where they would refer bills given their current language. The parliamentarians report that they receive such inquiries "almost daily," as policy entrepreneurs try crafting language that maximizes the territory gained while minimizing the chances of bills being referred to the "wrong" committees. Parliamentarian Charles Johnson writes,

> Some astute students of the House rules think that a ruling, a germaneness precedent, for instance, can be found on either side of a given issue, that the Parliamentarian can virtually help or hinder a Member with the precedents he cites or fails to cite. That opinion oversimplifies the matter. The office can properly apply one germaneness precedent or line of precedent rather than another, depending on the language of the bill and its relationship to the specific language of the amendment. The fact that a member comes to us first to seek an opinion isn't necessarily to his advantage, but exploring his options early is.[4]

Formally, letters citing a string of bill referrals are sent to the Speaker, though aides for the last four Speakers say that the letters are almost immediately routed to the parliamentarian.

The parliamentarian considers the merit of precedent-based arguments, and letters that are found to be persuasive are kept to help guide future referrals in the issue area. "Memoranda of Understanding" have also been negotiated among committees on a few issues to state plainly where jurisdictions lie, though such memoranda are rare. In 1991, Speaker Foley announced that a memorandum of understanding had been written to distinguish between "taxes" (which are in the Ways and Means Committee's jurisdiction) and "user fees" (which are attached to services—such as admittance to the national parks—that are in other committees' jurisdictions).[5] Similarly, a Memorandum of Understanding released at the start of the 104th Congress spelled out how the former Merchant Marine and Fisheries turf would be divided.[6]

When William Brown was parliamentarian, he kept an old cardboard box next to his desk in H-211 of the Capitol Building. The box held especially persuasive letters that offered guiding interpretations of referral precedents. When exploring and citing legislative histories, it was the goal of policy entrepreneurs to have their versions of the House rules "accepted" into this worn box of precedents.

Invest in Gaining Expertise

Before introducing a jurisdictionally ambiguous bill, policy entrepreneurs are apt to hold oversight and investigatory hearings to see whether the committee should really move into the new issue area. Committees may hold investigatory hearings on virtually any issues they choose, even ones clearly in the jurisdiction of other committees. Rule X(2) instructs committees to watch that laws within their jurisdiction are "being implemented and carried out in accordance with the intent of the Congress," but it does not say that a committee cannot determine if this is happening for laws in another committee's jurisdiction as well. Accordingly, "Committees that lack legislative but have some claim to oversight jurisdiction, real or tenuous, often stake claims by holding hearings and influencing the development of policy."[7]

Formally, it takes a bill referral to change the law, but policies can be influenced informally by timely oversight from a committee without statutory or common law jurisdiction. Oversight hearings are sometimes a precursor to expanding jurisdictions because they are a signal to the rest of the House—and to the parliamentarian—that a committee is developing expertise in a policy area. Committees are also increasingly likely to hold oversight hearings to publicize problems through the national media. In their study of these hearings, Jeffery Talbert, Bryan Jones, and Frank Baumgartner explain that

> nonlegislative hearings are important in jurisdiction-grabbing because there are few restrictions on the topics that any subcommittee may investigate. Committee leaders are adept at using nonlegislative hearings in order to claim future legislative referrals. This threat is often enough to cause rival committees to act to protect their own jurisdictional claims.[8]

Throughout the summer of 1992, House Banking Committee Chairman Henry Gonzalez (D-TX) held investigatory hearings charging that the Bush administration supplied arms and intelligence to Iraq right up to the eve of the Kuwait invasion. The Banking Committee has very tenuous jurisdiction related to such issues, but their hearings got the attention of the White House nonetheless.[9] Similarly, in 1990 the Commerce Committee began hearings into academic research overhead expenses filed by Stanford University with the Office of Naval Research, which is in the jurisdiction of the Armed Services Committee.[10] The results—all accomplished without a bill referral to the committee of jurisdiction—brought down Stanford's president Donnald Kennedy and caused every research university in the country to review its books. At the height of President Reagan's defense buildup in the 1980s, John Dingell called hearings to publicize cost overruns and $700 hammers. Though not in the committee's jurisdiction, the hearings caused a public reexamination by the Pentagon of their procurement policies. Also, following revelations in 1989 of political favoritism in grant programs run by the Department of Housing and Urban Development, a half dozen subcommittees—few with direct legislative jurisdiction—clamored to hold hearings in front of national television audiences.

The frequency of oversight hearings increased dramatically following the 1973 "Subcommittee Bill of Rights," which "mandates that legislation be referred to subcommittees; that subcommittees be able to meet, hold hearings, and report legislation; and that each have adequate staff and budget."[11] It is in subcommittees that most legislative legwork gets done, and it is there that policy entrepreneurs begin staking out claims to policy turf. During the 1980s, almost all substantive hearings in the House Commerce Committee were held at the subcommittee level, which is a far cry from the late 1940s when the full committee held most hearings. The percentage of subcommittee hearings that were unassociated with a bill referral (such hearings are sometimes used to investigate issues outside of a committee's jurisdiction) rose from below 20 percent before 1973 to more than 50 percent throughout the 1980s. Committees also produce "prints" about issues they are investigating. In 1986, for example, Commerce produced two committee prints discussing and documenting unfair trade practices by foreign countries—an issue close to the Ways and Means' jurisdiction over "reciprocal trade agreements" but also a target issue for John Dingell and for James Florio (D-NJ).[12] And in 1990, the Ways and Means Committee published a 93-page print on crack cocaine,[13] an issue more likely to fall in Commerce or Judiciary territory.

It is not entirely clear what will happen to the frequency of investigatory hearings in the wake of committee staff reductions. The first session of the 104th Congress actually recorded an increase in the total hours that House committees held hearings, though much of that revolved around the Contract with America. Still, with more hearings being held by task forces, we should see a reduction in nonlegislative hearings soon—perhaps returning to levels more consistent with the 1960s than the 1980s. Recall, however, that legislators in the 1960s were just as jurisdictionally expansive as their successors.

Policy entrepreneurs sometimes avoid holding investigatory hearings—thereby avoiding signaling to the House a committee's interest in an issue—when (1) an entrepreneur does not want to risk agitating another committee's tendency to protect issues close to its jurisdiction, (2) when the entrepreneur is certain that an amending strategy will send the bill to the "right" committee without demonstrating additional expertise, and (3) when the entrepreneur has already made up his or her mind (and does not need to convince other committee members) about the wisdom of moving into a new issue area. These three elements were in place as the Commerce Committee moved into insurance issues in the early 1980s. Regulation of insurance companies was wide open to a jurisdictional grab by several committees, including the Banking Committee. Dingell wanted the issue, and he mapped out an amending strategy to get it. One Commerce Committee aide said that with a "hot" issue like insurance regulation, one does not want to hold preparatory and investigatory hearings before introducing a jurisdictionally ambiguous bill because "You don't want to tip off anybody. You sneak up on little cat's feet. And then you hit them. You don't hint. You bludgeon."

Policy entrepreneurs rely on staff to help move a committee into new issue areas. One person in charge of hiring and firing committee staffers said that "after you know what you want to do [for example, what issues policy entrepreneurs want to pursue], you go out and get the very best personnel you can." The Commerce Committee staff is recognized as among the best in Washington, in part because the committee has a large enough budget to make good hires.[14] That was true under Chairman John Dingell, and it is true under his successor, Republican Thomas Bliley.

Besides Commerce, other committees that regularly play the jurisdiction game have hired highly skilled staff. The 1990 House Science Committee's Subcommittee on Science, Research, and Technology is typical. Its 11-member staff included, among others, Grace Ostenso (Wisconsin Ph.D. with a background in nutrition research), Raphael

Panitz (New York University Ph.D.), James Turner (Yale Divinity School and Georgetown Law), James Wilson (West Virginia Ph.D. and retired Air Force Captain), and David Goldston (former New York State assemblyman and science journalist).[15] With personnel like this, the subcommittee had the expertise to launch investigations into a variety of jurisdictionally ambiguous science issues.

Committee staff budgets are set through yearly requests to the House Oversight Committee. Occasionally, the documents provided by committees to support budget increases contain detailed outlines of jurisdictionally ambiguous issues that the committee would like to pursue. One committee staffer explained, "We're always looking to see what areas are going to be hot areas. As staff director, I need to know where to direct attention, and we need a budget for that. We prepare as best we can." In 1983 and 1985, the Commerce Committee's budget requests so plainly laid out a policy agenda for the committee that they were published as committee prints.[16] The 1983 Commerce staff budget request helped set the stage for the committee's move into insurance regulation. "The business of insurance is large, financially complex, national and increasingly international in character. Is State regulation equal to the task?" It was a rhetorical question, and the Commerce Committee moved quickly to fill the jurisdictional gray area that had left insurance companies largely unregulated at the federal level since the McCarran-Ferguson Act in 1945.

Some committee chairs and staff directors see the role of expertise differently than what I have just described. Committees are in struggle with other committees to produce a bill that the parliamentarian will refer to them, but one's definition of what might constitute "expertise" partly depends on how established an issue is. One staff director said,

> I don't know if "expertise" is the right way to think about this. [The parliamentarians] do ask whether this is an area where the committee has done work, if it's a good area for the committee. But who has "expertise" on competitiveness? People don't even know what the problem is. The parliamentarians certainly *do* care about the committee's background and experience. If that's "expertise," then OK, but there aren't "experts" on some of these issues. Some committees are just more expert than others.

The goal, then, is to *establish* a pool of expertise, which enhances the policy entrepreneur's reputation and makes other members of the House more willing to defer to the know-how on the committee and subcommittee. Background, experience, and expertise buy policy entrepreneurs leeway to pursue their goals.

Argue for Sequential Referrals or Additional Initial Referrals

Since 1975, the parliamentarian has had the option of referring one bill to more than one committee. From 1975 through 1994, there were three types of multiple referrals: split (in which a bill is divided by section or title and then referred to committees), joint (also called concurrent, in which the same bill goes to two committees with instructions that the committees only work on issues within the jurisdiction of their committee), and sequential (where a bill is referred to a second committee only after it has been reported out of another committee that has primary jurisdiction).[17] The 1995 Gingrich reforms got rid of joint referrals, replacing them with a modified sequential referral called "additional initial" referrals.

Some scholars, notably Collie and Cooper (1989), have speculated that joint (or concurrent) referrals amount to jurisdictional free-for-alls, and through multiple referrals committees sacrifice autonomy over an issue for jurisdiction over issues in other committees. In fact, however, joint referrals are carefully written by the parliamentarian to limit committees to issues within the jurisdiction of the committee.

Successful jurisdictional poaching was relatively rare within joint referrals, and this point was emphasized time and time again in interviews with committee staff. This was not for lack of trying, because once a committee worked on part of a bill, members could be expected to imagine ways of legislating on another committee's turf. This was understood by all the players, so competing committees were especially vigilant. Multiple referrals heightened everyone's sensitivity to the jurisdiction game, because members feared that undefended turf would be quickly exploited by another committee receiving the same bill. "Border cops" patrolled daily listings of bills looking for breaches.

Partly because of constant monitoring by the staffs of other committees, joint referrals respected established jurisdictional boundaries; so the parliamentarian gradually stopped making split referrals. In effect, then, only two types of multiple referrals were used from 1975 through 1994—joint and sequential—and the jurisdiction game was played differently for each type. Under some circumstances, policy entrepreneurs use joint referrals to write "strategically ambiguous" bills and to move into jurisdictionally ambiguous areas. The dominant strategic use of multiple referrals, however, is to *protect* committee jurisdictions from other policy entrepreneurs. One Agriculture Committee staffer called multiple referrals "insurance policies" against the likes of John Dingell.

Even though multiple referrals are often used as insurance policies to protect jurisdictions, if a legislator wants jurisdiction over part of an issue that is very close to another committee's jurisdiction, he or she may craft a bill that is strategically ambiguous in order to get a joint referral. By crafting a bill that includes vaguely worded sections with some (often tenuous) links to a committee's jurisdiction, policy entrepreneurs can claim that they are working on "their" part of a joint referral and are not really poaching. An example illustrates this. Though the Commerce Committee has long had statutory jurisdiction over "interstate and foreign commerce," by the early 1980s they had not worked on trade bills for many decades. Trade agreements were under the jurisdiction of the Ways and Means Committee. Dingell, however, sought protection for U.S. automobile manufacturers (many based near his Detroit-area district) from "unfair" Japanese trade practices.

With his staff director, Dingell planned a strategy to redefine trade issues in terms of fairness and U.S. industrial competitiveness. As I have mentioned, trade issues had long been framed in terms of how free—not how fair—markets were. Dingell set up two special subcommittees, one on trade with China and one on trade with the Pacific Rim, and he hosted a series of investigatory hearings focusing on fairness. To move "fairness" legislation along in the House, a bill would have to be multiply referred with Ways and Means, but Commerce did not want Dan Rostenkowski, the Ways and Means chair, to foresee how large of a jurisdictional grab Dingell planned. They did not want to appear too eager for a trade bill. Accordingly, Dingell enlisted the help of an interest group, the Labor and Industry Coalition on International Trade, LICIT, to be sure that Ways and Means would report their half of the multiply referred bill. One Commerce staffer recalls,

> So we went to the LICIT people and said, "Look, we think we can help you. But to help you, we're going to need your help too. We're going to put together a bill in the next Congress, and that bill is going to have a lot of our jurisdiction in it. But *you're* going to have to go sell it to Ways and Means. None of our people are going to put it in until the big people on Ways and Means get used to it." When they did, we introduced it. You know, the chairman [Dingell] introduced it. It was multiply referred to Ways and Means and Commerce . . . Then what we did was fly the bill through the committee . . . The bill had a life of its own, and when Rostenkowski finally moved their part of it out, everyone knew we were behind it. Everyone knew Big John Dingell meant business on trade.

By writing a strategically ambiguous bill and having it multiply referred, John Dingell gained a "seat at the table when important decisions are made" about trade. The Commerce Committee has been a part of all subsequent trade bills, but Commerce was certainly not the only committee carving out a piece of the trade jurisdiction in the early 1980s. The 1986 Omnibus Trade Bill included portions of bills passed out of six committees, including Foreign Affairs, Banking, Commerce, Education and Labor, and Agriculture.[18]

Fragmentation—live and well on trade issues—is common in Congress, and it has been exacerbated by multiple referrals because committees are keen to use such referrals to protect their turf from possible assaults. Regardless of the ensuing fragmentation, multiple referrals of all types usually promote communication and coordination across committees, and they allow "a single up or down vote on [a bill]. Multiple referrals thus become a flexible tool of the leadership for protecting certain exchanges across subcommittees from falling apart on the floor."[19]

The opportunity for committees to request *sequential* referrals has heightened jurisdictional protectionism. One of the most important jobs of "border cops" on committees is to read through descriptions of referred bills and decide whether part of their turf is involved. If it is, then the committee chair may ask the parliamentarian to have the bill rereferred after the first committee reports the bill (if it is reported at all). More likely than requesting a sequential referral, however, two or more committees will hold informal meetings to negotiate the contents of a "potentially sequential" bill. One staff director explained, "I'll just get on the phone and say 'Hey, we have a problem with this,' and we have the staff work it out if they can." Informal agreements of these kinds have become very common in the 1990s affecting, according to interviewees, most of the major legislation that now passes through the House. One staff director boasted that he does so much negotiation on "potentially sequential bills" that he has the telephone numbers of all of the other committee staff directors memorized. A generation ago, before multiple referrals, we would have been unlikely to find such quick communication across committees.

With potentially sequential bills, going to the parliamentarian for a rereferral is a last-step threat. Border cops worry—needlessly, say the parliamentarians—that if they ask for and fail to get a sequential referral, then their committee may lose jurisdiction over an issue. A top committee aide explained,

> If we can negotiate our issues and avoid asking for a sequential referral, that's what we do . . . It's like the courts system. There are a series of appeals. If we fail at the staff level, then it can be bumped up to the subcommittee chairman, and maybe the full committee chairman, then

maybe to the leadership . . . If we still can't get things resolved, we may escalate the dispute and call the Parliamentarian. And going to the Parliamentarian is like going to the Supreme Court, and we try to avoid that. Because if you lose there, you've lost. You've lost forever.

There are strong incentives, then, for committees playing the jurisdiction game defensively to negotiate among committees and avoid sequential referrals. The increase in coordination among committees since multiple referrals was mentioned by a majority of interviewees. On some occasions, deals are cut over specific amendments that may be offered to bills on the floor, which is partially responsible for the increased percentage of restrictive rules written since 1975.[20] Further, committee reports now routinely include "statements of agreement" saying that one committee—in declining to ask for a sequential referral on a bill touching on part of its jurisdiction—is not relinquishing jurisdiction over the issue.[21] And recently some committee calendars (Ways and Means, for example) include lists under the title "Bills and Resolutions Referred to Other Committees Containing Provisions over Which Jurisdiction Has Been Asserted."

Other Strategies

Besides amending public laws, citing referral precedents, gaining expertise, and writing strategically ambiguous bills, policy entrepreneurs have been inventive with less typical strategies to gain jurisdiction. Five more strategies are discussed below.

First, closely related to the amending and precedence-citing strategies, committees use *clever drafting* of bill titles and preambles to influence how the parliamentarian views a bill and to minimize the chances of raising the suspicions of other committees. Charles Tiefer recounts the drafting techniques by three committees that were referred three slightly different bills on nuclear waste disposal in the early 1980s. Science and Technology drafted its preamble to "emphasize national policy: the bill was 'to establish a Federal policy with respect to the disposal of high-level radioactive waste.'" The Interior Committee emphasized "where the waste was going (i.e., public lands): the bill was 'to provide for repositories for the disposal of high-level radioactive waste.'" Energy and Commerce focused its preamble on nuclear energy, which was in its jurisdiction.[22] The result was that three bills on essentially the same general subject were reported out of three committees, but each committee successfully staked a claim to at least part of the turf. Similarly, in the 102d Congress, the House Judiciary Committee was referred a bill reregulating the "baby Bells" (which is normally under the jurisdiction of House Commerce) because the bill was crafted to emphasize antitrust laws (which is in Judiciary's jurisdiction).[23]

With the 1995 elimination of concurrent referrals and the innovation of additional initial referrals, clever drafting is likely to gain in prominence as a turf war strategy. Before 1995, committees might be content to draft legislation "close enough" to their turf that they could get multiple referral. Now policy entrepreneurs have to be more certain in the wording of their bills to ensure that their committee will be deemed "primary" by the parliamentarian.

Second, some committee entrepreneurs have tried to claim jurisdiction over issues based on the way that the *Appropriations Committee* consolidates issues into subcommittees. Appropriations bills bundle programs together, and some have argued to the parliamentarian (almost always unsuccessfully) that this constitutes a precedent that confers jurisdiction. Further, the 1974 Budget and Impoundment Control Act established budget reconciliation procedures. If the Budget Committee asks a committee to respond to reconciliation instructions covering an issue that overlaps jurisdictions, this could later be used to support a committee's jurisdictional claims. This is considered a "weak claim" by the parliamentarian, but that message has apparently not sunk in to policy entrepreneurs who continue making it.

Third, one might *shift agency oversight* of an issue into an agency over which a policy entrepreneur's committee has jurisdiction. In 1987, John Dingell tried this tactic after receiving complaints from constituents about misleading advertising by airlines. Commerce (through its jurisdiction over interstate communications and consumer protection) had a claim to most advertising, but advertising by airlines was overseen by the Department of Transportation, which is in the Public Works Committee's territory. Hidden in a bill authorizing 1988–90 funding for the Federal Trade Commission was a provision shifting oversight of airline advertising from the DOT to the FTC. When Dingell's attempted maneuver was discovered, "Public Works leaders sent a letter to House colleagues with the headline: 'Has the Energy and Commerce Committee Ever Tried to Steal Your Jurisdiction?'—a question to which many members could have, at least silently, responded, 'Yes.' "[24] Dingell was trounced on the floor and failed to gain jurisdiction. His attention to the issue, however, had an impact on the tenacity with which DOT began monitoring airline advertising. In pursuing an issue that was in another committee's jurisdiction, Dingell violated one of the rules of the jurisdiction game. The overwhelming majority of jurisdictional grabs are made for issues that are not in *any* committee's jurisdiction because members are eager to avoid the kind of conflict and public thrashing Commerce took on airline advertising.

A fourth strategy is to gain representation on a *House-Senate conference committee*.[25] If issues are settled in the conference committee that are beyond the jurisdictional scope of a member's committee, the member might later argue before the parliamentarian that the issue "belongs" in his or her committee. The parliamentarian has called seats on conference committees a "very weak precedent," and in January 1991 Speaker Foley announced that conference appointments should not be viewed as conferring jurisdiction. Nonetheless, some members still believe there is some value in trying to claim issues raised in conference committees, and this is spurred on by the Senate's tendency to add nongermane language in conferences.

Finally, fifth, some members join special issue caucuses to establish their expertise in an issue area, expertise that may later buttress either a committee appointment or a bill referral. In 1990, there were forty-two Joint and House caucuses, and several of these focused on issues that overlap committee jurisdictions, including the Arts Caucus, the Caucus for Women's Issues, the Human Rights Caucus, and the Export Task Force. Funding for House caucuses was cut in 1995, but they continue to exist, now largely subsidized by special interest groups. Judy Schneider of the Congressional Research Service advises members that the "House and Senate parliamentarians may take into account the committee assignments and generally acknowledged policy expertise of a measure's sponsor."[26]

These final five strategies are much less frequently used than the first three—amending public laws, citing referral precedents, and establishing expertise—but one should not underestimate the creativity of policy entrepreneurs. Since the late 1980s, for example, some committees have started holding hearings on specific bills *before* those bills are even introduced. One can imagine policy entrepreneurs doing this on jurisdictionally ambiguous bills to demonstrate to the parliamentarian that the committee is serious about an issue and is developing expertise that the rest of the House may value.

Create Subcommittees to Consolidate Gains

While standing committee jurisdictions are fixed in the Rules and in referral precedents, subcommittee jurisdictions can be easily modified because they are overseen by the majority caucus within each committee. The full House gets no direct control over subcommittee jurisdictions. This gives entrepreneurs flexibility to craft subcommittees in ways that will emphasize certain issues. And as a result, the jurisdictions of many subcommittees have gone through tremendous flux.

From 1981 through 1991 in the House, eighty-two (of a total of 135) subcommittees were either created anew or underwent name changes to reflect modifications of their charters.[27] On 14 of the 22 standing committees in operation during the 1980s, a majority of the subcommittees had their jurisdictions changed by the full committee.[28] During that decade, subcommittee names were changed 19 times in the Small Business Committee, 13 in Interior, and nine in Science and Technology.

The reasons for modifying subcommittees are varied, and they usually coincide with a change in leadership either of the full committee or the subcommittee. The subcommittee lineage of House Commerce is typical. In 1951, the Transportation Subcommittee became the Aviation Subcommittee, reflecting the committee's preoccupation with airport construction and airline regulation. In 1975, the Commerce and Finance Subcommittee was renamed Consumer Protection and Finance, which simply codified the subcommittee's long-standing consumer protection jurisdiction. In 1987, the Commerce, Consumer Protection and Competitiveness Subcommittee was created to show the full committee's rising interest in "competitiveness" issues. Finally, facing a mandatory reduction in the number of subcommittees in 1995, the committee consolidated two panels, making the subcommittee on Commerce, Trade and Hazardous Materials. This final name change was no accident, for under Republican leadership, the full committee was not expected to prosecute a consumer protection agenda.

Subcommittees can be used to consolidate jurisdiction gains and to give an institutional focus to staff and member expertise. The institutional assets afforded subcommittee chairs makes it easier for them to launch into new issue areas, and subcommittee creations reflect a commitment on the part of the full committee to the new issue. They also tend to institutionalize fragmentation. In the 102d Congress (1991–92), for example, three subcommittees claimed jurisdiction over aspects of economic strategy,[29] and four held partial jurisdiction over health.[30] Nine subcommittees dealt with the environment,[31] and seven subcommittees oversaw energy issues.[32]

This last issue—energy—provides a good example of how a subcommittee can be used to consolidate jurisdictional gains. Energy turf was wide open following the 1973 Arab oil embargo. Pieces of the energy jurisdiction were spread out over many committees, and no single panel had yet handled issues like energy conservation, energy research, and a national energy strategy.[33] The Commerce Committee's claim to energy policy was no stronger than the claims of a dozen other committees, and they built off their jurisdiction over the regulation of "interstate oil compacts" to get into oil pricing problems. In 1975, John Dingell, then a mid-ranking Democrat on the committee, formed the Energy and Power Subcommittee, and he moved quickly to build on referral precedents and recast the committee as the preeminent energy panel in the House. By 1980, the Energy and Power Subcommittee had so firmly established jurisdiction over energy issues that the name of the full committee was changed from Interstate and Foreign Commerce to Energy and Commerce. In the 93d Congress (1973–74), the committee devoted less than 3 percent of its total effort in hearings to these energy issues. But with a subcommittee established in 1975, activity jumped to nearly 15 percent from 1975 to 1976. This fivefold increase was made possible by concentrating member and staff expertise about energy issues in the new subcommittee.

T he principle guiding all of these referral strategies, and the follow-on subcommittee consolidations, remains the parliamentarian's "weight of the bill." That, in turn, leads committees to emphasize their expertise at every turn. Lobbyists, too, know how the jurisdiction game is played, and several specialize in predicting how the parliamentarian will view things. One lobbyist explained:

> Judge Oliver Wendell Holmes once said that in the study of the law, it is as important to study the judge as it is to study the statute. We used to call Lew Deschler "the Judge," by the way, but he was the only one around, so we had to shop committees instead . . . There are certain committees, by their very nature, by the way they're made up, that advocate programs for or against [the interests of certain of my clients.] . . . People like to get subjects before people that are the most friendly.

Of course, one reason why interest groups and politicians want their petitions heard in a friendly forum may be so that their issues will receive the biggest budget requests. Maybe groups "committee shop" to protect established programs, which take on a perpetual life of their own in congressional budgets. Maybe these strategies are a subterfuge for handing out goodies to narrowly defined constituencies, at the expense of the whole. It is to these possibilities—and the struggle between distributive politics theories and informational theories—that we now turn.

S I X

Flying Trains
and
Turf Wars

O n a February night in 1960, Dr. James R. Powell of the Brookhaven National Laboratory on Long Island was stuck in traffic on the Bronx–Whitestone Bridge when he had an idea how to ease traffic congestion. He devised a plan to use magnets to "levitate and propel a vehicle down a guideway."[1] Thus the magnetically levitated train was conceived. Along with a colleague at Brookhaven, Powell received the first patent on "maglev" technology, and an international race to develop viable high-speed rail was in high gear by the late 1960s.

Powell's invention has been in development ever since, and, as we will see, the innovation posed an intriguing (and I believe typical) jurisdictional ambiguity. In the late 1980s when maglev trains were taken up in Congress, the issue seemed to fall somewhere between the House Commerce Committee's authority over railroads and the House Public Work's transportation turf more generally. Legislators on both panels wanted to claim the issue, partly to help direct where federal dollars would flow. In interviews, staffers on Commerce and on Public Works recounted arguments they made to the parliamentarian when precedent-setting referrals were being considered. One Commerce Committee staffer explained,

> We assert that maglev trains are the natural evolution of the railroad, which is clearly in our jurisdiction. Public Works has jurisdiction over mass transit, so they say that maglev trains are a part of mass transit. And we say that it's not really mass transit but part of the long distance carrying system, which means trains, which is in our jurisdiction. Then Public Works comes along and says "well, it's not sitting on a rail. It's flying. A moving maglev train is like the glide path of an airplane, and we have

jurisdiction over airplanes." We think that's ludicrous, but they're insisting that the height off the ground that something is "flying" doesn't make much difference—it's still flying. I've heard all these arguments. We go back and forth.

Public Works staffers chuckled at their own idea of calling the train an airplane, but it was not a bad strategy.

In this chapter, I use the maglev train example as one test of the theory outlined in Chapter 1. The maglev case is used to show how the theory can be operationalized, and I do not intend to generalize too far beyond it. I chose the maglev case primarily because it is fun to tell and because staffers on Commerce and Public Works mentioned it several times. It is also relatively easy to develop measures of "informational" and "distributive" benefits derived from various jurisdictional arrangements. In the late 1980s, there was very little expertise in Congress about maglev. It will be interesting to see how predictions based on "informational efficiency" hold up under low levels of expertise. Before returning to Dr. Powell's invention and the turf war it inspired, we will revisit the theory and puzzle about testing it.

Operationalizing the Theory of Jurisdictional Change

Recall that there are two steps in most turf wars. First, a policy entrepreneur on a committee claims territory by proposing a jurisdictionally ambiguous bill. Second, the parliamentarian refers the precedent-setting bill based on jurisdictional proximity. I have argued (and this is the persistent message I heard on Capitol Hill) that the parliamentarians use the "weight of the bill" decision rule because "that is where the experts are." Such a process of jurisdictional evolution apparently helps maintain the informational efficiency of the committee system. At least that is what members of Congress, staffers, and the parliamentarians *say,* but we should not take their comments at face value. Does anything happen on Capitol Hill that is not touched—at least a little— by self-serving motives born of the constant drive to get reelected? Perhaps not. Turf wars are no exception, especially when lawmakers are trying to figure out which issues to pursue.

To test the theory, one would like to take a specific jurisdictionally ambiguous issue before it reaches Capitol Hill and predict which members (and therefore which committees) will be contestants for bill referrals. Based on (1) a member's constituency interests, (2) a member's expertise, (3) committee resources and expertise available to a member, and (4) the degree of jurisdictional proximity of the new issue to a committee's current jurisdiction—one would like to predict which members (and committees) will engage in prereferral activities (such as holding preparatory hearings, publicizing problems, and sponsoring bills) that increase their chances of winning jurisdiction.

Committees and entrepreneurs build up reputations for being "players" on some issues, which attract other like-minded members to their panels. More important, committee resources and expertise grow over time. It is no coincidence that the House Commerce Committee staffs some of the most expensive House subcommittees and also has a large jurisdiction. Ideally, one would model a historical feedback loop from committee successes to committee resources.

At step one—before a jurisdictionally ambiguous bill is introduced —the turf wars story yields some specific predictions. Lawmakers are more likely to become policy entrepreneurs if:

—their constituents have a stake in the jurisdictionally ambiguous issue,

—the lawmakers have personal expertise in the jurisdictionally ambiguous issue,

—committee staffers have expertise in the ambiguous issue area, and

—the lawmakers sit on jurisdictionally proximate committees because they anticipate how the parliamentarian is likely to refer bills.

At step two, we predict that the parliamentarian gives a bill to the committee best able to handle it, based on three things:

—the committee's jurisdictional proximity to the ambiguous issue,

—the expertise among members on the committee, and

—committee resources (such as staff expertise).

The best scenario for testing these hypotheses raises problems. First, one needs a representative sample of jurisdictionally ambiguous bills. This is difficult to produce because committees win by arguing that jurisdictionally ambiguous bills are not really so ambiguous after all.[2] Further, it is often hard to measure constituency interests. In Chapter 3 we learned about consumer protection, but during the early 1960s that phrase—and the issue—did not exist. "Consumer protection" took on the meaning it has today in part because of the specific bills that were referred in the House to the Commerce Committee, the Agriculture Committee, and the Banking Committee. One would have been hard-pressed to measure district-level interests related to regulating deceptive advertising or support for improved product labeling laws. It was the same with a hot "new" issue in the early 1990s: competitiveness. What, exactly, does competitiveness mean as a policy issue? It is still being defined by the committees staking claims, among them Agriculture, Banking, Commerce, and Science.

It is easier to measure the district-level impact of a bill for distributive programs than for legislation tapping into emerging issues or public goods—like the environment. We have, once again, a sample selection problem because if we only look at issues for which constituency measures are easily attainable, we may very well give too much play to the role of constituency interests that are rooted in distributive politics.[3]

Finally, it is also difficult to measure a committee's expertise in an issue area. The easiest way is to look at what subcommittees a member serves on. The 17 members of the old House Subcommittee on Oceanography and Great Lakes were likely experts on oceanography and the great lakes. The problem is that subcommittee memberships are highly correlated with jurisdictional proximity. Other measures of expertise might be drawn out of congressional biographies; however, typical biographies only identify a few general issue areas related to a member's background. Farmers are likely to be interested in farming issues, broadly defined. Bankers are likely to be interested in banking issues, broadly defined. Since the best test of the theory is at the bill level, such generalities do not help much.

Magnetically levitated trains seem an appropriate first test of the theory because virtually everyone on the committees that were involved pointed to the "trains" as a fundamentally jurisdictionally ambiguous issue. With maglev, also, there were several clearly identifiable entrepreneurs holding hearings, writing editorials, and holding forth on the House floor. Further, because a small set of contractors had a big stake in maglev technologies, it is fairly easy to trace the specific benefits that each district would have received had Congress helped get maglev off the ground.

Magnetically Levitated Trains

To the Japanese and Germans, it was a mystery why the U.S. Congress waited until the early 1990s to invest heavily in maglev technologies. Following James Powell's innovations, most of the technology's early developments were made in the United States under the direction of Dr. Henry Kolm at the Massachusetts Institute of Technology. Dubbed the "magneplane," Kolm's 1/25th- scale model hummed down an aluminum test track at 56 miles per hour in 1974. A full-scale model with identical technology could have gone 250 miles per hour.[4] Maglev systems use significantly less energy per passenger mile than automobiles or short-haul aircraft, and per mile of new construction they cost less to build than highways. Pollution per passenger mile is significantly reduced with maglev systems, and maintenance costs are far less than for roads and bridges.[5] From 1966 through 1975, the U.S. government spent $3 million on maglev research, but the Office of Management and Budget canceled all funds in early 1975, and virtually all research stopped in the United States when private industries failed to develop and refine the technology. Maglev funding in that earlier era was run through several federal offices (including the Pentagon), and no House or Senate committee staked a claim to the turf.

While maglev research disappeared in the United States by the late 1970s, public-private partnerships in England, West Germany, and Japan funded significant breakthroughs. The Japanese and West German governments each spent more than $1 billion on maglev by 1990, and their investment is apparently beginning to pay off.[6] Since the early 1980s, Walt Disney officials have been planning to build a 13-mile maglev line between the Orlando International Airport and Walt Disney World in central Florida. Construction might begin by the year 2000, and conservative estimates place the cost in the billions, and some state funding may still be needed.[7] The technology will have to be purchased from Germany, and because banks in the United States are unfamiliar with maglev systems a large part of the financing is being underwritten by Japanese banks. According to a 1991 Office of Technology Assessment report, two other maglev lines were thought likely to begin construction by 2000. One was a 19-mile line connecting downtown Pittsburgh with the airport, and a more ambitious project being partially financed by Bechtel Corporation was a proposed 265-mile link between Anaheim, California, and Las Vegas, Nevada.[8] All of these projects, now greatly delayed, will depend heavily on imported materials and technology.

After being out of view in this country for more than a decade, maglev research was back on the congressional agenda by the late 1980s for two reasons. First, the Orlando, Las Vegas, and Pittsburgh projects were widely cited as evidence that American industries had lost their competitiveness as companies failed to invest in research and development programs.[9] Second, Paul Chu and his colleagues at the University of Houston announced a series of major breakthroughs in the late 1980s in high-temperature superconductors. Superconducting materials produce powerful magnetic fields with very little energy, and suddenly it seemed possible that American industries could leapfrog to the forefront of maglev technology.[10]

During the late 1980s, Japan's maglev project was plagued by technical difficulties, including a spectacular fire that destroyed their primary test vehicle in late 1991.[11] Those difficulties, along with West Germany's heavy costs of reunification, seemed to give the United States a window of opportunity. The Japanese, however, overcame a long list of technical hurdles, announcing major cost savings in the technology during the mid-1990s.[12] Though German investment in maglev flagged during the early 1990s, the government now pledges to install a high-speed rail link service between Hamburg and Berlin by 2004.[13] In the United States, maglev became a victim of budget cuts in the mid-1990s, leading Transportation Secretary Fredrico Pena to say, "I would not be surprised if 10 or 15 years from now we begin buying [maglev] back from our competition." Still, the picture looked bright in the late 1980s, and committees braced for the turf war to come. The issue seemed very attractive, even lucrative for some districts. The question was how Congress would respond to the new opportunities to get into the maglev race.

WHICH COMMITTEES FOUGHT FOR TURF?

We should see policy entrepreneurs arising on committees that are jurisdictionally proximate to maglev trains. Sometimes the links are tenuous. Place yourself in the late 1980s, before House committee names were changed in 1995. The House Committee on Banking, Finance, and Urban Affairs had authority over urban development and could write special regulations designed to site maglev trains in some cities. The House Commerce Committee had jurisdiction over railroads, while the Public Works Committee handled almost all transportation legislation except railroads. The Committee on Space, Science, and Technology had jurisdiction over "scientific research, development, and demonstration" and could claim maglev projects in the R&D phase.

Most of the initial entrepreneurial action came from the Senate side, and mainly from Daniel Patrick Moynihan (D-NY), but the House was silent. Maglev was first raised in Congress in a serious way in 1987, and most of the turf issues were settled by 1992. In 1991, House committees helped push through maglev provisions in the Intermodal Surface Transportation Efficiency Act of 1991, authorizing $725 million for a prototype development project.[14] That promise of money was a major victory for the maglev industry, though it proved short-lived. Money can be authorized, but nothing is spent until it is appropriated. Maglev funds had to run the gauntlet of the House Appropriations Transportation subcommittee, chaired by the appropriately named Representative Robert Carr. Heavily funded by the automobile industry and representing Flint, Michigan, Carr sat on the funds in the name of deficit reduction. There has been little money forthcoming ever since.

Potential policy entrepreneurs anticipate that the parliamentarian uses the "weight of the bill" decision rule, which means that the parliamentarian tends to favor committees that are jurisdictionally proximate. Knowing this, an entrepreneur will not invest the time and effort needed to try to get a bill referral if his or her committee's current jurisdiction is not even "close" to the new issue. It is hard to imagine, for example, how a potential entrepreneur on the House Standards of Official Conduct Committee might stake a plausible claim to maglev. Even so, we need to be able to test the claim that jurisdictional proximity matters when potential entrepreneurs are deciding whether to get involved, and for this we need to be able to measure jurisdictional proximity.

I measured jurisdictional proximity by looking at two things. First, I read through *Deschler's Precedents of the U.S. House of Representatives* to see which committees might be able to point to referral precedents on issues related to maglev trains. This is admittedly subjective, but it is not time consuming and it is easily reproducible.[15] Of the 22 standing House committees from 1987 through 1992, five had some plausible claim to jurisdictional proximity by this first measure: Energy and Commerce, Public Works, Science, Banking, and Ways and Means. A second measure was based on the federal agencies that committees oversaw. Three agencies have given maglev prominent attention since the late 1980s, making for what the *Wall Street Journal* has correctly labeled a "turf battle" within the executive branch over the emerging technology. These three agencies—the Department of Transportation, the Department of Energy, and the Army Corps of Engineers—were also the most active members of President Bush's advisory committee on the future of maglev.[16] To measure the degree of proximity, I give a committee one point for each of the three agencies that they oversaw, and I give them one point for each of the proximate issues found in *Deschler's Precedents.*

Using these two measures of jurisdictional proximity, seven committees, or about a third of those in the House, could have staked some plausible claim to part of the maglev turf in the late 1980s.[17] The two committees, Commerce and Public Works, raised most often in interviews also have the highest proximity scores, with four points each. Ways and Means (with one point) shows up on the list because research and development projects often receive special tax incentives, which would have to include the committee. Banking (one point) has an opening through its jurisdiction over urban development because it is likely that city centers will benefit the most from reduced congestion. And one can imagine Armed Services (two points) staking a claim through the Army Corps of Engineers and through increased R&D work done at Department of Energy installations, such as the one in Los Alamos, New Mexico, that were formerly used for strategic weapons research. Jurisdictional proximity is a matter of degrees, and it should be modeled that way. The probability that an entrepreneur will emerge on a committee is a function of how close the committee's jurisdiction already is. While it is less likely that an entrepreneur will emerge on Armed Services than Commerce, it is not impossible.

Whether a policy entrepreneur on a jurisdictionally proximate committee wants to launch a turf war is related to constituency interests, the member's expertise in the issue, committee resources, and staff expertise that can be brought to bear on the issue. Based on these factors, and based on a committee's jurisdictional proximity, one would like to be able to predict the probability that any given member will emerge as a policy entrepreneur on an issue.[18]

Entrepreneurs want to engage in activities that anticipate how the parliamentarian refers ambiguous bills, so lawmakers try to demonstrate their committee's informational advantages, and they emphasize the links between the committee's current jurisdiction and the new issue. More specifically, we can expect policy entrepreneurs to engage in three prereferral activities that we can measure by looking carefully at public records: publicizing a problem, holding preparatory hearings, and sponsoring legislation.

First, entrepreneurs publicize jurisdictionally ambiguous issues in many ways, including writing editorials and giving House floor speeches. Through "extensions of remarks" and other means, members talk about issues even when no legislation is pending. When comments about an issue are made outside of the debate over a bill, this is a signal to the House, to the parliamentarian, and to a member's constituents that an entrepreneur is interested in an issue. To find entrepreneurs on maglev trains, I used the database Legi-Slate and searched through every word printed in the *Congressional Record* from January 1987 through June 1992. I looked for three phrases: maglev, magnetically levitated trains, and high-speed rail. I ignored all comments associated with a referred bill, because at this stage of the theory we care only about *pre*referral activities. Members were given two points for every floor speech that was primarily about maglev trains, both pro and con.[19]

Second, members may call preparatory hearings on subjects outside of their jurisdiction, and policy entrepreneurs do this as a way of publicizing problems and gaining expertise. Such hearings are at the pre-referral stage and are not called to discuss a specific bill. Like highlighting issues on the floor, these hearings are signals to the House, the parliamentarian, and a member's constituents that a committee is interested in an issue. Two preparatory hearings were held on maglev trains, one in 1987 and one in 1990.[20] Because our theory is at the individual level, we need to account for whether specific members participated in these prereferral hearings. To do this, I used a ruler and measured the total centimeters of printed text attributed to each member participating in the hearings. Points for participating in the hearings ranged from zero to three.[21]

Third, policy entrepreneurs sponsor legislation after tailoring their bills to improve their chances of getting the referrals they want. From 1987 through 1992, 13 members introduced bills relating to maglev trains, and I gave each primary sponsor four points in the index of entrepreneurial activity.[22] Cosponsors were given one point. The three indicators of prereferral entrepreneurial activity were added together to become our dependent variable in a multivariate test of the theory's first stage.

More than 500 people served in the House of Representatives during the six-year turf war on maglev trains. There were 113 of these who had some prereferral entrepreneurial activity, but a small group of members scored particularly high: Joe Kolter (D-PA) 14, Robert Mrazek (D-NY) 11, Robert Torricelli (D-NJ) 10, and James Hayes (D-LA) 8. These four legislators were also identified as the strongest maglev supporters in the House during interviews with maglev lobbyists. To anyone who knew Representative Kolter in the early 1980s, it would not be surprising that he emerged as a maglev entrepreneur. In a floor speech on April 23, 1991, Kolter said that when he first arrived in Congress in 1983,

> [a] senior legislator indicated that the first thing that I ought to do is to throw myself body, heart, and soul into something that I really liked, some form of legislation. That was easy. My first love has always been high-speed magnetic levitation rail . . . High-speed rail transport was a new idea then. Many were skeptical. Many were hostile. Now, so many are jumping on our bandwagon that those days—just 9 years ago—seem hard to believe.[23]

Likewise Robert Mrazek, who sat on the relevant Appropriations Subcommittee on Transportation, took up an interest in maglev trains shortly after entering the House in 1983. While Kolter's interests stem from a longtime fascination with the technology, however, Mrazek's attention to the issue was more closely linked to his district. Grumman Corporation, the aerospace giant based near Mrazek's district, employed thousands of his constituents.

In the multivariate model below, constituency interests in maglev trains are indicated by two things. First, all congressional districts in which maglev systems were expected to be operating by the year 2000 were identified with the aide of a 1991 Office of Technology Assessment report.[24] I gave the legislator from each district with a maglev terminal three points on a "constituency interests" index. Neighboring congressional districts within a 50-mile radius of a likely maglev terminal were given one point. This criterion tapped legislators in 18 congressional districts. Second, I identified all of the major corporations with an active interest in maglev research and development, and points were given for having them in a district as well.[25]

Of the 524 members who served at any time from 1987 through 1992, constituency interests were discerned for 79, or about 15 percent. At the top of the list was William Coyne (D-PA) 14, in whose district the Pittsburgh airport project was planned. Westinghouse Electric Corporation was among Coyne's constituents, and AEG Westinghouse Transportation Systems is headquartered nearby in the twentieth congressional district. There is a strong bivariate relationship between the presence of constituency interests in a district and a member's level of prereferral entrepreneurial activity. Among the 79 members with district interests in maglev, the average level of prereferral activity was 1.52. Among the members with no recorded constituency interest in maglev, the average level of prereferral activity was 0.31.

Assessing member expertise and committee staff expertise in an issue area presented additional challenges.[26] I began by selecting an initial list of House committee staffers who have been involved in the maglev issue.[27] In 1991 telephone interviews, I asked these staffers to rate member and staff knowledge about the maglev issue. Because entrepreneurial behavior needs to be modeled before a committee has gained jurisdiction over an issue, I tried to get the respondents to talk about the members and staffers who had expertise in maglev two to four years earlier—before it became visible on the agenda.[28] From the initial list of staffers, I used a snowball sample to contact all of the staffers mentioned.[29]

There were low levels of knowledge about maglev among legislators in the late 1980s. Asked to rate members' maglev expertise from zero to five, where zero was no expertise at all, only 11 members were mentioned by any staffer as having even the slightest personal expertise in the issue, and, chamber-wide, the average level of expertise was a mere

0.042.[30] Staffers were also asked for whom they felt they worked on the maglev issue so that the staffer's expertise ratings could be attributed to specific members. I use this measure of staff expertise as a proxy for institutional position, because these experts are, for the most part, available only to committee and subcommittee chairs.

The model to be estimated has entrepreneurial activity (EN) as a dependent variable. The independent variables are constituency interests in maglev (CI), jurisdictional proximity (JP), personal maglev expertise (PE), and committee staff maglev expertise (SE). We also expect that jurisdictional proximity matters even if members have strong constituency interests or high levels of expertise. This is reflected in two interaction terms. Testing the first step of the theory, then, the model to be estimated is $EN = B_0 + B_1CI + B_2JP + B_3(JP*CI) + B_4PE + B_5(JP*PE) + B_6SE + U$.

The findings,[31] reflected in table 6.1, confirm the powerful influence of jurisdictional proximity on the likelihood of entrepreneurial activity. Constituency interests and personal expertise also matter. Jurisdictional free-for-alls do not involve every member with a district-level stake in new issues. Rather, constituency interests are mediated through jurisdictional proximity and members are participating selectively.

Table 6.1 OLS Model of Prereferral Entrepreneurial Activity on Maglev Trains, 1987–1992

Independent Variable	Mean of Variable	Range of Variable	Estimated Coefficient (S.E. in Parenthesis)
Constituency Maglev Interests (CI)	0.23	0–7	0.23* (0.08)
Jurisdictional Proximity (JP)	1.23	0–4	0.10* (0.03)
Interaction (JP*CI)	0.34	0–20	0.17* (0.04)
Personal Maglev Expertise (PE)	0.04	0–3	2.36* (0.47)
Interaction (JP*PE)	0.13	0–12	−0.14 (0.23)
Staff Maglev Expertise (SE)	0.04	0–4	−0.00 (0.14)
Intercept			0.11

Note: $N = 524$, S.E. = Standard Error, Ave. $Y = 0.43$, $r^2 = 0.39$, Range $Y = 0–14$.
*$p < 0.01$.

Most of the expectations about entrepreneurial behavior that arise from our theory are supported by the results from the maglev case. The fact that any one of the relationships is statistically discernible suggests that more than "just personalities" is involved. Indeed, the influence of constituency interests is strong and in the expected direction. Members with relevant industries in their districts and with proposed maglev sites in their districts are, all else equal, more likely to engage in pre-referral entrepreneurial behavior. This result is right in line with the distributive politics tradition.

Entrepreneurial activity, however, depends on much more than constituency interests. As the first interaction term indicates, constituency interests are more likely to be acted on when they are found in conjunction with jurisdictional proximity. When a member was on a committee, like Public Works or Commerce, that was already jurisdictionally close to maglev, that member was much more likely to pursue district interests. This is because members anticipate the decision rules that the parliamentarian uses. No matter how much their districts might benefit from maglev, members on jurisdictionally distant committees are less likely to become entrepreneurs because they know that their chances of a bill referral are slight indeed.

A member's expertise about maglev technologies also appears to have had an important impact on which members pursue the issue. A handful of members have been thinking and writing about maglev issues for more than a decade, and it is not surprising that these members have been at the front of the line asking for more federal involvement. It may be, however, that the measurement of "personal expertise" is endogenous because interviewees may have had difficulty untangling their own assessment of a member's expertise from how visible that member has been on the issue.

While the results from the maglev case give us some confidence in the model, two things were unexpected. First, the interaction between jurisdictional proximity and personal expertise was not statistically discernible.[32] Second, the level of committee staff expertise available to a member was unrelated to entrepreneurial activity. My interviews lead me to expect subcommittee chairs and ranking members to be much more active as entrepreneurs, but the evidence from this single case does support the claim. Staff expertise is primarily available to committee and subcommittee chairs. The discrepancy between my interviews and the maglev case probably has more to do with the nature of maglev than the nature of turf wars. Maglev was first pushed by a few members trying to make a name for themselves. Only later did subcommittee chairs and the ranking minority members get on board.

Which Committees Won?

On maglev trains, constituency interests and jurisdictional proximity were both important in determining which members became entrepreneurs. At the second stage of the theory, the House parliamentarian decides which committees receive a bill—thereby conferring jurisdiction. The theory's predictions are clear here. The parliamentarian refers bills based on jurisdictional proximity, which is a surrogate for committee expertise.[33]

From spring 1990 through spring 1992, 16 House bills or resolutions were introduced that touched on aspects of magnetically levitated trains.[34] An important referral precedent followed the April 18, 1990, introduction of H.R. 4549, the Magnetic Levitation Transportation and Competitiveness Act of 1990. That bill, sponsored by Robert Mrazek (D-NY), was to "establish programs to promote the development and construction of magnetic levitation transportation systems and to establish a Magnetic Levitation Transportation Administration in the Department of Transportation."

As we showed earlier, seven House committees could have claimed some jurisdictional proximity to the maglev issue: Energy and Commerce, Ways and Means, Interior, Banking, Science and Technology, Public Works and Transportation, and Armed Services.

H.B. 4549 was not crafted to force a referral to any specific committee, and it did not amend a public law, so this is a good bill to assess what the parliamentarian weighed when referring the bill.[35] H.R. 4549 is also useful because it was jointly referred. In this example, I want to distinguish among committees with relatively higher expertise and relatively higher constituency interest. I have not designed this case study to distinguish among the specific committees that eventually won referrals. Rather, I am interested in how the "winning" committees compare—as a group—to the committees left out of the action on maglev.

H.R. 4549 was given a joint referral to Energy and Commerce, Public Works and Transportation, and Science and Technology. The joint referral indicates that the parliamentarians did not discern a primary committee of jurisdiction, allowing each of the three committees to extend incrementally their borders on the dimension most jurisdictionally proximate. Science and Technology, for example, extended their authority over the research and development aspects of maglev, while Commerce gained authority over implications of maglev on the rail system more generally. The giving of a joint referral does not render the jurisdiction game invalid. Far from it. The parliamentarian could have sent H.R. 4549 to five or six committees, but there was something distinctive about the three committees that finally received jurisdiction. What was distinctive? Was it that those three committees have the biggest constituency stakes in maglev, as distributive theory would predict?

The suspects—constituency interest, member expertise, staff expertise, and jurisdictional proximity—here become independent variables helping us understand the bill referral. To get committee level indicators, I summed across the individual level scores for the members of every committee. This yielded committee scores of constituency interests, member expertise, and the other variables. The range on these variables is large. No one on the Rules Committee or on the D.C. Committee, for example, registered any district interests in maglev from 1987 through 1992. In contrast, members on Banking, Finance and Urban Affairs totaled a score of 22 index points on the constituency interests measure. That is equivalent to eight major maglev industries and three proposed maglev lines among committee members. In a distributive politics world, members on the Banking Committee should have demanded high funding levels for maglev, and if jurisdictional change reflects such pressures, the Banking Committee should have received a bill referral. For the seven committees that either had some claim to jurisdictional proximity or engaged in prereferral activity on maglev issue, table 6.2[36] shows the relationship between committee characteristics and the referral of H.R. 4549.

As the theory of jurisdictional change predicts, on maglev issues the parliamentarian rewarded committees based on jurisdictional proximity and expertise. At this critical stage of the model—when Congress's committee jurisdictions are essentially decided—the institution embraced informational efficiency, even at the risk of denying high demanders. Recall that the measures of member and staff expertise were designed to tap knowledge about maglev technologies before a bill was referred. Among the three committees that received H.R. 4549, the average member expertise score was 9.0, far higher than the average, 0.5, among the four contending committees that did not get a bill referral. The contrast between the committees that did and did not get jurisdiction is just as striking when one looks at the committee staff expertise that could be brought to bear on maglev issues.

In the first stage when entrepreneurs were deciding whether to get involved in the maglev issue, both jurisdictional proximity and district-level interests played a powerful role. But using the parliamentarians' "weight of the bill" decision rule, constituency interests seem less relevant. A committee (like Banking) may be a high demanding prefer-

Table 6.2 Committee Characteristics and Maglev Bill Referrals

	Maglev Bill Referral (N = 3)	No Maglev Bill Referral (N = 4)
Constituency interests		
High	Science and Technology	Ways and Means Armed Services Banking
Medium	Energy and Commerce Public Works	None
Low	None	Interior
Ave. score	13.67	16.75
Member expertise		
High	Science and Technology Public Works	None
Medium	Energy and Commerce	Armed Services
Low	None	Ways and Means Banking Interior
Ave. score	9.0	0.5
Staff expertise		
High	Science and Technology Public Works Energy and Commerce	None
Low	None	Ways and Means Banking Armed Services Interior
Ave. score	8.0	0.0
Jurisdictional proximity		
High	Public Works Energy and Commerce	None
Medium	Science and Technology	Armed Services
Low	None	Ways and Means Interior Banking
Ave. score	3.33	1.25

ence outlier for maglev funds, but that makes little difference if that committee cannot also claim jurisdictional proximity and expertise. *For the maglev case, the four committees that did not receive jurisdiction actually had, on average, a bigger district-level stake in the issue than the three committees that won jurisdiction.* For the maglev case, the lesson seems clear. Turf was given to committees that could be low-cost specialists.

Though we should not generalize beyond a single case, the empirical evidence from the maglev case matches what members and staffers on Capitol Hill said I should expect. Entrepreneurial legislators got involved in the issue for several reasons, including constituency interests, personal expertise, and in anticipation that their committee might actually get a referral. The parliamentarian sent H.R. 4549 to the three committees that—as a group—held the most expertise and were the most jurisdictionally proximate. With that referral decision, the parliamentarian bypassed four plausible committees, even though those committees—as a group—had stronger constituency interests in the issue.

SEVEN

Governing through Fragmented Committees

Picture yourself in George Brown's position at the end of 1990. A California Democrat and a fixture in the House since 1972, you were unexpectedly handed the chairmanship of the House Science Committee when Glenn Anderson (D-CA) was ousted from Public Works and Science Chairman Robert Roe (D-NJ) took over for Anderson. Following the Christmas recess, you would be leading one of Congress's least respected committees. Your panel was so fraught with problems that an Appropriations subcommittee had taken over developing space programs because Science members could not even pass their own authorizing bills. Whatever innovative spark there was on the committee when you joined a generation earlier was almost extinguished. Now you found yourself surrounded by a highly homogeneous lot, as committee colleagues were drawn from districts representing either the National Aeronautics and Space Administration or the Department of Energy. A homogeneous committee membership is more likely to be satisfied with its turf, and you think that is a problem. You want your committee to regain its former glory. You want new issues, and you want new blood. What do you do?

Call your trusted advisers together and imagine what jurisdictionally ambiguous issue lies just beyond the horizon. Then chart a series of bill referrals to claim as much of the issue as possible. Amend a public law already in your turf, but be willing to introduce fresh legislation if needed. In order to land a more heterogeneous membership, advertise your committee among young colleagues as a place where new things are happening, and bring them on board to help you push for your vision of the committee's emerging turf. Focus on new members who have some expertise in science policy—like rare physicists, chemists, and engineers. Discourage potential new members with obvious constituent links to NASA and DOE, for these members are too likely to be satisfied with the status quo. Finally, bolster your committee's staff with expertise in the new issue area, and showcase their skills through committee reports which are available to the whole House and might be seen (not coincidentally) by the parliamentarian.

That, in brief, is precisely what George Brown did, and it surprised his colleagues who never before thought of him as a policy entrepreneur. However, Brown's new issue—American competitiveness—was just too compelling to ignore.[1] Brown had long been interested in competitiveness issues, introducing a 1987 bill along those lines called "America's Living Standards Act." His 1990 elevation to the chairmanship gave him the opportunity he had been looking for. In an excited phone call with committee staff, he repeated the word several times. Competitiveness. Brown visualized turning his moribund panel into the House's home for competitiveness. Over the next four years, he succeeded on almost every turf war he launched, incrementally securing referrals related to the scientific research and development components of American competitiveness.[2] The committee's transformation was so successful that in late 1994 the new Republican majority briefly toyed with changing the panel's name to the Committee on Science and Competitiveness.

There is nothing spectacular about the George Brown story, expect perhaps that his committee was almost renamed to reflect the accomplishment. Policy entrepreneurs on House and Senate committees know how turf wars are won. By this point in the book, so do you. Jurisdictions are not rigid. Those brief reform periods, like the one Newt Gingrich orchestrated in January 1995, have never settled turf once and for all. Again, it does not take an act of Congress to change the status quo. As a former assistant parliamentarian explained,

> You have the status quo, yes, but the status quo is reached by a negotiation process, and the players change, and the bills change, and the national issues change, and the old 'status quo' doesn't necessarily hold anymore. The way the rules are written, just about every committee has a fishing and a hunting license to extend the borders of their jurisdiction.[3]

However, wittingly or not, George Brown and his brand of policy entrepreneurs have left the U.S. Congress with highly fragmented committee jurisdictions. It is not likely that there will soon emerge a national competitiveness policy with a single voice and vision. There are too many committees involved to define—precisely—just what

competitiveness is or might be. Since turf wars are won and lost on incremental plots of territory, fragmentation is almost inevitable. The
more important, the more pressing, and the more politically rewarding
a new issue is, the more committees it will attract, and the more fragmentation there will be.

This closing chapter touches on the opportunities and challenges of
jurisdictional fragmentation, but I offer no hard and fast rules or solutions. Fragmentation, most journalists and politicians agree, is bad. It is
bad for building a consensus around policy solutions. It is bad for coordinating activities between the House and Senate, between the Congress and the White House, and between the federal and state
governments. Writing in the 1880s, Woodrow Wilson once called committees "dim dungeons of silence;"[4] jurisdictional fragmentation simply gives bills more places to die. Today bills are larger, more complex.[5]
The 1990 amendments to the Clean Air Act passed through seven
House committees, and the 1988 Omnibus Trade Act included provisions from 23 House and Senate Committees.[6] Conference committees
are larger than ever. One cannot come to terms with the reasons for
crafting these "mega bills" without addressing the jurisdiction game
and its impact on the institution.

Optimal Fragmentation

Congress's scattered approach to policymaking, often unfocused and
uncoordinated, has its costs and benefits, which we will outline shortly.
First, though, imagine that there exists some optimal level of fragmentation. Below this level, committees would find whole policy areas in
their exclusive control, with little need to consult other panels. Above
this level, the political process might grind to a halt as committee after
committee takes turns forming policy. I do not know precisely what the
optimal level of fragmentation may be, and this is a question that would
benefit from careful consideration by formal modelers. I do know,
however, that the optimal level is considerably greater than zero, for a
committee system without fragmentation strikes me as a sterile and
lackluster creation.

If we could conceive of a "fragmentation equilibrium," I do not
know just what it would look like, but it may well tend toward an informationally efficient system. The more fragmented a committee's turf
becomes, the more heterogeneous its membership, and the more its
members' preferences mirror those of the parent chamber. One result
of the jurisdiction game is that committees with large policy territories
are more likely to win, and a small minority of panels eventually end up

handling a majority of the legislation. That has happened in the House, the Senate, and in every state legislature I've explored. On its face, this seems anything but informationally efficient. However, large committees with growing jurisdictions also have large and well-paid staffs, so they are best able to handle new issues. What may at first appear to be an inefficient way of handing out new turf may be rewarding heterogeneous committees instead.

Whatever the optimal level of fragmentation is, it must be related to how difficult or complex a problem happens to be. For discrete proposals in which solutions are easily mapped onto likely outcomes, there is little to be gained by fragmenting the issue among committees. There has never been much of a tussle over which committees should oversee the national parks, and for good reason. The Resources Committee has the background and expertise to handle the job. However, George Brown's issue—competitiveness—is something else entirely. When information is low, when an emerging issue is not clearly defined, a certain amount of fragmentation should be encouraged. Writes Heinz Eulau, "jurisdictional conflicts can be seen as first signals that a given piece of legislation may involve a great variety of complex and technical issues whose solution calls for bargaining and expertise."[7] In designing an informationally efficient legislature, this quest for expertise is key.

The notion of a "fragmentation equilibrium" should be thought of in terms of an idealized legislative organization in which jurisdictions are fluid, not fixed. My experience has been that the current reform-minded House members have an equilibrium—however fuzzily articulated—in mind. They understand the costs and benefits of jurisdictional fragmentation and tend to support what they call "Goldilocks" reforms: not too hard (on fragmentation) and not too soft either. These distinctions are not very helpful, but they do underscore an appreciation among political practitioners for the benefits of having jurisdictions with some degree of fragmentation and fluidity.

Costs of Fragmentation

Fragmentation is more pervasive today than at any time since the 1946 act. The 1995 reforms made nary a dent. In some instances (such as giving authority over the Trans-Alaska Oil Pipeline to the Resources Committee), the 1995 reforms made fragmentation worse. Name any general policy area that has become a hot topic since World War II, and one finds several committees claiming different parts of the action. While there are more than 125 federal programs aimed at helping children and their families, the direction of those programs is shared among 13 House committees.[8] Until recently, such fragmentation was used to justify the continuation of select committees, like the Select Committee on Children, Youth and Families, and the Select Committee on Hunger. The policy impact of such panels is limited, however, because they are not allowed to report legislation; furthermore, the new Republican leadership closed the doors of many select committees, even though they helped coordinate across fragmented policy areas. Barred by the House rules from reporting legislation, select committees always played second-fiddle to the standing committees.

Select committees, often indirectly funded by outside interest groups, have been largely replaced by Speaker-controlled task forces, but the rationale for task forces—overcoming fragmentation—is the same argument made on behalf of select committees. House task forces flourished in the 104th Congress, fueled to a great extent by the enthusiasm of first-term Republicans eager to circumvent the standing committees. Newt Gingrich's Medicare reforms were formed within Republican-only task forces, but died a painful public death by the revelation of shortcomings that would have likely surfaced in the committees of jurisdiction.[9] Time will tell, but I suspect that the use of task forces peaked in the 104th Congress. While task forces may be alluring to leaders eager for control over what comes out of committees, and while task forces may be attractive as devices for coordinating across fragmented issues, until task forces gain the track record of expertise found on standing committees, and until task forces are allowed to report legislation, the policy relevance of standing committees will be unchallenged.

Jurisdictions become fragmented as committees try to redefine settled issues. The 1988 Omnibus Trade Act included provisions from 23 different House and Senate committees. Although the committees shared jurisdiction over the general area of trade policy, each committee took their own slant on different parts of the bill, like a patchwork quilt. The Ways and Means Committee's jurisdiction over trade predates the national income tax when U.S. customs houses provided much of the federal government's revenue. Naturally, all tariff legislation went to the committee as well, and the debate within Ways and Means has traditionally been over how *free* trade ought to be.[10] Other House committees have made inroads into the general area of trade by designing bills that tap a new dimension—*fair* trade. In the midst of the trade turf war, one *National Journal* headline read, "Strategic Value of Introducing Trade Bill May Be More Important than Passage."[11] If that is the political environment in which the world's largest economy formulates trade policies, then the costs of fragmentation might be global.

From May 1983 through April 1992, 112 hearings were held in the House that tackled either "free trade" or "fair trade" issues.[12] The Congressional Information Service publishes paragraph-long descriptions of the subjects discussed in the hearings. Of the 112 hearings during this period, the words "free trade" (and not the words "fair trade") appeared in the descriptions of 82 hearings. The overwhelming majority of these hearings were held by the Ways and Means Committee, though the Agriculture Committee was sometimes involved as well. In 24 of the 112 hearings, the words "fair trade" (and not the words "free trade") were used to describe the hearings. Most of these cases involved the Commerce Committee and the Banking Committee. Only six of the 112 hearings dealt with both "free trade" and "fair trade." So while there are several committees that have jurisdiction over trade policy, the lower the level of one's analysis, the more clearly the lines of authority become.

From the public manager's perspective, one of the biggest costs of fragmentation is having to keep multiple committees appraised of what an executive branch agency is doing. Virtually identical reports and testimonies might be given to a half-dozen panels, and each committee will routinely demand that public managers fill out questionnaires, progress statements, and answers to countless time-consuming questions. Without jurisdictional fragmentation, congressional liaison offices throughout the executive branch would be gutted, which would please any number of assistant secretaries, deputy secretaries, and deputy assistant secretaries in offices around Washington.

Worse than the problem of duplication, public managers in Washington fear jurisdictional fragmentation because their multiple masters occasionally give conflicting demands. It is not uncommon for House and Senate committees to have competing ideas about what should be done, but that can be written off to the differing nature of the two bodies. More vexing is what happens when two or more committees in the same chamber give opposing orders. Sometimes these conflicts appear trivial, but they can tie up an agency's decision making for months. In the early 1980s, for example, Army Undersecretary James Ambrose got caught in a power struggle between the House Defense Appropriations Subcommittee and the House Armed Services Committee. The Appropriations subcommittee chair, Joseph Addabbo (D-NY), ordered the Pentagon to issue a single 9mm handgun instead of allowing each of the armed services to buy their own peculiar weapons. Lawmakers on the House Armed Services Committee told Ambrose to do no such thing. The resulting stalemate consumed attention for months and threatened to delay the entire authorization for President Reagan's defense buildup.[13]

That executive branch bureaucrats sometimes serve multiple masters is not entirely the Congress's fault. Bureaucrats protect their turf in much the same ways that legislators do, and executive branch reorganization plans notoriously fall short of consolidating similar programs under a single agency's umbrella. Writes Richard Neustadt, "Both organizationally and in terms of personnel the new bureaucracy is a projection of committee jurisdictions, or more precisely, since 1946, of standing subcommittee jurisdictions . . . Of course, committee jurisdictions have been influenced, in turn by organizational developments downtown."[14] Concludes William Morrow, "If major strides are made in the direction of a program or function orientation within the executive branch, the probability is that congressional committee reshuffling will follow."[15]

As we have seen, Congress's reliance on the "weight of the bill" decision rule was a direct response to earlier threats (first from floor majorities, then from partisan Speakers) to the collective benefits that committee systems can provide. Now, ironically, the committee system appears threatened by rampant fragmentation—especially since the appearance of multiple referrals in 1975. To hear some critics tell it, fragmentation has all but destroyed the effectiveness of committees so that the Congress cannot speak with a strong and coherent voice about any national problems at all.[16] There are too many cooks. Hedrick Smith puts it plainly. "Fragmentation," he writes, "often leaves our politicians wallowing in deadlock because the government lacks the cohesion to form the durable coalitions needed to resolve the nation's most demanding problems."[17] With "too many" committees involved in "too many" issues because of jurisdictional fragmentation, pressure groups have more points of access to pursue their special interests. So if a special interest group loses in one committee, it can go to another, and then another—evoking among some observers fears that policies are being influenced by narrow special interests as they never have before.[18]

Committee jurisdictions have always been fragmented to some extent, and committees have long been criticized for failing to address issues that overlap committee boundaries. Recent frustrations with legislative impasses, I think, have more to do with divided government, with the ways campaigns are financed, and with a huge budget deficit than with the practice of dividing general policy areas into several committees based on policy expertise. Certainly, jurisdictional fragmentation has some of the drawbacks raised by critics. It often is difficult to hear Congress speaking with one voice about complex issues. Fragmentation often does slow down legislation—especially when sequential referrals are used. And more interest groups do gain access to the policy process as the number of committees with jurisdiction over parts of an issue increases. Still, there are several reasons why one might prefer a jurisdictionally fragmented committee system.

Benefits of Fragmentation

When different aspects of complex issues are handled in multiple committees, the expertise and experience in each committee can be tapped. When committees share bills under sequential referrals and "additional initial referrals," they do not share full jurisdiction because the language of the referrals limits a committee to the parts of the bills that are already in its jurisdiction. Some degree of fragmentation may be informationally efficient *because* there are "more people at the table when important decisions are being made." When issue fragments are patched together (like the 1992 energy package), the final vehicle is likely to have been shaped by a collection of panels that, as a whole, is more heterogeneous and less biased than any single committee.

Moreover, when an issue is fragmented among several committees, the committees are not islands unto themselves. Especially since committees have been able to request sequential referrals, coordination among committees over larger issue areas has increased dramatically. Heightened communication between committees before bills go to the floor helps build a consensus behind new initiatives. The handful of members, staffers, and lobbyists on Capitol Hill who can recall what turf wars looked like before multiple referrals almost invariably mention this increase in communication. So while more committees are involved in more things, this does not mean they are not communicating. Explains one staff director, "I go right to the other committee and say 'hey, we've got to work this out.' That's also what the Speaker's people and the Rules committee staff expects us to do. Why let the floor decide these things? There's no reason at all."

Fragmentation has hastened the dismantling of so-called iron triangles by increasing the points at which interest groups can access Congress.[19] When an interest group community only needs to focus on one House and one Senate committee, a close and usually cooperative relationship often develops. As Baumgartner and Jones have shown, policy monopolies structure political agendas, influence the tone of media coverage, and help write the script for usually favorable public hearings.[20] The destruction of these issue monopolies, and the related jurisdictional fragmentation, makes it more likely that new voices will be heard. Still, the conventional wisdom is that there are too many voices already being heard on these committees. That is the message of Jonathan Rauch's popular analysis, *Demosclerosis: The Silent Killer of American Government.*[21] It is hard to say how many interest groups are "too many," but I would err on the side of overwhelming Congress with points of view rather than restricting, as Congress has done in the past, access to a handful of well-financed interests.[22]

Although we hear, time and again, that jurisdictional fragmentation slows down the political process, that is not necessarily so. Turf wars are not fought in moderation, as two or more panels usually race to establish referral precedents. Some observers consider the 1990s battle over telecommunications deregulation to be a rush to judgment by panels hurrying to get a piece of the action.[23] One former Commerce Committee staff director articulated his "lightening strategy" by repeating his motto several times in an interview. "Blitz it," he said. "When you see something and you know you can get it past the parliamentarian, blitz it."

Finally, the communication and coordination between committees necessitated by fragmentation means that an ever-more-representative subset of the whole House is crafting legislation before it comes to the floor. Serious disputes are almost always settled before the Rules Committee might get involved. Explains one Rules staffer, "The Rules Committee doesn't pretend to be the policy experts. That would usurp the legislative role of the other committees. So Rules would probably demand that before a bill is given a rule the two sides come together and reconcile their differences." This reconciling of differences—before the whole chamber gets its turn—might be spurred by distributive or nondistributive coalitions.

Fragmentation receives lip service in Washington, but the odds are long that anything substantial will be done to consolidate turf and coordinate issues between the House and Senate. Perhaps the 1995 innovation of "additional initial" referrals will decrease the patrols of border cops, though the loss of concurrent referrals will inevitably inspire still more clever drafting to ensure that a bill goes to the "correct" lead committee. Furthermore, it is often in the interests of the House and Senate leadership to perpetuate committee fragmentation. When coordination is needed among committees, the leaders step in. If a task force is created, its short life is more dependent on the House Speaker and Senate Majority Leader than on any standing committee chair.

When sequential referrals are necessary—as is increasingly the case— the Speaker gets to set time limits on committee activities, effectively creating a one person discharge petition. Given a choice between no jurisdictional fragmentation and the patchwork quilt of conflicts we have today, House and Senate leaders would likely prefer fragmentation. Solving the problems they create give those leaders more power to shape the policy outcomes.

Several intriguing questions remain unresolved, not the least of which is what the rise of the Republican Caucus in the House will do to the entrepreneurial spirit of its members. More fundamentally, though, we might aspire to a better sense for how the referral system, with the parliamentarian as a neutral arbiter, is perpetuated. Why does the parliamentarian's role remain unchallenged when the individual-level payoffs for winning the jurisdiction game can be so high? There are plenty of examples in which legislators "defect" from what might be collectively rational. Many even get elected to Congress by ridiculing the institution, which helps render it more ineffective. What is special about the parliamentarian's referral process that keeps it going? I have a two speculations.

First, inertia weighs heavy once aspects of an organization are institutionalized. The parliamentarians help socialize new members of Congress and teach them about the rules. Doing so, they try to emphasize their role as guardians of the rules. Around the mid-1910s when the parliamentarian took center stage in the referral process, there were members who could clearly remember how referrals bogged down the business of the House before 1890, and everyone could remember what Speaker Cannon did with referrals in his hands. The parliamentarian was also institutionalized during the progressive era with the help of Democrats and anti-Cannon Republicans. The progressive era was marked by calls to take many decisions out of the hands of political parties and political appointees. The long service of Lewis Deschler was also surely important as his tenure spanned nine Speakers and several changes in the party control of the House.

Second, institutions are maintained when alternatives to the status quo are so onerous that the status quo is reinforced. One would expect to see occasional deviations from reliance on the parliamentarians when members flirt with Speaker or partisan control over referrals. One such flirtation was mentioned by several staffers. In 1987, Speaker Wright cut a deal with Claude Pepper (D-FL), chairman of the House Rules Committee, to bring a long-term health care bill to the floor. The bill bypassed the committees of jurisdiction (Commerce and Ways and Means). "Rostenkowski and Dingell were outraged," writes John

Barry. "The Rules Committee had enough power dictating procedure; it was not supposed to produce substance, especially substance in their jurisdictions."[24] Pepper's bill was defeated on the floor, and its demise can be traced clearly to the precedent that could be set by passing such an improperly referred bill.[25] Occasional scares like the 1987 "Pepper Bill" may go a long way to maintaining the present referral system. Likewise, when Speaker Gingrich was reportedly considering replacing Charles Johnson with a partisan appointee, members imagined what the system would look like. When Johnson was retained, there was an audible sigh of relief on Capitol Hill.

If governing through fragmented committees is an inevitability, then perhaps we should make the best of it. If you were George Brown, that is what you would have done. And that is not such a bad thing. Legislative entrepreneurs breath life into legislatures and help governments embrace new problems. Organizational change in Congress is ongoing, and, with respect to committee jurisdictions, turf wars tend to be resolved in ways that maintain the informational integrity of the committee system.

NOTES

Introduction

1. Lawrence C. Evans & Walter J. Oleszek, ,"Reform Redux: Jurisdictional Change and the New Republican House" (paper delivered at the annual meeting of the Midwest Political Science Association, Chicago, April 7, 1995a).

2. Personal interview, Cambridge, MA., April 5, 1995.

3. Roger H. Davidson & Walter J. Oleszek, *Congress against Itself* (Bloomington: Indiana University Press, 1977); Frank R. Baumgartner & Bryan D. Jones, *Agendas and Instability in American Politics* (Chicago: University of Chicago Press, 1993.)

4. Jeffery C. Talbert, Bryan D. Jones, & Frank R. Baumgartner, "Nonlegislative Hearings and Policy Change in Congress," *American Journal of Political Science* 39 (May 1995): 383–406; Bryan Jones, Frank Baumgartner, & Jeffery Talbert 1993; Frank Baumgartner, & Bryan Jones 1993; Charles R. Shipan, "Individual Incentives and Institutional Imperatives: Committee Jurisdiction and Long-Term Health Care," *American Journal of Political Science* 36 (1992): 877–885; Roger H. Davidson, & Walter J. Oleszek, "From Monopoly to Management: Changing Patterns of Committee Deliberation," in Roger H. Davidson, ed., *The Postreform Congress* (New York: St. Martin's Press, 1992).

5. Nelson W. Polsby, "The Institutionalization of the U.S. House of Representatives," *American Political Science Review* 62 (March 1968): 156.

6. Gary W. Cox and Mathew D. McCubbins, *Legislative Leviathan: Party Government in the House* (Berkeley: University of California Press, 1993), 12–13.

7. Roger Davidson & Walter Oleszek, *Congress and Its Members*, 2d edition (Washington: Congressional Quarterly Press, 1981), 216–219; or *Congress against Itself*, 1977; and ibid., "Adaptation and Consolidation: Structural Innovation in the U.S. House of Representatives," *Legislative Studies Quarterly*, 1 (1976): 37–665; For an equally clear distinction between the formal rules and parliamentary precedents, see Lewis A. Froman, Jr., *The Congressional Process: Strategies, Rules, and Procedures* (Boston: Little, Brown, 1967), 36–37. Another good (though dated) overview of jurisdictional infighting because of

ambiguity is George Goodwin, Jr., *The Little Legislatures,* (Amherst: University of Massachusetts Press, 1970), 33-34.

8. C. Lawrence Evans & Walter J. Oleszek, "Congressional Tsunami? Institutional Change in the 104th Congress" (paper delivered at the annual meeting of the American Political Science Association, Chicago, 1995a).

9. Donald M. Freeman, "The Making of a Discipline," in William Crotty, ed., *Political Science: Looking to the Future,* volume 1 (Evanston: Northwestern University Press, 1991), 15-44; David Ricci, *The Tragedy of Political Science* (New Haven: Yale University Press, 1984); Maurice Cowling, *The Nature and Limits of Political Science* (Cambridge: Cambridge University Press, 1963).

10. Robert A. Dahl, "The Behavioral Approach in Political Science: Epitaph for a Monument to a Successful Protest," *American Political Science Review* 55 (1961): 763-772.

11. One nice example is the early evolution of standing committees in the U.S. Congress. See Gerald Gamm & Kenneth Shepsle, "Emergence of Legislative Institutions: Standing Committees in the House and Senate, 1810-1825," *Legislative Studies Quarterly* 14 (1989): 39-66. Also see James G. March & Johan P. Olsen, *Rediscovering Institutions: The Organizational Basis of Politics* (New York: Free Press, 1989).

12. Arthur Maass, *Congress and the Common Good* (New York: Basic Books, 1983), 95.

13. The referral strategy of introducing an ambiguously worded bill is discussed briefly in Nelson W. Polsby, *Congress and the Presidency,* 2d edition (Englewood Cliffs, NJ: Prentice-Hall, 1971), 91-93. Still, other scholars barely mention the bill referral process. Two of the best texts on Congress pay little attention to jurisdictional change. The referral process receives one sentence in William Keefe & Morris Ogul's *Congress and the Legislative Process,* 5th edition (Englewood Cliffs, NJ: Prentice-Hall 1981); and it is not discussed in Randall Ripley's *Congress: Process and Policy,* 2d edition (New York: W. W. Norton, 1978).

14. Sarah A. Binder, "A Partisan Theory of Procedural Change: Creation of Minority Rights in the House, 1789-1991 (paper delivered at the annual meeting of the Midwest Political Science Association, Chicago, 1992); Keith Krehbiel, *Information and Legislative Organization* (Ann Arbor: University of Michigan Press, 1991); Douglas Dion, "Majority Rule, Minority Rights, and the Politics of Procedural Change" (paper delivered at the annual meeting of the American Political Science Association, San Francisco, 1990); Weingast & Marshall 1988.

15. Talbert, Jones, & Baumgartner 1995.

16. Barry R. Weingast, "A Rational Choice Perspective on Congressional Norms," *American Journal of Political Science* 23 (1979): 245-262; Kenneth A. Shepsle & Barry R. Weingast, "The Institutional Foundations of Committee Power," *American Political Science Review* 81 (1987): 85-104; David P. Baron & John A. Ferejohn, "Bargaining in Legislatures," *American Political Science Review* 83 (1989a): 1181-1206.

17. Thomas W. Gilligan & Keith Krehbiel, "Organization of Informative Committees by a Rational Legislature," *American Journal of Political Science* 34 (1990): 531–564; Keith Krehbiel 1991; Bruce Bimber, "Information as a Factor in Congressional Politics," *Legislative Studies Quarterly* 16 (1991): 585–606.

18. Gary W. Cox & Mathew D. McCubbins 1993; David W. Rohde, *Parties and Leaders in the Postreform House* (Chicago, University of Chicago Press, 1991).

19. For example, Janet Hook, "Extensive Reform Proposals Cook on the Front Burner," *CQ Weekly Report* (June 6, 1992): 1579–1585.

20. Gary W. Cox & Mathew D. McCubbins 1993, 252, 255.

21. Eric Schickler and Andrew Rich, "Controlling the Floor: Parties as Procedural Coalitions in the House" (paper delivered at the annual meeting of the American Political Science Association, Chicago, August 31, 1995).

22. Weingast & Marshall 1988, 132–163.

23. For a general review, see Kenneth A. Shepsle & Barry R. Weingast, "Positive Theories of Congressional Institutions," *Legislative Studies Quarterly* 19 (1994): 149–179; Krehbiel 1991; Gilligan & Krehbiel 1990.

Chapter One

1. Spencer Rich, "Senate Chairmen in Tug of War over Health Plan; Two Panels Battle for Jurisdiction—and Power," *Washington Post* (November 24, 1993): A1; Alissa Rubin, "Jurisdictional Power Struggle Slows Overhaul in Senate," *CQ Weekly Report* (November 27, 1993): 3274. For a more general analysis, see Frank R. Baumgartner & Jeffery C. Talbert, "From Setting a National Agenda on Health Care to Making Decisions in Congress," *Journal of Health Politics, Policy and Law* 20 (Summer 1995): 437–445.

2. Evans & Oleszek 1995c.

3. *Congressional Record* (June 18, 1992): H4872.

4. Juliet Eilperin, "House Bills Bypass Committee Process," *Roll Call* (March 18, 1996): 1; Jackie Koszczuk, "Regained Footing," *Players, Politics and Turf of the 104th Congress* (supplement to no. 12) (March 23, 1996): 9.

5. Richard F. Fenno, *The Emergence of a Senate Leader: Peter Domenici and the Reagan Budget* (Washington, DC: Congressional Quarterly Press, 1991), xi.

6. Steven H. Gifis, *Law Dictionary* (New York: Barron's Educational Series, 1984), 254.

7. "Caught in Turf Battle, Bank Powers Bill Dies," *1988 Congressional Quarterly Almanac*, volume 44 (Washington, DC: Congressional Quarterly Press, 1989), 230–241; John Cranford, "Banking Overhaul Losing Ground to Complexity, Controversy," *CQ Weekly Report* (November 2, 1991): 3182–3185.

8. William L. Morrow, *Congressional Committees* (New York: Charles Scribner's Sons, 1969), 24.

9. Rich 1993, A1.

10. The jurisdictions of committees, wrote Woodrow Wilson in 1885, "overlap at many points, and it must frequently happen that bills are read which

cover just this common ground. Over the commitment of such bills sharp and interesting skirmishes often take place." See Woodrow Wilson, *Congressional Government: A Study in American Politics* (Baltimore: Johns Hopkins Press, 1981 [1885]), 63.

11. Jon Healey, "Panel Vote Sets Up Clash," *CQ Weekly Report* (May 20, 1995): 1412; Al Kamen, "Smoothing Bumps in Highway Jurisdiction," *Washington Post*, (July 2, 1993): A17; John Mintz, "Victory in a Battle with the Bells: Brooks Wins Control of Turf for Regional Phone Companies," *Washington Post* (August 14, 1992): B1; Holly Idelson, "Miller vs. Dingell," *CQ Weekly Report* (May 23, 1992b): 1438; Steven Pressman, "Ex-Im Bank Measure Moves as Deadline Nears," *CQ Weekly Report* (September 27, 1986): 2323; ibid., "Beyond the Hoopla, Looking for Options," *CQ Weekly Report* (November 22, 1986a): 2936–2940; Julie Rovner, "Pepper Bill Pits Politics against Process," *CQ Weekly Report* (June 4, 1988): 1491–1493; "Waste Hauling Measures," *1989 Congressional Quarterly Almanac,* volume 45 (Washington, DC: Congressional Quarterly Press, 1990), 379–380; Paul Starobin, "Parliamentarian 'Screwed Up': Jurisdictional Fight Stalls Drunken-Driving Bill," *CQ Weekly Report* (September 24, 1988): 2668; "Coal-Slurry Bill Renewed," *1989 Congressional Quarterly Almanac,* volume 45 (Washington, DC: Congressional Quarterly Press, 1990), 681–682; David S. Cloud, "Bill Gives FDA Nod to Oversee Rish," *CQ Weekly Report* (February 24, 1990): 585; Julie Rovner, "Rights Bill Linkage, Turf Spats Slow ADA Progress in House," *CQ Weekly Report* (February 24, 1990): 600; Alyson Pytte, "House OKs Bomb-Detector Bill with Funding Compromise," *CQ Weekly Report* (September 23, 1989): 2454–2455.

12. On various aspects of the appropriations process, see D. Roderick Kiewiet & Mathew D. McCubbins, *The Logic of Delegation: Congressional Parties and the Appropriations Process* (Chicago: University of Chicago Press, 1991); Charles Stewart, *Budget Reform Politics: The Design of the Appropriations Process in the House of Representatives, 1865–1921* (New York: Cambridge University Press, 1989). For a recent account of a jurisdictional battle between Appropriations and Interior, see Phillip A. Davis, "Policy Dispute Delays Bill on Interior Spending," *CQ Weekly Report* (July 4, 1992): 1940.

13. Krehbiel 1991; Joseph Cooper, *Congress and Its Committees: A Historical Approach to the Role of Committees in the Legislative Process* (New York: Garland Publishing, 1988); Richard L. Hall, "Participation and Purpose in Committee Decision Making," *American Political Science Review* 81 (March 1987): 105–127; Steven S. Smith & Christopher J. Deering, *Committees in Congress,* 2d edition (Washington, DC: Congressional Quarterly Press, 1990); Richard F. Fenno, *Congressmen in Committees* (Boston: Little, Brown, 1973).

14. Heinz Eulau, "Committee Selection," in Gerhard Loewenberg, Samuel C. Patterson, & Malcolm E. Jewell, eds., *Handbook of Legislative Research* (Cambridge, MA: Harvard University Press, 1985); Kenneth A. Shepsle, *The Giant Jigsaw Puzzle* (Chicago: University of Chicago Press, 1978).

15. Melissa P. Collie & Joseph Cooper, "Multiple Referral and the 'New'

Committee System in the House of Representatives," in Lawrence C. Dodd & Bruce I. Oppenheimer, *Congress Reconsidered,* 4th edition (Washington, DC: Congressional Quarterly Press, 1989), 253.

16. Thomas Stratmann. "The Effects of Logrolling on Congressional Voting." *American Economic Review* 82 (1992): 1162–1176.

17. John Ferejohn, "Logrolling in an Institutional Context," in Gerald C. Wright, Leroy N. Rieselbach, & Lawrence C. Dodd, eds., *Congress and Policy Change* (New York: Agathon Press, 1986); Gary W. Cox & Mathew D. McCubbins 1993.

18. Margaret E. Kriz, "Poison Gamesmanship," *National Journal* (April 18, 1992): 930–933. An unrelated "surf-and-turf war" shaped our national policies on fish inspections. For comment, see the *Congressional Record* (October 24, 1990): H13471.

19. Interview by author, June 13, 1991.

20. By linking civil rights with legal issues in the House—instead of tagging it to the commerce clause as in the Senate—House Speaker John McCormack kept the bill away from the House Commerce chair Orren Harris, a civil rights opponent from Arkansas. See Froman 1967, 36–37.

21. T. R. Reid, *Congressional Odyssey: The Saga of a Senate Bill* (New York: W. H. Freeman & Co., 1980); in the early 1980s, Domenici scored another important jurisdictional fight, wrestling handling of Reagan's economic package into the Senate Budget Committee, which he chaired, and away from Senator Mark Hatfield's Appropriations Committee and Senator Robert Dole's Finance Committee. This jurisdiction grab is recounted in Hedrick Smith, *The Power Game: How Washington Works* (New York: Ballantine Books, 1989), 285–286; Fenno 1991, passim.

22. Donald Simon, "Senator Kennedy and the Civil Aeronautics Board, "Case no. C14-77-157, John F. Kennedy School of Government, Harvard University, 1977.

23. John M. Barry, *The Ambition and the Power* (New York: Viking Penguin, 1989).

24. Charles Tiefer, *Congressional Practice and Procedure: A Reference, Research, and Legislative Guide* (New York: Greenwood Press, 1989), 111.

25. For a general treatment on how conditions become defined as problems, see John W. Kingdon, *Agendas, Alternatives, and Public Policies* (Boston: Little, Brown, 1984), 115–119.

26. Philip Marwill, "Environmental Turf," *CQ Weekly Report* (January 20, 1990): 151.

27. Steven S. Smith, *Call to Order: Floor Politics in the House and Senate* (Washington, DC: Brookings Institution, 1989a), 170. For a similar argument and an attempt at estimating the ideal points of committee and noncommittee members, see Keith Krehbiel & Douglas Rivers, "The Analysis of Committee Power: An Application to Senate Voting on the Minimum Wage," *American Journal of Political Science* 32 (1988): 1151–1174.

28. David P. Baron & John Ferejohn, "The Power to Propose," in Peter C. Ordeshook, ed., *Models of Strategic Choice in Politics* (Ann Arbor: University

of Michigan Press, 1989b). Also 254–256 of Krehbiel 1991. A committee's power also comes from the selective blocking of legislation.

29. John F. Manley, *The Politics of Finance: The House Committee on Ways and Means* (Boston: Little, Brown, 1970).

30. See Judy Schneider's discussion in Donald C. Bacon, Roger H. Davidson, & Morton Keller, eds., *The Encyclopedia of the United States Congress* (New York: Simon & Schuster, 1995), 426–430.

31. For a good introduction to collective goods, see David L. Weimer & Aidan R. Vining, *Policy Analysis: Concepts and Practice,* 2d edition (Englewood Cliffs, NJ: Prentice Hall, 1992), 41–62; and Paul A. Samuelson, "Diagrammatic Exposition of a Theory of Public Expenditure," *Review of Economics and Statistics* 37 (1955): 37:350–356.

32. Morris P. Fiorina, "Universalism, Reciprocity, and Distributive Policy-Making in Majority Rule Institutions," in John Crecine, ed., *Research in Public Policy Analysis and Management* (Greenwich, CT: JAI Press, 1981); Weingast 1979, 245–262.

33. Krehbiel 1991.

34. Mancur Olson, *The Logic of Collective Action* (Cambridge, MA: Harvard University Press, 1965); Thomas S. McCaleb & Richard E. Wagner, "The Experimental Search for Free Riders: Some Reflections and Observations," *Public Choice* 47 (1985): 479–490.

35. The logic here is similar to Dodd's interpretation of the effects on Congress of legislative careers. Fragmentation (and lower collective productivity) result from the individual-level motivations of legislators. See Lawrence C. Dodd, "The Cycles of Legislative Change: Building a Dynamic Theory," in Herbert F. Weisberg, ed., *Political Science: The Science of Politics* (New York: Agathon Press, 1986).

36. Davidson & Oleszek 1977, 218.

37. *Congressional Record* (September 20, 1994): H9226.

38. Wayne L. Francis, *The Legislative Committee Game: A Comparative Analysis of Fifty States* (Columbus: Ohio State University Press, 1989), 8–9.

39. Gamm & Shepsle 1989, 62–63.

40. At times, however, the DC Committee has tried to make the capital a model city for some new policies. For example, the committee was among the first to hold a hearing on consumer protection within the city, and they pushed for a mass transit system that would be the envy of the country. Still, its legislative jurisdiction rarely extended beyond the district's boundaries.

41. Not coincidentally, there has been no pressure at all to increase the size of these two committees. More "popular" committees occasionally allow their size to grow instead of turning down requests for new members to join. See Michael Munger, "Allocation of Desirable Committee Assignments: Extended Queues versus Committee Expansion," *American Journal of Political Science* 32 (1988): 317–344; and Charles Stewart III, "The Growth of the Committee System, from Randall to Gillett," in Allen D. Hertzke & Ronald M. Peters, Jr. eds., *The Atomistic Congress: An Interpretation of Congressional Change* (Armonk, NY: M. E. Sharpe, 1992).

42. The Agriculture Committee is unlikely to face demands from members to move its jurisdiction into new areas because the members are drawn from homogeneous districts that roughly match what the committee is doing. Still, the committee *does* have the jurisdictional base to move into new areas if policy entrepreneurs decide to do so. This is alluded to in a discussion of the reasons why Thomas Foley gave up his chairmanship of Agriculture to become the Democratic party's whip. "A man like John Dingell, chairman of Energy and Commerce, or Rostenkowski of Ways and Means, or certainly Coelho, would not have given up a chairmanship for a third-ranking job. Instead they would have used their chairmanship to build an empire. Foley could have. His committee involved world trade and world politics . . . it involved the financial system and securities . . . it involved rural development and infrastructure. *A vast empire could be built on such a base . . . He did not set forth an agenda and pursue it . . . He did not root around in the dirt, dig his nails in, and create things.*" See Barry 1989, 135 (emphasis added).

43. The concept of a discretionary agenda is articulated in Jack L. Walker, "Setting the Agenda in the U.S. Senate: A Theory of Problem Selection," *British Journal of Political Science* 7 (October 1977): 423–445.

44. Davidson & Oleszek 1977, 60–61.

45. Fenno 1973; Hall 1987, 105–127. For implications of taking reelection as the primary goal, see David R. Mayhew, *Congress: The Electoral Connection* (New Haven: Yale University Press, 1974).

46. Fenno 1973, 1.

47. Ibid., 2, 5, 9.

48. Richard Hall, *Participation in Congress* (New Haven: Yale University Press, 1996); David C. King, "Representation through Participation in Committee Hearings" (paper delivered at the annual meeting of the Midwest Political Science Association, Chicago, 1989).

49. Shepsle 1978, 5. Also see Barbara Hinckley, "Policy Content, Committee Membership, and Behavior," *American Journal of Political Science,* 19 (1975): 543–558.

50. Shepsle 1978, 231–232. Shepsle's conclusion on this point pertains mainly to freshmen seeking initial committee assignments. The electoral value of "good" assignments is minimal, according to Charles Bullock, "Freshman Committee Assignments and Re-Election in the United States House of Representatives," *American Political Science Review* 66 (1972): 996–1007. Nonetheless, legislators believe that committee assignments are important to them for both electoral and policy reasons. See Charles Clapp, *The Congressman: His Work as He Sees It* (Garden City, NY: Anchor Books, 1964).

51. Some states delegations have proprietary claims on seats. For example, from 1899 through 1992, New York Democrats have held a seat on Ways and Means every Congress but one (1953–1954). See Christopher J. Froke, "State Delegations and the U.S. House Committee System: Ways and means in the 20th Century" (paper delivered at the annual meeting of the Midwest Political Science Association, Chicago, 1992). Also Charles S. Bullock, "The Influence of State Party Delegations on House Committee Assignments," *Midwest Jour-*

nal of Political Science 15 (1971): 525–546; David E. England & Charles S. Bullock, "Prescriptive Seats Revisited," *American Journal of Political Science* 30 (1986): 496–502.

52. Michael Munger 1988, 317–344; Goodwin 1970, 64–79, 110–117; Tiefer 1989, 87–98. Scholars interested in this should be sure to look at the proposal for "voluntary rotation" among committees proposed in an appendix to a 1973 House report. See House Select Committee on Committees, *Committee Structure and Procedures of the House of Representatives: Working Draft of Report of the Select Committee on Committees,* 93d Congress, 1st session (December 7, 1973) (Washington, DC: Government Printing Office, 1973), 81–84.

53. Norman J. Ornstein, Thomas E. Mann, & Michael J. Malbin, *Vital Statistics on Congress: 1991–1992* (Washington, DC: Congressional Quarterly Press, 1992), 114–115.

54. Krehbiel 1991, 264–265.

55. S. L. Shakdher, *System of Parliamentary Committees* (New Delhi, India: S. L. Shakdher, Secretary-General, Lok Sabha, 1974), 1–6.

56. Weingast & Marshall 1988. Also see Barry R. Weingast & Mark J. Moran, "Bureaucratic Discretion or Congressional Control? Regulatory Policymaking by the Federal Trade Commission," *Journal of Political Economy* 91 (1983): 765–800.

57. Ferejohn describes the "institutionalization" of a logroll as one possible solution, giving the development of the Food Stamp program as an example. See Ferejohn 1986. In the same vein, Shepsle writes that each legislator "in effect, trades off influence in policy areas of less interest to his or her constituents in exchange for extraordinary influence in those areas central to their economic and social life; it is an institutional logroll." "Representation and Governance: The Great Legislative Trade-Off," *Political Science Quarterly* 103 (Fall 1988): 472.

58. Weingast & Marshall 1988 148.

59. Ibid., 146.

60. Personal interview, June 18, 1991.

61. Weingast & Marshall 1988, 146–147.

62. Fiorina 1981.

63. Krehbiel 1991, 74.

64. Thomas W. Gilligan & Keith Krehbiel, "Organization of Informative Committees by a Rational Legislature," working paper no. P-88-13, Hoover Institution, 1988, 13.

Chapter Two

1. Oliver Wendell Holmes, *The Common Law* (Cambridge, MA: Harvard University Press, 1963 [1881]), 7. Also see Karl N. Llewellyn, *The Bramble Bush* (New York: Oceana, 1960).

2. *Rules and Orders of the House of Representatives* (Washington, DC: Government Printing Office, 1867), 181.

3. There is an interesting exception to the tendency for statutory jurisdic-

tions of this period to be vague. The Merchant Marine and Fisheries Committee's statutory jurisdiction was added to the rules in 1877 and written as "The merchant marine, including all transportation by water, Coast Guard, life-saving service, lighthouses, lightships, ocean derelicts, Coast and Geodetic Survey, Panama Canal, and fisheries." These were specifically stated because they were issues carved out of the Commerce Committee's jurisdiction.

4. Another committee with jurisdiction over some commerce issues, the Committee on Industrial Arts and Expositions (made a standing committee in 1903) was dissolved in 1927, and its jurisdiction was absorbed by the Judiciary Committee. Though absorbing the Expeditions Committee, the statutory jurisdiction of the Judiciary Committee did not change a word. It was enough for the speaker to proclaim that the committee's jurisdiction had changed. See Clarence Cannon, *Cannon's Procedure in the House of Representatives of the United States,* volume 7, 3d edition (Washington, DC: Government Printing Office, 1935), 840.

5. Figure 3.1 is summarized from Charles E. Schamel & Donnald K. Anderson, *Guide to the Records of the United States House of Representatives at the National Archives, 1789–1989* (Washington, DC: Government Printing Office, 1989), 73, 201.

6. George B. Galloway, *Congress at the Crossroads* (New York: Thomas Y. Crowell Co., 1946), 340.

7. Schickler & Rich 1995. The following changes in statutory jurisdiction are drawn from table 2 in Schickler & Rich 1920, recentralize Appropriations; 1924, create World War Veterans, along with minor changes to Civil Service and Irrigation and Reclamation; 1927, merge 11 Expenditures Committees and abolish five minor committees; 1929, create Memorials Committee; 1935, Merchant Marine jurisdiction over radio was given to Commerce, and Commerce jurisdiction over water transportation and related matters was transferred to Merchant Marine; 1939, jurisdiction of Pensions, Invalid Pensions, and Veterans Affairs adjusted; 1944, expand World War Veterans' jurisdiction; 1945, creation of the House UnAmerican Activities Committee; 1946, Legislative Reorganization Act; 1946, Joint Atomic Energy Committee created; 1953, minor changes to Armed Services jurisdiction to account for creation of the Defense Department; 1954, Atomic Energy Committee consolidated; 1958, Science and Astronautics created, and national Bureau of Standards shifted from Commerce to the new committee; 1967, Standards and Conduct Committee created; 1967, Veterans Committee given jurisdiction over veterans' cemeteries from Interior; 1969, clarify HUAC jurisdiction and change its name to Internal Security; 1971, Banking and Finance given jurisdiction over impact on the economy of tax exempt foundations and charitable trusts; 1971, Small Business made permanent Select Committee; 1974, creation of the Budget Committee and related budget jurisdiction changes; 1974, Hansen-Bolling reforms; 1972, permanent Select Committee on Aging created; 1975, abolish Internal Security Committee and strip Standards and Conduct of its jurisdiction over campaign contributions; 1977, abolish Joint Atomic Energy and strip Standards and Conduct of its jurisdiction over lobbying; 1977, permanent Select In-

telligence Committee created; 1980, Energy jurisdiction reforms; 1983, tighten Ways and Means jurisdiction over tax matters; 1993, dissolve Select Committee.

8. *Congressional Record* (January 22, 1959): 1027.

9. House Committee on Energy and Commerce, *180 Years of Service: A Brief History of the Committee on Interstate and Foreign Commerce* (Washington, DC: Government Printing Office, 1975), 9. Also see Walter Oleszek, *Congressional Procedures and the Policy Process,* 4th edition (Washington, DC: Congressional Quarterly Press, 1995), 96–100.

10. Lewis Deschler & William Holmes Brown, *Procedure in the U.S. House of Representatives* (Washington, DC: Government Printing Office, 1982), quoted in Evans & Oleszek 1995c, 6.

11. Interview by author. June 14, 1991.

12. Edward H. Levi, *An Introduction to Legal Reasoning* (Chicago: University of Chicago Press, 1949), 1.

13. Melvin A. Eisenberg, *The Nature of the Common Law* (Cambridge, MA: Harvard University Press, 1988).

14. Tiefer 1989); John L. Zorack, *The Lobbying Handbook: A Comprehensive Guide to Lobbying* (Washington, DC: Professional Lobbying and Consulting Center, 1990).

15. Cannon 1963.

16. For a thoughtful discussion about jurisdictional fragmentation, see Morrow 1969, 21–28.

17. Asher Hinds, *Hinds' Precedents of the House of Representatives* (Washington, D.C.: Government Printing Office, 1907), volume 7: sections 1725, 1851, and volume 4: sections 4025, 4117. The Committee on Territories (1825–1846) also had substantial jurisdiction over Alaska.

18. Fred I. Greenstein, *Personality and Politics: Problems of Evidence, Influence, and Conceptualization* (Princeton: Princeton University Press, 1987).

19. The story has been retold by staffers on Commerce and other committees. One variation depicts Dingell's boast as a threat to the Science, Space, and Technology Committee's territory. Another variation has Dingell telling this to a former astronaut.

20. *Congressional Quarterly Almanac,* volume 43 (Washington, DC: Congressional Quarterly Press, 1988), 357.

21. Michael Barone & Grant Ujifusa, *The Almanac of American Politics, 1988* (Washington, DC: National Journal, 1987), 615.

22. Rochelle L. Stanfield, "Plotting Every Move," *National Journal* (March 26, 1988): 792.

23. Munger 1988, 317–344.

24. David Maraniss, "Powerful Energy Panel Turns on Big John's Axis," *Washington Post* (May 15, 1983), cited in Roger H. Davidson, Walter J. Oleszek, & Thomas Kephart, "One Bill, Many Committees: Multiple Referrals in the U.S. House of Representatives," *Legislative Studies Quarterly* 13 (1988): 13.

25. It also helps to have a committee membership that is a nonpartisan microcosm of the House. The lack of partisan bickering on Energy and Com-

merce came up again and again in interviews with staffers from several commit-tees. "Republican loyalty to chairman Dingell is plentiful at the staff level as well. A GOP staff member, asked to rate the chairman's performance at a re-cent oversight hearing, cited a new version of the Republic '11th command-ment' prohibiting criticism of other Republicans: Thou shalt not speak unkindly of chairman Dingell." Christopher Madison, "Dingell's Heat Wave," *National Journal* (July 7, 1990), 1658. Although Commerce was perceived by committee members and staffers to be essentially nonpartisan (especially so before the early 1990s), Commerce Committee bills often sparked bitter parti-san divisions on the House floor. I do not have an explanation for this.

26. The Commerce Committee has long had some claim over trade (Hinds 4:4097), but the turf has been fallow for most of this century. When Commerce pursued trade again in the early 1980s, Representative Dingell used tactics of-ten reserved for entirely "new" issues.

27. On these types of strategies, see William Riker, *The Art of Political Ma-nipulation* (New Haven: Yale University Press, 1986). On the Ways and Means Committee's reactions to the Commerce Committee's attempts to redefine the issue, see Christopher Madison, "Strategic Value of Introducing Trade Bill May Be More Important than Passage," *National Journal* (January 14, 1984): 63–65. On trade issues in the Congress during the early 1980s, see Don Bonker, *America's Trade Crisis: The Making of the U.S. Trade Deficit* (Boston: Houghton Mifflin, 1988).

28. Baumgartner & Jones 1993.

29. Coleen Cordes, "New Head of a House Science Panel Plans Activist Role," *Chronicle of Higher Education* (January 2, 1991): A20. On other Sci-ence Committee changes, see "Brown Beefs Up Science Committee," *Science* (February 15, 1991b): 733.

30. Cordes 1991.

31. Staggers (D-WV) served as chair from 1966 to 1981. Harris (D-AK) was chair from 1957 to 1965.

32. In interviews with committee staff, personalities were usually cited as the main reason why some committees are more likely to play the jurisdiction game. I argue that there is much more involved. Dingell himself acknowledges this and credits the jurisdictional legacy passed down from previous chairs as the basis for his success. "Not a day passes," Dingell has said, "in which I do not thank Sam Rayburn for what he did with this committee." Rayburn was the chair of Commerce before joining the House leadership. Dingell is quoted in Barry 1989, 204.

33. Paul Teske & Mark Schneider, "A Theory of the Bureaucratic Entre-preneur: The Case of City Manager" (paper delivered at the annual meeting of the Midwest Political Science Association, Chicago, 1992). Also see Mark Schneider, Paul Teske, & Michael Mintrom, *Public Entrepreneurs: Agents for Change in American Government* (Princeton: Princeton University Press, 1995b): chapter 5; Israel M. Kirzner, *Competition and Entrepreneurship* (Chi-cago: University of Chicago Press, 1973); and Joseph Schumpeter, *Capitalism, Socialism, and Democracy* (New York: Harper & Row, 1942).

34. Joel T. Kaji & Michael Mintrom, "Selling Ideas: A Strategic Analysis of Policy Entrepreneurship" (Department of Political Science, State University of New York, Stony Brook June 1995, typescript, 21.

35. Carol S. Weissert, "Policy Entrepreneurs, Policy Opportunities and Legislative Effectiveness," *American Politics Quarterly* 19 (1991): 262–274. Weissert argues that policy entrepreneurs only arise on highly salient issues— which are few. I disagree. Entrepreneurs exploit jurisdictional gaps to define new issues and to redefine old ones. These issues need not be highly salient except, perhaps, to the entrepreneur.

36. Ross K. Baker, "Fostering the Entrepreneurial Activities of Members of the House," in John J. Kornacki, ed., *Leading Congress: New Styles, New Strategies* (Washington, DC: Congressional Quarterly Press, 1990).

37. Jameson Doig & Edwin Hargrove, eds., *Leadership and Innovation: A Biographical Perspective on Entrepreneurs in Government* (Baltimore: Johns Hopkins University Press, 1987).

38. Teske and Schneider 1992; and Mark Schneider & Paul Teske 1992, 737–747.

39. Quoted in Burdett Loomis, *The New American Politician: Ambition, Entrepreneurship, and the Changing Face of Political Life* (New York: Basic Books, 1988), 168.

40. Miller changed the name to Natural Resources from Interior and Insular Affairs in 1993.

41. Phil Kuntz, "Interior to Feel Firmer Touch after Udall's Gentle Hand," *CQ Weekly Report* (April 27, 1991): 1052 (emphasis added).

42. Holly Idelson, "House Gives Energy Bill Big Win; Lengthy Conference Expected," *CQ Weekly Report* (May 30, 1992a): 1530–1532.

43. *House Journal,* December 14, 1795:376.

44. Charles E. Schamel & Donnald K. Anderson 1989, chapter 7; House Committee on Energy and Commerce, *Legislative Journal of the Committee of Commerce and Manufacturers: December 14, 1795 to March 3, 1797* (Washington, DC: Government Printing Office, 1988). For less than a week while the House was in session in 1975, the committee was known as the Committee on Commerce and Health, reflecting a growing health agenda, but Chairman Harley Staggers (D-WV) instructed that the name be changed back to Interstate and Foreign Commerce (H.Res. 5, 94th Congress).

45. Steven S. Smith & Christopher J. Deering 1990. Also see Terry O. Sullivan, *Procedural Structure* (New York: Praeger, 1984).

46. Cannon's *Procedure* has been replaced by Deschler's *Precedents,* which does not list common law issues separately.

47. In some respects, this approach is a decedent of Lawrence C. Dodd & Richard L. Schott's *Congress and the Administrative State* (New York: John Wiley & Sons, 1979): 168–179; and David E. Price's *Policymaking in Congressional Committee: The Impact of "Environmental" Factors.* (Tucson: Institute of Government Research, University of Arizona, 1979) uses of hearings. The closest similarities are to Baumgartner & Bryan D. Jones 1993. My coding differs in that I specifically look at the distinction between common law and statu-

tory issues, and I record how and when new issues are linked in a hearing to existing issues.

48. Data here only cover through 1958 because jurisdiction over the Bureau of Standards was transferred to the newly created Committee on Science and Astronautics (now Science, Space, and Technology) on July 21, 1958.

49. In the late 1800s, the committee staked a claim to adulterated food by reporting bills "preventing the shipment of adulterated food, drugs, or cattle in interstate commerce." See House Committee on Energy and *180 Years of Service: A Brief History of the Committee on Interstate and Foreign Commerce* (Washington, DC: Government Printing Office, 1975), 7.

50. Subjects in figure 2.3 were categorized in the following manner. Health included public health and quarantine generally, drug abuse, alcohol abuse, and children's health. Communications included the regulation of interstate and foreign communications generally, telephones, telegraphs, radios, and television. Ground transportation included regulation of interstate railroads, hazardous materials transportation, regulation of interstate buses, regulation of interstate trucks, regulation of interstate pipelines, railroad labor, railroad retirement, railroad unemployment. Securities and exchanges included SEC issues generally and mergers and acquisitions. Air transportation included civil aeronautics (primarily accident investigations and airport construction) and postal rates on airmail. Other statutory issues not otherwise classified included interstate and foreign commerce generally, barriers to foreign trade, the Weather Bureau, interstate oil compacts and petroleum and natural gas (except on public lands), inland waterways, the Bureau of Standards, standardization of weights and measures, the metric system, the regulation of interstate transmission of power (except the installation of connections between government water power projects), war claims, committee housekeeping, and general oversight hearings.

51. Talbert, Jones, & Baumgartner 1995, 383–405. Since the mid 1970s, only about half of the Committee's hearings have focused on referred bills, but during the period from 1947 to 1974, 83 percent of the hearings addressed referred bills.

52. During this period, the U.S. Supreme Court expanded the federal government's reach through the Commerce Clause. See, for example, *United States v. Darby* (1941) and *Katzenbach v. McClung* (1964).

53. Interview with the author. June 26, 1991.

54. Stephen Jay Gould, *Wonderful Life: The Burgess Shale and the Nature of History* (New York: W. W. Norton, 1989).

55. The discussion that follows is similar, in some respects, to the "path dependency" literature in economics. Though I do not draw on this literature directly, see Kurt Dopfer, "Toward a Theory of Economic Institutions: Synergy and Path Dependency," *Journal of Economic Issues* 25 (1991): 535–550; W. Brian Arthur, "Self-Reinforcing Mechanisms in Economics," in P. W. Anderson, Kenneth Arrow, & David Pines, eds., *The Economy as an Evolving Complex System: The Proceedings of the Evolutionary Paths of the Global Economy Workshop*, volume 5 (Santa Fe: Addison-Wesley Press, 1988); Paul

A. David, *Technical Choice Innovation and Economic Growth* (New York: Cambridge University Press, 1975).

56. House Committee on Energy and Commerce 1988, 5.

57. The Merchant Marine and Fisheries Committee was created in 1877; the Rivers and Harbors Committee was created in 1883.

58. Referred on March 23, 1796; House Committee on Energy and Commerce 1988, 117. This was the first public bill sent to the committee; four private bills were referred earlier.

59. U.S. Public Health Service Office of Administrative Management 1976, 1–2. The hospital service was paid for by a tax on sailors' wages, though the tax was often uncollected and the hospital service was underfunded and ineffective during its first three decades.

60. Ibid., 2.

61. The title "Surgeon General" was given to the primary administrator of the Marine Hospital Service, and he wore a Coast Guard uniform. The emblem of the Public Health Service still includes an anchor, reflecting its history in maritime safety.

62. Louis C. Hunter 1949, 541. Hunter warns that this estimate is based on newspaper reports that likely inflated the fatalities, but the number of deaths was high nonetheless, and the public outcry was loud.

63. Hinds 1907, 4:743.

64. H.J.Res. 219, 98th Congress; House Committee on Energy and Commerce, *Hosting the 1986 Soccer World Cup,* 98th Congress, 1st session (Washington, DC: Government Printing Office, 1983a). The committee gained jurisdiction over the Winter Olympics in 1972, and was a bill on the Moscow Olympics in 1980, as well as bolls related to the 1984 and 1988 Olympics. Also in sports, the committee examined organized crime links to boxing in 1965 (an issue that could just as easily have been claimed by the Judiciary Committee), and in 1983 the committee reported on the need for uniform safety regulations for boxing matches among the states.

65. This followed the creation by Commerce of the House Special Subcommittee on Traffic Safety. In a fairly typical pattern, the committee first received a bill, HR 9836 in the 84th Congress, establishing Interstate Commerce Commission authority over the transportation safety regulations for migrant farm workers. This was justified at the federal level because migrant farm workers often cross state lines. See House Interstate and Foreign Commerce Committee, *Transportation of Migrant Farm Workers,* 84th Congress, 2d session (Washington, DC: Government Printing Office, 1956b). One month later the Traffic Safety Subcommittee conducted investigatory hearings into other safety problems. See House Committee on Interstate and Foreign Commerce, *Traffic Safety,* 84th Congress, 2d session (Washington, DC: Government Printing Office, 1956a).

66. House Committee on Interstate and Foreign Commerce, *Unburned Hydrocarbons,* 85th Congress, 2d session (Washington, DC: Government Printing Office, 1958b).

67. This amendment was in the form of HR 2105, which regulated vehicles

transported in interstate commerce. See House Committee on Interstate and Foreign Commerce, *Clean Air Act Amendments,* 89th Congress, 1st Session (Washington, DC: Government Printing Office, 1965b). Of course, the fact that "clean air" ended up on the Commerce Committee does not mean that Congress quickly enacted sweeping legislation. John Dingell has often worked to protect the automobile industry interests at the expense, some claim, of clean air.

68. House Committee on Interstate and Foreign Commerce, *Clean Air Act Amendments,* 94th Congress, 1st session (Washington, DC: Government Printing Office, 1975).

69. Ibid., *National Automobile Research Act,* 96th Congress, 2d session (Washington, DC: Government Printing Office, 1980).

Chapter Three

1. David S. Cloud, "GOP, to Its Own Great Delight, Enacts House Rules Changes," *CQ Weekly Report* (January 7, 1995a): 13–15.

2. For example, see Joseph Cooper, *Congress and Its Committees: A Historical Approach to the Role of Committees in the Legislative Process* (New York: Garland, 1988).

3. Gabriel Kahn, "Dreier, Frosh Take on Committee Reform," *Roll Call* (June 12, 1995).

4. Kurt Shillinger, "Efficiency-Minded Reformers Hit Snags," *Christian Science Monitor* (February 14, 1995): 1.

5. Interview with the author, March 14, 1996.

6. Joint Committee on the Organization of Congress, *Committee Structure,* 103d Congress, 1st session (Washington, DC: Government Printing Office, 1993).

7. Kirk Victor, "Mr. Smooth," *National Journal* (July 8, 1995): 1761.

8. David S. Cloud, "Shakeup Time," *CQ Weekly Report, Supplement* (supplement to no. 12) (March 25, 1995b), 10.

9. Janet Hook & David S. Cloud, "A Republican-Designed House Won't Please All Occupants," *CQ Weekly Report* (December 3, 1994), 3430. Also see C. Lawrence Evans & Walter J. Oleszek 1995c.

10. The meaning of the words "efficient" and "effective" cannot be divorced from one's political views. Alexander Hamilton, as secretary of the treasury in Washington's first administration, complained that it would be inefficient to create a House Ways and Means Committee to oversee the national treasury, and he pushed hard to keep the purse in the executive's hands by waving the efficiency flag. Among the 1946 reformers, one's view of what an effective legislature might look like was strongly related to whether one chafed at President Franklin Roosevelt's programs. A strong president seemed to imply a weak Congress, which was more troubling to Republicans than Democrats in the 1940s.

11. George B. Galloway, *The Legislative Process in Congress* (New York: Thomas Y. Crowell Co., 1955); Leroy N. Rieselbach, *Congressional Reform:*

The Changing Modern Congress (Washington, DC: Congressional Quarterly Press, 1994).

12. The quotation is from Roger H. Davidson, David M. Kovenock, & Michael K. O'Leary, *Congress in Crisis: Politics and Congressional Reform* (Belmont, CA.: Wadsworth Publishing Co., 1966), 3. Also see Charles Lindblom, "Some Limitations on Rationality: A Comment," in Carl J. Friedrich, ed., *Rational Decision* (New York: Atherton Press, 1964), 224–228.

13. Davidson et al. 1966, xii.

14. Charles Henning, *The Wit and Wisdom of Politics* (Golden, CO: Fulcrum, 1989), 233.

15. Richard Bolling, *House Out of Order* (New York: E. P. Dutton & Co., 1965), 110.

16. John A. Perkins, "Congressional Self-Improvement," *American Political Science Review* 38 (1944): 499–511; Hadley H. Cantril, ed., *Public Opinion, 1935–1946* (Princeton: Princeton University Press, 1951); Robert C. Byrd, *The Senate, 1789–1989: Addresses on the History of the United States Senate,* (Washington, DC: Government Printing Office, 1988); Roger H. Davidson, "The Advent of the Modern Congress: The Legislative Reorganization Act of 1946," *Legislative Studies Quarterly* 15 (1990): 357–374.

17. Quoted in Robert M. La Follette, "A Senator Looks at Congress," *Atlantic Monthly* 174 (July 1943): 91.

18. Byrd 1988, 540.

19. Committee on Congress, American Political Science Association, *The Reorganization of Congress* (Washington, DC: Public Affairs Press, 1945), 5. Also see Donald R. Matthews, "American Political Science and Congressional Reform," *Social Science History* 5 (1981): 91–120.

20. Galloway 1955, 591.

21. Ibid. 1946, 351.

22. The 1946 LRA's most important accomplishment has nothing to do with these two reform elements, and it is often overlooked. That is, the 1946 Act set in motion the professionalization (and proliferation) of congressional staff (Dodd & Schott 1979; Davidson 1990).

23. Galloway 1961, 57.

24. Randall B. Ripley, "Power in the Post–World War II Senate," *Journal of Politics* 31 (1969): 474; Nelson W. Polsby, Miriam Gallaher, Barry S. Rundquist, "The Growth of the Seniority System in the U.S. House of Representatives," *American Political Science Review* 63 (1969): 787–807.

25. Excluded were: Disposition of Executive Papers, Elections 1, 2, and 3, Enrolled Bills, the Library committee, Memorials, Printing, and the Committee on UnAmerican Activities.

26. Hinds 1908, sections 4084, 4:4087–4089, 4083.

27. George Robinson, "The Development of the Senate Committee System" (Ph.D. dissertation, New York University, 1954), 389–390.

28. By 1955, 63 percent of all chairmanships in the House were held by southerners. See Ornstein, Mann, & Malbin 1992, 116.

29. Galloway 1955, 312; Smith & Deering 1990, 43.

30. Madeline Wing Adler, "Congressional Reform: An Exploratory Case" (Ph.D. dissertation, University of Wisconsin, 1969).

31. Davidson et al. 1966, 192.

32. Congressional Quarterly Almanac, 1974, volume 30 (Washington, DC: Congressional Quarterly Press, 1975), 634.

33. Davidson & Oleszek, 1977.

34. Mark V. Nadel, *The Politics of Consumer Protection* (New York: Bobbs-Merrill, 1971).

35. House Committee on Interstate and Foreign Commerce, *Food Additives*, 85th Congress, 1st session (Washington, DC: Government Printing Office, 1957a).

36. Ibid., *Automobile Labeling*, 85th Congress, 2d session (Washington, DC: Government Printing Office, 1958a).

37. Ibid., *Cigarette Labeling and Advertising*, 89th Congress, 1st session (Washington, DC: Government Printing Office, 1965a); ibid., *National Commission on Product Safety Extension and Child Protection Act*, 91st Congress, 1st session (Washington, DC: Government Printing Office, 1969a); ibid., *Review of Electronic Products Radiation Hazards*, 91st Congress, 1st session (Washington, DC: Government Printing Office, 1969b).

38. Evans & Oleszek, 1995a, 9; C. Lawrence Evans, "Committees and Health Jurisdictions in Congress" (College of William and Mary, 1994, typescript).

39. House Committee on Interstate and Foreign Commerce, *Medical School Inquiry*, 85th Congress, 1st session (Washington, DC: Government Printing Office, 1957b).

40. Ibid., *Humane Treatment of Animals used in Research*, 87th Congress, 2d session (Washington, DC: Government Printing Office, 1962).

41. Ibid., *Drug Abuse Control Amendments of 1965*, 89th Congress, 1st session (Washington: Government Printing Office, 1965c).

42. Ibid., *Travel in the United States*, 80th Congress, 2d session (Washington, DC: Government Printing Office, 1948).

43. Davidson & Oleszek 1977, 54.

44. Walker's 1985 survey of interest groups finds that organizations focusing on transportation tend also to monitor energy issues, but health and human services, education, government organization, civil rights, housing, agriculture, and national security issues are emphasized less by transportation groups than my most other interest group subsystems. See Jack L. Walker, *Mobilizing Interest Groups in America: Patrons, Professions, and Social Movements* (Ann Arbor: University of Michigan Press, 1991), 72.

45. Kingdon 1984, 125.

46. Present and former staffers on the House Public Works and Transportation Committee maintain that Rep. Staggers promised to let Public Works have jurisdiction over railroads after Staggers left office. The deal was not written down, and when Rep. Dingell took the Commerce chair in 1981, he did not feel beholden. In interviews in the early 1990s, Commerce staffers said they never heard of such a deal, though Public Works staffers remained bitter.

47. Charles O. Jones & Randall Stahan, "Crisis Response in Washington: The Case of Oil Shocks," *Legislative Studies Quarterly* 10 (1985): 151–179.

48. House Select Committee on Committees, *Final Report, Committee Reform Amendments of 1974,* H.Rept. 93-916. 93d Congress, 2d session (March 21, 1974a), quoted in Davidson and Oleszek 1977, 53.

49. One of the members I interviewed explained that "energy" referred to the jurisdiction, and "power" to Rep. Dingell.

50. In 1973, Dingell hosted hearings that had to be held at the full-committee level because no appropriate subcommittee was yet in place. That initial foray proved critical, both in terms of staking a claim to the issue and in demonstrating the need for a new subcommittee. See House Committee on Interstate and Foreign Commerce, *Energy Emergency Act,* 93d Congress, 1st session (Washington, DC: Government Printing Office, 1973).

51. Eric M. Uslaner, *Shale Barrel Politics: Energy and Legislative Leadership* (Stanford: Stanford University Press, 1989), 154.

52. C. Lawrence Evans & Walter J. Oleszek, "The Joint Committee on the Organization of Congress," in James A. Thurber and Roger H. Davidson, eds., *Remaking Congress: Change and Stability in the 1990s* (Washington, DC: Congressional Quarterly Press, 1995b).

53. Evans & Oleszek 1995a, 10.

54. Shillinger February 14, 1995, 1.

55. David Dreier, "News Conference with Rep. David Dreier (R-CA)," Federal Information Systems Corporation, December 2, 1994.

56. Quoted in ibid., 12.

57. Ibid., 12. David Hosansky, "GOP Bid to Reform Committees Faces Intraparty Skepticism," *CQ Weekly Report* (November 19, 1994): 3324–3325. Hook & Cloud, December 3, 1994. 3430–3435.

58. Victor, July 8, 1995, 1761; Nancy Roman, "Dingell Panel Cuts Would Anger Heir to Chairmanship," *Washington Times* (November 16, 1994): A3.

59. Roger H. Davidson, "The 104th Congress and Beyond," in Roger H. Davidson & Walter J. Oleszek, *The 104th Congress: A Congressional Quarterly Reader* (Washington: Congressional Quarterly Press), 4.

60. Hook & Cloud 1994, 3431.

61. Representative Don Young of Alaska took over as chair of the Resources Committee, and he was especially eager to land the trans-Alaska pipeline in his turf. Jurisdiction over all other pipelines, and pipeline policies more generally, remain with the Commerce Committee.

62. Victor 1995, 1761.

63. Chitra Ragavan, "House Energy and Commerce Committee to Lose Influence," *All Things Considered,* National Public Radio, Washington, DC, broadcast December 28, 1994.

64. Paul Connolly, "GOP Gets Energy Panel in Its Cross-Hairs," *Oil Daily* (December 5, 1994): 1.

65. Interview with the author. August 12, 1995.

66. "Slight Change Expected in House Jurisdiction over Energy Matters," *Inside F.E.R.C.* (December 12, 1994): 1.

67. "House Commerce Committee Alone in Telecommunications Jurisdiction," *Common Carrier Week* 11, no. 49 (December 12, 1994); "Markey Looks to Maintain Agenda in New Role," *Television Digest* 23, no. 49 (December 5, 1994): 3.

68. "Financial Services Industries Could Gain from New GOP Plan," *Bank Letter* 17, no. 45 (November 14, 1995): 1.

69. Victor 1995, 1761.

Chapter Four

1. For a review and extensions, see Douglas Dion, "The Robustness of the Structure-Induced Equilibrium," *American Journal of Political Science* 36 (May 1992): 462–482. Also see Keith Krehbiel, "Spatial Models of Legislative Choice," *Legislative Studies Quarterly* 13 (1988): 259–319.

2. William Riker, "Implications from the Disequilibrium of Majority Rule for the Study of Institutions," *American Political Science Review* 73 (1980): 85–102.

3. See, for example, Robert H. Bates & William T. Bianco, "Cooperation by Design: Leadership, Structure, and Collective Dilemmas," *American Political Science Review* 84 (March 1990): 113–138; Mayhew 1974.

4. Robert Axelrod, *The Evolution of Cooperation* (New York: Basic Books, 1984); Gerald Marwell & Ruth E. Ames, "Experiments on the Provision of Public Goods: Resources, Interest, Group Size, and the Free Rider problem," *American Journal of Sociology* 84 (1979): 1135–1160.

5. Russell Hardin, *Collective Action* (Baltimore: Johns Hopkins University Press, 1982); Jon Elster, *The Cement of Society: A Study of Social Order* (New York: Cambridge University Press, 1989).

6. John L. Zorack 1990, 359.

7. Clarence Brown, a representative from Ohio, said on the House floor in 1974: "While I am fully aware that [the parliamentarian] has served at the pleasure of the speaker, he has served to the pleasure of the House itself. Without his rational stability, this body would not have been able to serve the people as well as it has for the last half century." See the *Congressional Record* (June 27, 1974): 21592.

8. Ted Siff & Alan Weil, *Ruling Congress: A Study of How the House and Senate Rules Govern the Legislative Process* (New York: Grossman, 1975), 27.

9. Barbara Sinclair, *Majority Leadership in the U.S. House* (Baltimore: Johns Hopkins University Press, 1983), 34; and ibid., *Legislators, Leaders, and Lawmaking: The U.S. House of Representatives in the Postreform Era* (Baltimore: Johns Hopkins, 1995), 67.

10. More often than not (though Roger Davidson and Walter Oleszek are the great exceptions), legislative scholars say nothing at all about the parliamentarians. I have scoured every major Congress text going back 20 years, and the parliamentarians are virtually invisible. That is in stark contrast to the prominence they receive in private interviews with legislators and their staffs.

11. For example, in Massachusetts, the chief clerks of the House and Senate

are explicitly given the job of referring bills to committees. The same goes for the Louisiana Senate, the Maine Senate and House, and the Tennessee Senate. Six states (California, Illinois, Kentucky, Nebraska, and Ohio) use a Rules or Steering Committee to refer bills. In theory, at least, all remaining state legislatures give referral duties to the Speaker. In practice, however, the chief clerks and parliamentarians play an important role in those Speaker-centered systems. American Society of Legislative Clerks and Secretaries, *Inside the Legislative Process* (Denver: National Conference of State Legislatures, 1988), 57–58.

12. Some states have partisan clerks. Some clerks handle adjudicate bill referrals. There is considerable state-by-state variation. We have a lot to learn about the sources of this variance and the institutional development of clerks and parliamentarians.

13. *Congressional Record* (March 30, 1995): H4023.

14. Janet Hook, "Parliamentarians: Procedure and Pyrotechnics," *CQ Weekly Report* (July 14, 1987): 1951–1987.

15. Ibid., "A New House Historian with a New Twist," *CQ Weekly Report* (January 7, 1995): 21; Juliet Eilperin, "First Firings Claim Top Managers, Including Heads of Food Service, OFEP, Post Office, Finance Office," *Roll Call* (December 22, 1994b): 3.

16. Juliet Eilperin, "Aftershocks: The New GOP Officers," *Roll Call* (November 17, 1994a): 47.

17. David S. Cloud, "GOP Picks Management Pros to Run House Operations," *CQ Weekly Report* 52 (December 17, 1994): 3559.

18. D. B. Hardeman & Donald C. Bacon, *Rayburn: A Biography* (Austin: Texas Monthly Press, 1987), 304.

19. Dan Rostenkowski (D-IL) said of Deschler, "His unparalleled knowledge of the House has been muted only by his disdain for the public eye. In a city that craves the limelight, he has excelled in its shadow." *Congressional Record* (June 27, 1974): 21592–21593.

20. Interview with the author, June 21, 1991.

21. *Congressional Record* (September 20, 1994): H9226.

22. The speaker *is* more involved in referrals now that he can set time limits on sequential referrals. This is discussed later in this chapter.

23. *Congressional Record* (September 20, 1994): H9227.

24. Ibid. (March 4, 1963): H3374. For a brief discussion on Deschler and former Speaker Longworth, see Ronald M. Peters, Jr., *The American Speakership: The Office in Historical Perspective* (Baltimore: Johns Hopkins University Press, 1990), 105.

25. *Congressional Record* (March 4, 1963), H3373 (emphasis added).

26. Ibid., H3377. Upon Deschler's retirement in 1974, members of the House again honored him for his service and impartiality. It was revealed that John Garner, former vice president and one-time candidate for the presidency, respected Deschler's work as an arbiter so much that he pledged to nominate him as Chief Justice of the Supreme Court if elected. See the *Congressional Record* (June 27, 1974): 21591.

27. Tiefer 1989, 110.

28. During the 101st (1989–1990) Congress, 11,824 House and Senate measures were introduced. Only a tiny percentage of these measures were not referred to committees (primarily in the Senate) so that they could be taken up immediately on the floor. Of all the measures introduced, 1,734 (14.7 percent) were reported out of committee, and 484 (4.1 percent) became public laws. See the January 3, 1991, *Congressional Record.*

29. Rule 22 (4) (a). Because so many bills are introduced on the first day of a new Congress, sometimes this one-day requirement is waived.

30. In 1966, Speaker John McCormack took to the floor and explained the referral of the 1967 Alaska Centennial bill to the Public Works Committee. See Lewis Deschler, *Deschler's Precedents of the U.S. House of Representatives, volumes 1–9* (Washington, DC: Government Printing Office, 1977), chapter 16, subsection 3.2.

31. Hinds 1907, 4: subsections 4365–4371; and 7: subsections, 1489, 2108–2113; Deschler 1977, chapter 16, subsection 3.14.

32. Deschler 1977, vii, viii.

33. Joseph Cooper, *The Origins of the Standing Committees and the Development of the Modern House* (Houston: Rice University Studies 1970), 56.3; ibid., *Congress and Its Committees: A Historical Approach to the Role of Committees in the Legislative Process* (New York: Garland 1988. Besides Cooper's works, there are several good overviews of history of committees, among them Dodd & Schott 1979, chapter 3; & Deering 1990, chapter 2; Robinson 1954. On the professionalization of House memberships and its consequences on the institution, see Polsby 1968, 62:144–168.

34. Ralph V. Harlow, *The History of Legislative Methods in the Period before 1825* (New Haven: Yale University Press, 1917), 145.

35. Ibid., 150.

36. Ibid., 155.

37. Richard Bolling, *Power in the House* (New York: E. P. Dutton & Co., 1968), 33.

38. Gamm & Shepsle 1989, 14:44.

39. Cooper 1970, 8–17.

40. Ibid., 47. Also see Peters 1990, 34–41.

41. Harlow 1917, 200.

42. Joseph Cooper & Cheryl D. Young, "Bill Introduction in the 19th Century: A Study of Institutional Change," *Legislative Studies Quarterly* 14, no. 1 (1989): 71, 72.

43. Private bills were essentially eliminated by the 1946 Legislative Reorganization Act.

44. For example, of 6,940 bills passed in the 59th Congress, only 692 were public bills. The remaining 6,248 were private. Hinds 1907, 4: subsection 3365.

45. The clerk's authority to refer *petitions* is codified in the Old House Rule no. 131. Informally, this also extended to other private bills and to bills affecting rivers and harbors (which automatically went to Commerce). For duties of the

clerk, see John M. Barclay, *Digest of the Rules of the House of Representatives U.S.* (Washington, DC: Government Printing Office, 1867), 38–46.

46. Cooper & Young 1989.

47. According to the 1837 House Rules, "Every bill shall be introduced on the report of a committee or by motion for leave. In the latter case, at least one day's notice shall be given of the motion." See Hinds 1907, 4: subsection 3365.

48. Lauros G. McConachie, *Congressional Committees: A Study of the Origins and Development of Our National and Local Legislative Methods* (New York: Thomas Y. Crowell Co., 1898), 120.

49. *The Congressional Globe* (January 14, 1854): 255. For a wide-ranging discussion of guano politics, see Jimmy M. Skaggs, *The Great Guano Rush* (New York: St. Martin's Press, 1994).

50. Wilbur Mills (D-AR), chair of the Ways and Means Committee throughout the 1960s and much of the 1970s, fought battles similar to George Houston's fights a hundred years earlier. "The results of transferring trade and tariffs to Foreign Affairs," said Mills in 1973, "would be . . . a signal that the House no longer considers it a revenue function and thus outside the purview of matters which must originate here." Quoted in Davidson & Oleszek 1977, 180.

51. McConachie 1898, 120.

52. DeAlva S. Alexander, *History and Procedure of the House of Representatives* (New York: Houghton Mifflin, 1916), chapter 15 and passim.

53. Morton Keller, *Affairs of State: Public Life in Late Nineteenth Century America,* (Cambridge, MA: Harvard University Press, 1977).

54. Douglas Dion 1990.

55. Bolling 1968, 31.

56. Ibid., 31–32.

57. In addition to the 1887 rules change on referrals, Carlisle used an important 1885 rules change that altered the appropriations process in the House primarily to pursue his interest in lowering tariffs. At odds with Samuel Randall, a Pennsylvania Democrat, chairman of the Appropriations Committee and former Speaker of the House, Carlisle spread the appropriations process out to other committees primarily to undermine Randall's power base and to make a tariff reform bill more likely. See Peters 1990, 60–61; and Stewart 1989, 119–128.

58. Peters, Jr., 1990, 62.

59. On Reed as speaker, see ibid., 62–73; Galloway 1961, 52–53; Mary Parker Follett, *The Speaker of the House of Representatives* (New York: Burt Franklin, 1902), passim; William A. Robinson & *Thomas B. Reed, Parliamentarian* (New York: Dodd, Mead, 1930); Thomas B. Reed, "Obstruction in the National House," *North American Review* 149 (1889): 421–428.

60. Peters 1990, 69.

61. Though the Rules plainly said that "an erroneous reference of a petition or *private* bill under this clause shall not confer jurisdiction" on the committee that receives the bill (Rule 22[2], emphasis added), the jurisdictional protection did not extend to *public* bills; so "erroneous" referrals of public bills established precedents that conferred jurisdiction on committees. See Hinds 1908, 4: subsections 4365–4371.

62. Cited in Bolling 1968, 59.

63. Follett 1902, 145.

64. *Rules of the House of Representatives,* 53d Congress, Rule 22 (3). The rules of the 53d Congress are reprinted as Appendix D in Follett 1902.

65. See, for example, Barclay 1867. Also *A Manual of Parliamentary Practice* (New York: Clark, Austin & Smith, 1856).

66. Peters 1990, 81–87; Charles O. Jones, "Joseph G. Cannon and Howard W. Smith: An Essay on the Limits of Leadership in the House of Representatives," *Journal of Politics* 30 (1968): 617–646.

67. For a good discussion of the Rules Committee from Reed to Cannon, see House Committee on Rules, *A History of the Committee on Rules: 1st to 97th Congress, 1789–1981,* 97th Congress, 2d session (Washington, DC: Government Printing Office, 1983), 55–93.

68. Peters, 1990, 83.

69. To the end, Cannon insisted that nothing good was accomplished by his defeat. "It seems to me, regarding the matter quite dispassionately, the Insurgents accomplished about as much as did that famous king of France who marched his forty thousand men up the hill and then marched them down again; doubtless to the profit of the shoemakers and the improvement of the sweet tempers of his soldiers." See L. White Busbey, *Uncle Joe Cannon: The Story of a Pioneer American* (New York: Henry Holt & Co, 1927), 269.

70. Peters 1990, chapter 3, passim; Jones 1968; Joseph Cooper & David W. Brady, "Institutional Context and Leadership Style: The House from Cannon to Rayburn," *American Political Science Review* 75 (1981): 411–425.

71. Clark left in 1917 for the army and World War I. For a brief discussion of this service and his time as clerk, see *Congressional Record* (May 15, 1918): H6553.

72. U.S. House of Representatives, *Clarence Andrew Cannon, Late a Representative from Missouri: Memorial Addressed Delivered in Congress,* 88th Congress, 2d session (Washington, DC: Government Printing Office, 1964), 43.

73. Polsby 1968, 157; Peters 1990, 92–97.

74. Clarence Cannon was a Missouri representative for more than 41 years until his death in 1964. He gained great power as chair (and ranking minority member) of the Appropriations Committee from 1941 until his death.

75. Quoted in Siff & Weil 1975, 26.

76. Reprint of a letter to Speaker Carl Albert, *Congressional Record* (June 27, 1974): 21590. In the eighth case, when the Speaker was overruled by a floor majority, that was the result that the Speaker wanted in order to correct an erroneous precedent.

77. House Select Committee on Committees, *Monographs on the Committees of the House of Representatives,* 93d Congress, 2d session (December 13, 1974b), (Washington, DC: Government Printing Office, 1974), 150–151.

78. Rule 21 (5) (b). According to people who were at the Democratic caucus when the rule was written, there was little debate over it because it only seemed to codify what had long since been established. But Dan Rostenkowski (D-IL) has used the clause to raise points of order against bills containing "user

fees." Many committee chairs saw this not as jurisdictional protection by Ways and Means but as a power grab by Rostenkowski. In late 1990, a "memorandum of understanding" was completed that is supposed to spell out the differences between user fees and taxes (see the *Congressional Record* [January 3, 1991]), but some members are now arguing about whether the agreement pertains only to new user fees (like ones at national parks), or old user fees as well (such as gas taxes going to the Highway Trust Fund).

79. A former parliamentarian acknowledged that there may be *some* value in parliamentarian shopping on things *other* than bill referrals, such as "what points of orders lie in appropriation bills, what's germane and what's not, and there are [committee staff] who know who'll be a strict constructionist."

80. Speaker Albert is quoted in House Select Committee on Committees 1973, 57.

81. Adler 1969), chapters 3–5; on jurisdictions, see 197.

82. House Select Committee on Committees 1974b, 5.

83. Ibid., 1973, 1. Also see Davidson & Oleszek 1977, 50–57.

84. House Select Committee on Committees, 1973, 57–58.

85. Garry Young, "Coordination and Legislative Organization: The Case of Multiple Referral" (University of Missouri, 1994c, typescript), 8–10.

86. Oleszek 1995, 100–103; Garry Young, "Committee and Party Behavior under Single and Multiple Referral," Paper delivered at the annual meeting of the Midwest Political Science Association, Chicago, 1994b; ibid., "Committee Gatekeeping and Proposal Power under Single and Multiple Referral" (University of Missouri, 1994a, typescript).

87. Change in Rule 22 (4) (b) effective January 3, 1979.

88. Davidson, Oleszek, & Kephart 1988, 8.

89. Collie & Cooper 1989, 254.

90. Oleszek, Davidson, & Kephart, "The Incidence and Impact of Multiple Referrals in the House of Representatives," Congressional Research Service, Library of Congress, July 1986, 43, 46.

91. Ibid., 44. Collie & Cooper 1989 make much the same argument on 248.

92. Davidson, Oleszek, & Kephart 1988, 8. Evidence on the decline of split referrals comes from interviews with staffers close to the parliamentarian's office.

93. Oleszek, Davidson, & Kephart 1986, 11.

94. Ibid., 8.

95. Roger H. Davidson, "The Emergence of the Postreform Congress," in Roger H. Davidson, ed., *The Postreform Congress,* (New York: St. Martin's Press, 1992), 21.

96. Evans & Oleszek 1995a, 14.

Chapter Five

1. "Nixon Signs Comprehensive Bill to Regulate Pesticides," *Congressional Quarterly Almanac, 1972,* volume 27 (Washington, DC: Congressional Quarterly, 1973), 394–397.

2. Deschler 1977, vii.

3. Formally, letters are addressed to the Speaker, but they are passed on to the parliamentarian—usually unread by the Speaker.

4. Zorack 1990, 361.

5. *Congressional Record* (January 3, 1991).

6. Ibid., (January 30, 1995): H849.

7. Charles Tiefer 1989, 86. On oversight more generally, see Joel D. Aberbach, *Keeping a Watchful Eye: The Politics of Congressional Oversight* (Washington, DC: Brookings Institution, 1990); and Morris S. Ogul, *Congress Oversees the Bureaucracy* (Pittsburgh: University of Pittsburgh Press, 1976).

8. Talbert, Jones, & Baumgartner 1995, 385.

9. Elaine Sciolino, "Eccentric Still But Obscure No More, Texan Leads Inquiry on Iraq Loans," *New York Times* (July 3, 1992), A10. The committee's hearings have been ranging so far from its jurisdiction that one committee Republican, Representative Al McCandless from California, said, "I'm wondering if I've been promoted to Foreign Affairs."

10. The Commerce Committee has jurisdiction over the National Institutes of Health, which operates a similar research overhead program.

11. Leroy N. Rieselbach, *Congressional Reform* (Washington: Congressional Quarterly Press, 1986), 155. On participation in subcommittees, see Richard L. Hall & C. Lawrence Evans, "The Power of Subcommittees," *Journal of Politics* 52 (1990): 335–355. Also see Roger H. Davidson, "Subcommittee Government: New Channels for Policy Making," in Thomas E. Mann & Norman J. Ornstein, eds.), *The New Congress* (Washington, DC: American Enterprise Institute, 1981).

12. Florio chaired the Commerce, Consumer Protection, and Competitiveness Subcommittee. The subcommittee was created in 1987 to include "competitiveness" as an issue in the committee's jurisdiction, and it is under this label that Florio and Dingell launched into the trade jurisdiction.

13. House Committee on Ways and Means, *Enemy Within: Crack-Cocaine and America's Families*, 101st Congress, 2d session (June 12, 1990) (Washington, DC: Government Printing Office, 1990). This issue traditionally belongs to the Commerce Committee, but it was politically hot in 1990. This was especially true near Thomas Downey's (D-NY) Suffolk County district, and Downey chaired the Subcommittee on Human resources that produced the print.

14. In 1980, when the Energy Committee reforms were being debated, Jerry Patterson (D-CA) circulated a "Dear Colleague" letter pointing out that six of the seven most expensive subcommittees in the House were in the Commerce Committee.

15. *1990 Congressional Staff Directory* (Mount Vernon, VA: Staff Directories, Ltd., 1990).

16. House Committee on Energy and Commerce, *Subject and Policy Issues for Energy and Commerce Committee Review during the 98th Congress*, 98th Congress, 1st session (September 1983b), (Washington, DC: Government Printing Office, 1983b); ibid., *Subject and Policy Issues for Energy and Com-*

merce Committee Review during the 99th Congress, 99th Congress, 1st session (May 1985) (Washington, DC: Government Printing Office, 1985).

17. For an introduction to multiple referrals in the House, see Roger H. Davidson & Walter J. Oleszek, "From Monopoly to Management: Changing Patterns of Committee Deliberation," in Roger H. Davidson ed., *The Postreform Congress* (New York: St. Martin's Press, 1992).

18. Steven Pressman, "Over Reagan's Protest, House Votes Trade Bill," *CQ Weekly Report* (May 24, 1986c), 1154–1158.

19. Barry R. Weingast, "Fighting Fire with Fire: Amending Activity and Institutional Change in the Postreform Congress," in Roger H. Davidson, ed., *The Postreform Congress* (New York: St. Martin's Press, 1992), 163.

20. From 1975 through 1986, restrictive rules increased from 5.1 to 16.6 percent. Likewise, "multiple-committee" rules increased from 6.9 to 19.8 percent. On the effects of multiple referrals on rules, see Stanley Bach & Steven S. Smith, *Managing Uncertainty in the House of Representatives: Adaptation and Innovation in Special Rules,* (Washington, DC: Brookings Institution, 1988), 18–23, 73.

21. For an example, see "Exchange of Letters Concerning Markup of H.R. 2854, Agricultural Market Transition Act," *Congressional Record* (February 29, 1996): H1575.

22. Tiefer 1989, 115.

23. Mike Mills, "Two Powerful Chairmen Duel to Shape the Bells' Future," *CQ Weekly Report* (June 27, 1992): 1866–1868.

24. *Congressional Quarterly Almanac, 1987* (Washington, DC: Congressional Quarterly Press, 1988), 43:357.

25. On conference committees generally, see Lawrence D. Longley & Walter J. Oleszek, *Bicameral Politics: Conference Committees in Congress* (New Haven: Yale University Press, 1989).

26. Judy Schneider, "Committee Jurisdictions," in Donald C. Bacon et al., eds., *The Encyclopedia of the United States Congress* (New York: Simon & Schuster, 1995), 427.

27. Calculated by the author with the use of the *Congressional Staff Directory.* This number, 82, does not include the Budget Committee Task Forces.

28. Committees on which the subcommittees remained relatively stable were Armed Services, District of Columbia, Education and Labor, Post Office and Civil Service, Public Works and Transportation, Rules, Standards of Official Conduct, and Ways and Means.

29. Budget Committee (Economic Policy, Projections, and Revenues), Banking Committee (Economic Stabilization), Public Works Committee (Economic Development).

30. Commerce Committee (Health and the Environment), Education and Labor (Health and Safety), Veterans Affairs (Hospitals and Health Care), Ways and Means (Health).

31. Agriculture (Conservation, Credit and Rural Development), Budget (Community Development and Natural Resources), Commerce (Health and the Environment), Government Operations (Environment, Energy, and Natu-

ral Resources), Interior (Mining and Natural Resources), Merchant Marine and Fisheries (Fisheries and Wildlife Conservation and the Environment), Science (Environment), Small Business (Antitrust, Impact of Deregulation, and Ecology), Small Business (Environment and Employment).

32. Agriculture (Forests, Family Farms, and Energy), Appropriations (Energy and Water Development), Commerce (Energy and Power), Government Operations (Environment, Energy, and Natural Resources), Interior (Energy and the Environment), Interior (Water, Power, and Offshore energy Resources), Science (Energy).

33. Davidson & Oleszek 1977, 53, 60–61.

Chapter Six

1. Daniel Patrick Moynihan, "How to Lose: the Story of Maglev," *Scientific American* (November 1989): 130.

2. One Commerce Committee staffer said in an interview that his committee has not expanded its jurisdiction one inch; it has merely asserted its already existing authority over new issues. Everyone in the room laughed at the claim, but it shows how difficult it may be to decide what is jurisdictionally ambiguous and what is not.

3. John E. Jackson & David C. King, "Public Goods, Private Interests, and Representation," *American Political Science Review* 83 (December 1989): 1143–1164; David C. King 1989.

4. House Committee on Science, Space, and Technology, "High Speed Railroad Technology," 100th Congress, 1st session (April 3, 1987) (Washington, DC: Government Printing Office, 1987), 65–93.

5. Senate Committee on Environment and Public Works, *Benefits of Magnetically Levitated High-Speed Transportation for the United States,* report prepared by the Maglev Technology Advisory Committee, 101st Congress, 1st session (August, 1989) (Washington, DC: Government Printing Office, 1989); Gregory T. Pope, "Supertrain," *Popular Mechanics* (June 1988): 78–89, 114.

6. "Japanese Make Significant Gains in Maglev Technology," *Research & Development* 31 (February 1989): 64–66.

7. Christopher D. King, "Florida Rail Unit in Preliminary OK for Maglev," *Metalworking News* (July 3, 1989): 5–6; House Committee on Public Works and Transportation, *Development of High-Speed Transportation Corridors, Including Those Which May Utilize Magnetic Levitation Technology,* 101st Congress, 2d session (May 3, 1990) (Washington, DC: Government Printing Office, 1990), 136–143; Roger Roy, "Companies Vie to Get on Board Train Project," *Orlando Sentinel Tribune* (August 14, 1995): 12.

8. The OTA report is printed in House Committee on Public Works and Transportation, *High-Speed Rail Transportation,* 102d Congress, 1st session (October 16, 1991) (Washington, DC: Government Printing Office, 1991), 60–67; Gene Koprowski, "Pittsburgh Examines Maglev Transportation," *Metalworking News* (March 4, 1990): 4–5. The Las Vegas line is in some peril because

of money problems. See Kenneth Reich & Jeffrey A. Perlman, "Maglev Line Hopes Vanishing in the Air," *Los Angeles Times* (May 5, 1991): A3.

9. See, for example, Clement Work, "The Flying Train Takes Off: Maglev is Airborne, But American Business Is Not at the Controls," *U.S. News & World Report* (July 23, 1990): 52–53.

10. Robert Cassidy, "Japan's Open Door: Is the U.S. Missing Its Golden Opportunity?" *Research & Development* 30 (November, 1988): 81–84; Skip Derra, Superconductivity: Levitation Could Lead Way to Uses for Superconductors," *Research & Development* 30 (September 1988): 24.

11. David Swinbanks, "Maglev Burns Out in Japan," *Nature* (October 17, 1991): 592; John Van, "Why Maglev Won't Fly," *San Francisco Examiner* (August 9, 1992): E-14.

12. Atasushi Nakayama, "JAL First to Market with Maglev Train," *Nikkei Weekly* (August 7, 1995): 9; "Conference Report on H.R. 2002," *Congressional Record* (October 20, 1995).

13. "German Government Orders Construction of Maglev Railway," *Deutsche Presse-Agentur* (June 29, 1995).

14. For a summary, see Luther S. Miller, "1992 Outlook: Transit Hits the Bullseye," *Railway Age* 193 (January 1992): 56, 59.

15. As a check, I asked a friend, Joel Kaji, to repeat my exercise. I gave him a brief description of the maglev issue and asked him to pretend that he was a legislator trying to find links between committee turf and the issue. He read through *Dreschler's Precedents* and came up with the same committees that I did, though he credited two committees with more proximity. He thought that the Energy and Commerce Committee's statutory jurisdiction over "interstate and foreign commerce, generally" should count as an indicator of proximity, because the train lines could carry cargo between states. He also thought that "environmental R&D" should count for the Science Committee. These two additions would increase Commerce's proximity score to 5 and would increase Science and Technology's score to 3. If anything, these changes would increase the estimated impact of "jurisdictional proximity" in the models discussed below.

16. Jeffrey H. Birnbaum, "High-Speed Train Propelled by Magnets Attracts 'Peace Dividend' Funds and Defense Contractors," *Wall Street Journal* (May 10, 1990): A24. The National Aeronautics and Space Administration and the Environmental Protection Agency were also involved, but at a much lower level. It is also common for representatives from DOT, DOE, and the Army Corps of Engineers to appear at congressional hearings on maglev, while NASA and EPA officials are rarely involved.

17. Energy and Commerce, 4 ("Measures relating to the conservation of energy resources," Railroads," DOT, DOE); Public Works and Transportation, 4 ("Transportation, including civil aviation, except railroads," "Roads, and the safety thereof," DOT, DOE); Science, Space and Technology, 2 ("Scientific research, development, and demonstration," DOE); Armed Services, 2 (Army Corps of Engineers, DOE); Interior and Insular Affairs, 1 (DOE); Banking, Finance, and Urban Affairs, 1 ("Urban development"); Ways and Means, 1 ("Revenue measures generally").

18. Entrepreneurial activity is a type of political participation, and instead of directly modeling the probability of being an entrepreneur I model the propensity to engage in prereferral activity. I think of prereferral entrepreneurial activity as behavior on the high end of a participation scale, so my approach here is naturally influenced by Richard Hall's work. I considered trying to establish a point on the participation scale above which a member might be considered an "entrepreneur," but I had no good theoretical reason to pick one point on the scale as opposed to another. When other scholars have made arbitrary cleavages between "entrepreneurs" and "active supporters," their findings have seemed driven more by the way the distinction was made than by the underlying process. See Weissert 1991. Accordingly, I model the propensity to engage in prereferral entrepreneurial activity—not the probability of being an entrepreneur.

19. Scores from this were: Kolter (D-PA) 4, Hamilton (D-IN) 2, Gejdenson (D-CT) 2, Rostenkowski (D-IL) 2, and Packard (R-CA) 2.

20. House Committee on Science, Space, and Technology, 1987; House Committee on Public Works and Transportation, 1990.

21. Within each hearing document, I calculated the percentage of the total text attributed to each member. One point was given to each member participating up to 10 percent of the time. Two points were given for participating up to 25 percent of the time, and 3 points were given for participating at least 25 percent of the time. Scores were: McCurdy (D-OK) 3, Lewis (R-FL) 3, Mineta (D-CA) 3, Hayes (D-LA) 3, Sensenbrenner (R-WI) 2, Schuster (R-PA) 2, Costello (D-IL) 1, Jones (D-GA) 1, Cox (R-CA) 1, Payne (D-VA) 1, Kolter (D-PA) 1, Packard (R-CA) 1.

22. Sponsors include: Pepper (D-FL), Mrazek (D-NY), Torricelli (D-NJ), Walgren (D-PA), Kolter (D-PA), Panetta (D-CA), Cardin (D-MD), Swift (D-WA), Sangmeister (D-IL), Coyne (D-PA), Hayes (D-LA), Schumer (D-NY), and Valentine (D-NC).

23. *Congressional Record* (April 23, 1991); H-2448.

24. In 1990 there were three projects underway that were funded by state and local governments and companies. These include the Orlando International airport project, the Pittsburgh airport project, and Bechtel Corporation's 235-mile line between Anaheim, California, and Las Vegas, Nevada. A fourth line, then being planned as a federal demonstration project, would have linked Washington, DC, with Baltimore, Maryland.

25. Three sources were used to come up with a list of companies: (1) major contributors to the Council on Superconductivity and Competitiveness' Maglev 2000 Committee were identified; (2) financial supporters of Maglev USA, another trade group representing potential U.S. component makers; and (3) corporate members of the U.S. Senate's Maglev Technology Advisory Committee. To code constituency interests, I gave a legislator representing the districts that house the headquarters of these companies 2 points. If a company with a maglev interest had more than 5,000 employees, I gave neighboring districts within a 100-mile radius of the headquarters 1 point. If a company had fewer than 5,000 employees, legislators in neighboring districts within a 50-mile

radius received 1 point. Firms identified by at least one of the three criteria include: AEG Westinghouse Transportation Systems, Argonne National Laboratory, Babcock and Wilcox Company, Bechtel Corporation, Brookhaven National Laboratory, CSX Transportation Inc., General Dynamics Corporation, Grumman Aerospace Corporation, Intermagnetics General Corporation, Kaman Aerospace Corporation, Rust International, and Sverdrup Corporation. Three small companies that met the criteria were excluded because they employ fewer than 100 people: New Technology Products, The Magneplane Corporation, and Xerad. I checked this list with Wayne Thevenot, a lobbyist with Maglev USA, and he suggested that a complete sample of the maglev "players" would include three more companies, which I have added. These are: Morrison-Knudsen, KCI International, and Westinghouse. On Morrison-Knudsen's involvement in high-speed rail, see Robert McGough, "The Texas Cannonball," *Financial World* 160 (August 6, 1991): 20–22.

26. The approach I used is adapted from Richard Hall's studies of participation in committees. See his "Measuring Legislative Influence," *Legislative Studies Quarterly* 17 (May 1992): 205–232.

27. This list was drawn up with the help of Wayne Thevenot, a lobbyist for Maglev USA.

28. The questions were these:

1. I'm interested in which members of the House and which House staffers are knowledgeable about maglev. Try to think back two to four years ago when maglev was just getting on the agenda. Please try to clear your mind about what committees a person is on and think only about their maglev knowledge. I am interested in their technical knowledge, not their political know-how. Now, on a scale from 1 to 5, where 1 is a small level of knowledge about maglev and related technologies and where 5 is a wide-ranging knowledge and understanding about maglev, please name any member or staffer who comes to mind. [Answer.] Can you think of anyone else? [Probe until they can come up with no more names.]

2. As a staffer with some knowledge about maglev systems, to which member or members do you most often report? In other words, which members do you feel you're working for on the maglev issue?

29. I contacted 14 current or former committee staffers who were mentioned by at least one other person. I was unable to talk with one staffer, and two others refused to participate. The data in this section, then, are based on 11 interviews with people who were close to the maglev issue in the late 1980s, when it was just beginning to get on the congressional agenda.

30. Listed from the highest level of expertise to the lowest level: Ritter, Mineta, Roe, Valentine, Torricelli, Swift, Lewis, Hockbruckner, Mrazek, DeLay, Kolter.

31. The model was first developed as a multinomial logit, with three categories on the dependent variable (entrepreneur, participant, nonparticipant). This current specification, in OLS, yields the same conclusions and is easier to interpret.

32. Two reasons come to mind, one based on a measurement problem and

one based on the nature of expertise. Since so few members have personal expertise on the issue, the interaction term is highly colinear with the measure of personal expertise, which makes the estimate of the coefficient inefficient. On substantive grounds, it may be that "experts" care more about getting an issue on the congressional agenda than which committees ultimately control the issue.

33. This second stage calls for a multivariate approach. There may be times when jurisdictional proximity, member expertise, and staff expertise do not all point to the same committee, and only a multivariate analysis could help us untangle the relative importance of each. Since the unit of analysis here is a single bill referral, we will not be able to run a multivariate test.

34. 101st Congress: H.C.R. 232, H.R. 3714, H.R. 4515, H.R. 4549, H.R. 5535. 102d Congress: H.R. 422, H.R. 1087, H.R. 1452, H.R. 2102, H.R. 2619, H.R. 2761, H.R. 2878, H.R. 2914, H.R. 2941, H.R. 2950, H.R. 3348.

35. Robert Mrazek, the bill's sponsor, was on the Appropriations Committee, and he did not care very much about which committee gained jurisdiction over the authorization. Contrast this with H.R. 4515, which was sponsored by Commerce member Doug Walgren (D-PA). He crafted the bill to amend the Rail Safety and Service Improvement Act of 1982 which guaranteed a referral to Commerce. That bill was introduced on April 4, 1990—two weeks before H.R. 4549—but it dealt primarily with other forms of high-speed rail and did not clearly establish a maglev referral precedent.

36. Constituency Interests: $0-10$ = low, $11-15$ = medium, $16-22$ = high. Member Expertise: 0 = low, $1-5$ = medium, $6-14$ = high. Staff Expertise: 0 = low, >0 = high. Jurisdictional Proximity: $0-1$ = low, $2-3$ = medium, 4 = high.

Chapter Seven

1. Cordes 1991, A15, A20. "Brown Beefs Up Science Committee," 1991b, 733.

2. David I. Lewin, "Setting an Agenda for Competitiveness," *ASAP* 114, no. 7 (July 1992): 85.

3. Interview with the author, June 19, 1991.

4. Wilson, 1981 [1885].

5. The average length of a public bill has more than tripled since the early 1960s. See Norman J. Ornstein, Thomas E. Mann, & Michael J. Malbin, *Vital Statistics on Congress: 1991–1992* (Washington, DC: Congressional Quarterly Press, 1992), 156.

6. On the Clean Air Act generally, see Richard E. Cohen, *Washington at Work: Back Rooms and Clean Air* (New York: Macmillan, 1992).

7. Heinz Eulau, "The Committees in a Revitalized Congress," in Alfred de Grazia, ed., *Congress: The First Branch of Government* (Washington, DC: American Enterprise Institute, 1966), 215; cited in Morrow 1969, 22.

8. See Rep. Frank Wolf's comments on H.Res.51 (102d Congress), *Congressional Record* (February 6, 1991): H-919. Also see Rich Jaroslovsky, "Turf Wars over Child Care Portend a Possible Legislative Mess," *Wall Street Journal* (February 9, 1990): A1.

9. *Congressional Record* (July 25, 1995): H7554; *Congressional Record* (October 19, 1995): H10469.

10. Madison 1984, 63–65.

11. Ibid.

12. I arrived at this number, 112 hearings, by searching House hearings records using the Congressional Information Service's CD-ROM Masterfile. I searched on the hearing description fields for "free trade" or for "fair trade."

13. Harvey Simon, "Buying the Baretta: The Army's Dilemma," Case no. 848, John F. Kennedy School of Government, Harvard University, 1988.

14. Richard Neustadt, "Politicians and Bureaucrats," in David B. Truman, ed., *The Congress and America's Future* (Englewood Cliffs, NJ: Prentice-Hall, 1965): 108, quoted in Morrow 1969, 25.

15. Morrow 1969, 25.

16. Richard E. Cohen, "Crumbling Committees," *National Journal* (August 4, 1990): 1876–1881.

17. Smith 1989, 699.

18. Such complaints about Congress and the so-called deadlocks of democracy are by no means new among political scientists, though the theme seems to have been picked in the popular media. Theodore Lowi, *The End of Liberalism* (New York: W. W. Norton, 1969). Samples of recent criticisms in the popular press include: Haynes Johnson, "Washington Risks Irrelevance," *Washington Post* (November 29, 1991): A2; Adam Clymer, "An Institution under Duress; Congress's Committees Stumble, and Change," *New York Times* (November 10, 1991): 14; Charles R. Babcock & Richard Morin, "PAC Money Follows Those Who Control Its Interests," *Washington Post* (June 19, 1990): A19.

19. For a discussion of the role of iron triangles during their heydays in the 1940s and 1950s, see Henry Kariel, *The Decline of American Pluralism* (Stanford: Stanford University Press, 1961). For evidence on the connection between jurisdictions and the demise of iron triangles, see Baumgartner & Jones 1993).

20. Baumgartner & Jones, 1993.

21. Jonathan Rauch, *Demosclerosis: The Silent Killer of American Government* (New York: Random House, 1994).

22. Jack L. Walker 1991; Thomas L. Gais, Mark A. Peterson, & Jack L. Walker, "Interest Groups, Iron Triangles, and Representative Institutions in American National Government," *British Journal of Political Science* 14 (1984): 161–185.

23. Mills 1992, 1866–1868.

24. Barry 1989, 301.

25. Charles R. Shipan, "Individual Incentives and Institutional Imperatives: Committee Jurisdiction and Long-Term Health Care," *American Journal of Political Science* 36 (1992): 877–895.

BIBLIOGRAPHY

Aberbach, Joel D. 1990. *Keeping a Watchful Eye: The Politics of Congressional Oversight.* Washington, DC: Brookings Institution.

Adler, Madeline Wing. 1969. "Congressional Reform: An Exploratory Case." Ph.D. dissertation, University of Wisconsin.

Aldrich, John H. 1989. "Power and Order in Congress." In Morris P. Fiorina & David W. Rohde, eds., *Home Style and Washington Work: Studies of Congressional Politics.* Ann Arbor: University of Michigan Press.

Alexander, DeAlva S. 1916. *History and Procedure of the House of Representatives.* New York: Houghton Mifflin.

American Society of Legislative Clerks and Secretaries. 1988. *Inside the Legislative Process.* Denver: National Conference of State Legislatures.

Arthur, W. Brian. 1988. "Self-Reinforcing Mechanisms in Economics." In P. W. Anderson, Kenneth Arrow, & David Pines, eds., *The Economy as an Evolving Complex System: The Proceedings of the Evolutionary Paths of the Global Economy Workshop.* Volume 5. Santa Fe: Addison-Wesley Press.

Axelrod, Robert. 1984. *The Evolution of Cooperation.* New York: Basic Books.

Babcock, Charles R., & Richard Morin. 1990. "PAC Money Follows Those Who Control Its Interests." *Washington Post* (June 19): A19.

Bach, Stanley, & Steven S. Smith. 1988. *Managing Uncertainty in the House of Representatives: Adaptation and Innovation in Special Rules.* Washington, DC: Brookings Institution.

Bacon, Donald C., Roger H. Davidson, & Morton Keller, eds. 1995. *Encyclopedia of the United States Congress.* New York: Simon & Schuster.

Baker, Ross K. 1990. "Fostering the Entrepreneurial Activities of Members of the House." In John J. Kornacki, ed., *Leading Congress: New Styles, New Strategies.* Washington, DC: Congressional Quarterly Press.

Barclay, John M. 1867. *Digest of the Rules of the House of Representatives U.S.* Washington, DC: Government Printing Office.

Baron, David P., & John A. Ferejohn. 1989a. "Bargaining in Legislatures." *American Political Science Review* 83:1181–1206.

———. 1989b. "The Power to Propose." In Peter C. Ordeshook, ed., *Models of Strategic Choice in Politics.* Ann Arbor: University of Michigan Press.

Barone, Michael, & Grant Ujifusa. 1987. *The Almanac of American Politics, 1988.* Washington, DC: National Journal.

Barry, John M. 1989. *The Ambition and the Power.* New York: Viking Penguin.

Bates, Robert H., & William T. Bianco. 1990. *Cooperation by Design: Leadership, Structure, and Collective Dilemmas."* American Political Science Review* 84 (March): 113–138.

Baumgartner, Frank R., & Bryan D. Jones. 1993. *Agendas and Instability in American Politics.* Chicago: University of Chicago Press.

Baumgartner, Frank R., & Jeffery C. Talbert. 1995. "From Setting a National Agenda on Health Care to Making Decisions in Congress." *Journal of Health Politics, Policy and Law* 20 (Summer): 437–445.

Bimber, Bruce. 1991. "Information as a Factor in Congressional Politics." *Legislative Studies Quarterly* 16:585–606.

Binder, Sarah A. 1992. "A Partisan Theory of Procedural Change: Creation of Minority Rights in the House, 1789–1991." Paper delivered at the annual meeting of the Midwest Political Science Association, Chicago.

Birnbaum, Jeffrey H. 1990. "High-Speed Train Propelled by Magnets Attracts 'Peace Dividend' Funds and Defense Contractors." *Wall Street Journal* (May 10): A24.

Bolling, Richard. 1965. *House Out of Order.* New York: E. P. Dutton & Co.

————. 1968. *Power in the House.* New York: E. P. Dutton & Co.

Bonker, Don. 1988. *America's Trade Crisis: The Making of the U.S. Trade Deficit.* Boston: Houghton Mifflin.

Brown, William Holmes. 1991a. *Constitution, Jefferson's Manual, and Rules of the House of Representatives of the United States 102d Congress.* Washington, DC: Government Printing Office.

"Brown Beefs Up Science Committee." 1991b. *Science* (February 15): 733.

Bullock, Charles S. 1971. "The Influence of State Party Delegations on House Committee Assignments." *Midwest Journal of Political Science* 15:525–546.

————. 1972. "Freshman Committee Assignments and Re-Election in the United States House of Representatives." *American Political Science Review* 66:996–1007.

Busbey, L. White. 1927. *Uncle Joe Cannon: The Story of a Pioneer American.* New York: Henry Holt & Co.

Byrd, Robert C. 1988. *The Senate, 1789–1989: Addressed on the History of the United States Senate,* Washington, DC: Government Printing Office.

Cannon, Clarence. 1935. *Cannon's Procedure in the House of Representatives.* 3d edition (1963, 6th edition). Washington, DC: Government Printing Office.

Cantril, Hadley H., ed. 1951. *Public Opinion, 1935–1946.* Princeton: Princeton University Press.

Cassidy, Robert. 1988. "Japan's Open Door: Is the U.S. Missing Its Golden Opportunity?" *Research & Development* 30 (November): 81–84.

"Caught in Turf Battle, Bank Powers Bill Dies." 1989. *1988 Congressional Quarterly Almanac* 44:230–241. Washington, DC: Congressional Quarterly Press.

Chamberlin, Lawrence H. 1945. "Congress—Diagnosis and Prescription." *Political Science Quarterly* 60:437–445.

Clapp, Charles. 1964. *The Congressman: His Work as He Sees It.* Garden City, NY: Anchor Books.

Cloud, David S. 1990. "Bill Gives FDA Nod to Oversee Fish." *CQ Weekly Report* 48 (February 24): 585.

———. 1994. "GOP Picks Management Pros to Run House Operations." *CQ Weekly Report* (December 17): 3559.

———. 1995a. "GOP, to Its Own Great Delight, Enacts House Rules Changes." *CQ Weekly Report* (January 7): 13–15.

———. 1995b. "Shakeup Time." *CQ Weekly Report, Supplement* (supplement to issue 12) 53 (March 25): 9–10.

Clymer, Adam. 1991. "An Institution under Duress; Congress's Committees Stumble, and Change." *New York Times* (November 10): 14.

"Coal-Slurry Bill Renewed." 1990. *1989 Congressional Quarterly Almanac* 45:681–682. Washington, DC: Congressional Quarterly Press.

Cohen, Richard E. 1990. "Crumbling Committees." *National Journal* (August 4): 1876–1881.

———. 1992. *Washington at Work: Back Rooms and Clean Air.* New York: Macmillan.

———. 1993. "The Patchwork Quilt." *National Journal* (October 30): 2584.

Collie, Melissa P., & Joseph Cooper. 1989. "Multiple Referral and the 'New' Committee System in the House of Representatives." In Lawrence C. Dodd & Bruce I. Oppenheimer, eds., *Congress Reconsidered.* 4th edition. Washington, DC: Congressional Quarterly Press.

Committee on Congress, American Political Science Association. 1945. *The Reorganization of Congress.* Washington, DC: Public Affairs Press.

"Committee Reorganization." 1981. *Congressional Quarterly Almanac.* Volume 36. Washington, DC: Congressional Quarterly.

Congressional Directory, 79th Congress, 2d session. 1946. Washington, DC: Government Printing Office.

Congressional Directory, 80th Congress, 1st session. 1947. Washington, DC: Government Printing Office.

Congressional Quarterly Almanac, Volume 29. 1974. Washington, DC: Congressional Quarterly Press.

———. Volume 30. 1975. Washington, DC: Congressional Quarterly Press.

———. Volume 35. 1980. Washington, DC: Congressional Quarterly Press.

———. Volume 36. 1981. Washington, DC: Congressional Quarterly Press.

———. Volume 43. 1988. Washington, DC: Congressional Quarterly Press.

Connolly, Paul. 1994. "GOP Gets Energy Panel in Its Cross-Hairs." *Oil Daily* (December 5): 1.

Cooper, Joseph. 1970. *The Origins of the Standing Committees and the Development of the Modern House.* Volume 56, no. 3. Houston: Rice University Studies.

———. 1988. *Congress and Its Committees: A Historical Approach to the Role of Committees in the Legislative Process.* New York: Garland Publishing.

Cooper, Joseph, & David W. Brady. 1981. "Institutional Context and Leadership Style: The House from Cannon to Rayburn." *American Political Science Review* 75:411–425.

Cooper, Joseph, & Cheryl D. Young. 1989. " Bill Introduction in the 19th Century: A Study of Institutional Change." *Legislative Studies Quarterly* 14, no. 1: 67–106.

Cordes, Colleen, 1991. "New Head of a House Science Panel Plans Activist Role." *Chronicle of Higher Education* (January 2): A15, A20.

Cowling, Maurice. 1963. *The Nature and Limits of Political Science.* Cambridge: Cambridge University Press.

Cox, Gary W., & Mathew D. McCubbins. 1993. *Legislative Leviathan: Party Government in the House.* Berkeley: University of California Press.

Cranford, John. 1991. "Banking Overhaul Losing Ground to Complexity, Controversy." *CQ Weekly Report* (November 2): 3182–3185.

Dahl, Robert A. 1961. "The Behavioral Approach in Political Science: Epitaph for a Monument to a Successful Protest." *American Political Science Review* 55:763–772.

David, Paul A. 1975. *Technical Choice Innovation and Economic Growth.* New York: Cambridge University Press.

Davidson, Roger H. 1981. "Subcommittee Government: New Channels for Policy Making." In Thomas E. Mann & Norman J. Ornstein, eds., *The New Congress.* Washington, DC: American Enterprise Institute.

———. 1990. "The Advent of the Modern Congress: The Legislative Reorganization Act of 1946." *Legislative Studies Quarterly* 15:357–374.

———. 1992. "The Emergence of the Postreform Congress." In Roger H. Davidson, ed., *The Postreform Congress.* New York: St. Martin's Press.

———. 1995. "The 104th Congress and Beyond." In Roger H. Davidson & Walter J. Oleszek, *The 104th Congress: A Congressional Quarterly Reader.* Washington, DC: Congressional Quarterly Press.

Davidson, Roger H., David M. Kovenock, & Michael K. O'Leary. 1966. *Congress in Crisis: Politics and Congressional Reform.* Belmont, CA: Wadsworth Publishing Co.

Davidson, Roger H., & Walter J. Oleszek. 1976. "Adaptation and Consolidation: Structural Innovation in the U.S. House of Representatives." *Legislative Studies Quarterly* 1:37–65.

———. 1977. *Congress against Itself.* Bloomington: Indiana University Press.

———. 1981. *Congress and Its Members.* 2d edition. Washington, DC: Congressional Quarterly Press.

———. 1992. "From Monopoly to Management: Changing Patterns of Committee Deliberation." In Roger H. Davidson, ed., *The Postreform Congress.* New York: St. Martin's Press.

Davidson, Roger H., Walter J. Oleszek, & Thomas Kephart. 1988. "One Bill, Many Committees: Multiple Referrals in the U.S. House of Representatives." *Legislative Studies Quarterly* 13:3–28.

Davis, Phillip A. 1992. "Policy Dispute Delays Bill on Interior Spending." *CQ Weekly Report* (July 4): 1940.

Derra, Skip. 1988. "Superconductivity: Levitation Could Lead Way to Uses for Superconductors." *Research & Development* 30 (September): 24.

Deschler, Lewis, 1977. *Deschler's Precedents of the U.S. House of Representatives,* Volumes 1–9. Washington, DC: Government Printing Office.

Deschler, Lewis, & William Holmes Brown. 1982. *Procedure in the U.S. House of Representatives.* Washington, DC: Government Printing Office.

Dexter, Lewis Anthony. 1970. *Elite and Specialized Interviewing.* Evanston, IL: Northwestern University Press.

Dion, Douglas. 1990. "Majority Rule, Minority Rights, and the Politics of Procedural Change." Paper delivered at the annual meeting of the American Political Science Association, San Francisco.

―――. 1992. "The Robustness of the Structure-Induced Equilibrium." *American Journal of Political Science* 36 (May): 462–482.

Dodd, Lawrence C. 1986. "The Cycles of Legislative Change: Building a Dynamic Theory." In Herbert F. Weisberg, ed., *Political Science: The Science of Politics.* New York: Agathon Press.

Dodd, Lawrence C., & Richard L. Schott. 1979. *Congress and the Administrative State.* New York: John Wiley & Sons.

Doig, Jameson & Edwin Hargrove, eds. 1987. *Leadership and Innovation: A Biological Perspective on Entrepreneurs in Government.* Baltimore: Johns Hopkins University Press.

Dopfer, Kurt. 1991. "Toward a Theory of Economic Institutions: Synergy and Path Dependency." *Journal of Economic Issues* 25:535–550.

Dreier, David. 1994. "News Conference with Rep. David Dreier (R-CA)." Federal Information Systems Corporation, December 2.

Eilperin, Juliet. 1994a. "Aftershocks: The New GOP Officers." *Roll Call* (November 17): 47.

―――. 1994b. "First Firings Claim Top Managers, Including Heads of Food Service, OFEP, Post Office, Finance Office." *Roll Call* (December 22): 3.

―――. 1996. "House Bills Bypass Committee Process." *Roll Call* (March 18): 1.

Eisenberg, Melvin A. 1988. *The Nature of the Common Law.* Cambridge, MA: Harvard University Press.

Elster, Jon. 1989. *The Cement of Society: A Study of Social Order.* New York: Cambridge University Press.

England, David E., & Charles S. Bullock. 1986. "Prescriptive Seats Revisited." *American Journal of Political Science* 30:496–502.

Eulau, Heinz. 1966. "The Committees in a Revitalized Congress." In Alfred de Grazia, ed., *Congress: The First Branch of Government.* Washington, DC: American Enterprise Institute.

Eulau, Heinz. 1985. "Committee Selection." In Gerhard Loewenberg, Samuel C. Patterson, & Malcolm E. Jewell, eds., *Handbook of Legislative Research.* Cambridge, MA: Harvard University Press.

Evans, C. Lawrence. 1994. "Committees and Health Jurisdictions in Congress." College of William and Mary. Typescript.

Evans, C. Lawrence, & Walter J. Oleszek. 1995a. "Congressional Tsunami? Institutional Change in the 104th Congress." Paper delivered at the annual meeting of the American Political Science Association, Chicago.

———. 1995b. "The Joint Committee on the Organization of Congress." In James A. Thurber & Roger H. Davidson, eds., *Remaking Congress: Change and Stability in the 1990s.* Washington, DC: Congressional Quarterly Press.

———. 1995c. "Reform Redux: Jurisdictional Change and the New Republican House." Paper delivered at the annual meeting of the Midwest Political Science Association. Chicago, April 7.

Fenno, Richard F. 1973. *Congressmen in Committees.* Boston: Little, Brown.

———. 1991. *The Emergence of a Senate Leader: Peter Domenici and the Reagan Budget.* Washington, DC: Congressional Quarterly Press.

Ferejohn, John. 1986. "Logrolling in an Institutional Context." In Gerald C. Wright, Leroy N. Rieselbach, & Lawrence C. Dodd, eds., *Congress and Policy Change.* New York: Agathon Press.

"Financial Services Industries Could Gain from New GOP Plan." 1995. *Bank Letter* 17, no. 45 (November 14): 1.

Fink, Evelyn C., & Brian D. Humes. 1992. "Electoral Forces and Institutional Change in the United States House of Representatives, 1860–1894." Paper delivered at the annual meeting of the Midwest Political Science Association, Chicago.

Fiorina, Morris P. 1981. "Universalism, Reciprocity, and Distributive Policy-Making in Majority Rule Institutions." In John Crecine, ed., *Research in Public Policy Analysis and Management.* Greenwich, CT: JAI Press.

Follett, Mary Parker. 1902. *The Speaker of the House of Representatives.* New York: Burt Franklin.

Francis, Wayne L. 1989. *The Legislative Committee Game: A Comparative Analysis of Fifty States.* Columbus: Ohio State University Press.

Freeman, Donald M. 1991. "The Making of a Discipline." In William Crotty, ed., *Political Science: Looking to the Future.* Volume 1. Evanston: Northwestern University Press.

Froke, Christopher J. 1992. "State Delegations and the U.S. House Committee System: Ways and Means in the 20th Century." Paper delivered at the annual meeting of the Midwest Political Science Association, Chicago.

Froman, Lewis A., Jr. 1967. *The Congressional Process: Strategies, Rules, and Procedures.* Boston: Little, Brown.

Gais, Thomas L., Mark A. Peterson, & Jack L. Walker. 1984. "Interest Groups, Iron Triangles, and Representative Institutions in American National Government." *British Journal of Political Science* 14:161–185.

Galloway, George B. 1946. *Congress at the Crossroads.* New York: Thomas Y. Crowell Co.

———. 1955. *The Legislative Process in Congress.* New York: Thomas Y. Crowell Co.

———. 1961. *History of the House of Representatives.* New York: Thomas Y. Crowell Co.

Gamm, Gerald, & Kenneth Shepsle. 1989. "Emergence of Legislative Institutions: Standing Committees in the House and Senate, 1810–1825." *Legislative Studies Quarterly* 14:39–66.

"German Government Orders Construction of Maglev Railway." 1995. *Deutsche Presse-Agentur* (June 29).

Gifis, Steven H. 1984. *Law Dictionary.* New York: Barron's Educational Series.

Gilligan, Thomas W., & Keith Krehbiel. 1988. "Organization of Informative Committees by a Rational Legislature." Hoover Institution Working Paper no. P-88-13.

———. 1990. "Organization of Informative Committees by a Rational Legislature." *American Journal of Political Science* 34:531–564.

Goodwin, George, Jr. 1970. *The Little Legislatures.* Amherst: University of Massachusetts Press.

Gosselin, Peter G. 1993. "Kennedy Gains in Turf War on Health Bill." *Boston Globe* (November 23): 3.

Gould, Stephen Jay. 1989. *Wonderful Life: The Burgess Shale and the Nature of History.* New York: W. W. Norton.

Greenstein, Fred I. 1987. *Personality and Politics: Problems of Evidence, Inference, and Conceptualization.* Princeton: Princeton University Press.

Hall, Richard L. 1987. "Participation and Purpose in Committee Decision Making." *American Political Science Review* 81 (March): 105–127.

———. 1992. "Measuring Legislative Influence." *Legislative Studies Quarterly* 17 (May): 205–232.

———. 1996. *Participation in Congress.* New Haven: Yale University Press.

Hall, Richard L., & C. Lawrence Evans. 1990. "The Power of Subcommittees." *Journal of Politics* 52:335–355.

Hall, Richard L., & Bernard Grofman. 1990. "The Committee Assignment Process and the Conditional Nature of Committee Bias." *American Political Science Review* 84:1149–1166.

Hardeman, D. B., & Donald C. Bacon. 1987. *Rayburn: A Biography.* Austin: Texas Monthly Press.

Hardin, John. 1994. "Congressional Activity on National Health Insurance Proposals: An Example of How Political Change Influences Legislative Organization." Paper delivered at the annual meeting of the Midwest Political Science Association, Chicago, April 14.

Hardin, Russell. 1982. *Collective Action.* Baltimore: Johns Hopkins University Press.

Harlow, Ralph V. 1917. *The History of Legislative Methods in the Period before 1825.* New Haven: Yale University Press.

Healey, Jon. 1995. "Panel Vote Sets Up Clash." *CQ Weekly Report* 53 (May 20): 1412.

Heller, Robert. 1945. *Strengthening the Congress.* Washington, DC: National Planning Association.

Henning, Charles. 1989. *The Wit and Wisdom of Politics.* Golden, CO: Fulcrum.

Hertzke, Allen D., & Ronald M. Peters, Jr. 1992. "Introduction: Interpreting the Atomistic Congress." In Allen D. Hertzke & Ronald M. Peters, Jr., eds., *The Atomistic Congress: An Interpretation of Congressional Change.* Armonk, NY: M. E. Sharpe.

Hinckley, Barbara. 1975. "Policy Content, Committee Membership, and Behavior." *American Journal of Political Science* 19:543–558.

———. 1988. *Stability and Change in Congress.* 4th edition. New York: Harper & Row.

Hinds, Asher C. 1907. *Hind's Precedents of the House of Representatives.* Volumes 1–3. Washington, DC: Government Printing Office.

———. 1908. Volume 4.

Holmes, Oliver Wendell. 1963 [1881]. *The Common Law.* Cambridge, MA: Harvard University Press.

Hook, Janet. 1987. "Parliamentarians: Procedure and Pyrotechnics." *CQ Weekly Report* (July 14): 1951–1987.

———. 1991. "Former Rep. Richard Bolling Dies of Heart Attack." *CQ Weekly Report* (April 27): 1039.

———. 1992. "Extensive Reform Proposals Cook on the Front Burner." *CQ Weekly Report* (June 6): 1579–1585.

———. 1995. "A New House Historian with a New Twist." *CQ Weekly Report* (January 7): 21.

Hook, Janet, & David S. Cloud. 1994. "A Republican-Designed House Won't Please All Occupants." *CQ Weekly Report* 52 (December 3): 3430–3435.

Hosansky, David. 1994. "GOP Bid to Reform Committees Faces Intraparty Skepticism." *CQ Weekly Report* (November 19): 3324–3325.

"House Commerce Committee Alone in Telecommunications Jurisdiction." 1994. *Common Carrier Week* 11, no. 49 (December 12).

House Committee on Energy and Commerce. 1975. *180 Years of Service: A Brief History of the Committee on Interstate and Foreign Commerce.* Washington, DC: Government Printing Office.

———. 1983a. *Hosting the 1986 Soccer World Cup.* 98th Congress, 1st session. Washington, DC: Government Printing Office.

———. 1983b. *Subject and Policy Issues for Energy and Commerce Committee Review during the 98th Congress.* 98th Congress, 1st session (September). Washington, DC: Government Printing Office.

———. 1985. *Subject and Policy Issues for Energy and Commerce Committee Review during the 99th Congress.* 99th Congress, 1st session (May). Washington, DC: Government Printing Office.

———. 1988. *Legislative Journal of the Committee of Commerce and Manufacturers: December 14, 1795 to March 3, 1797.* Washington, DC: Government Printing Office.

House Committee on Interstate and Foreign Commerce. 1948. *Travel in the United States.* 80th Congress, 2d session. Washington, DC: Government Printing Office.

———. 1954. *Extending Exemption from Regulation to Agricultural Products Shipped by Air.* 83d Congress, 2d session. Washington, DC: Government Printing Office.

———. 1956a. *Traffic Safety.* 84th Congress, 2d session. Washington, DC: Government Printing Office.

———. 1956b. *Transportation of Migrant Farm Workers.* 84th Congress, 2d session. Washington, DC: Government Printing Office.

———. 1957a. *Food Additives.* 85th Congress, 1st session. Washington, DC: Government Printing Office.

———. 1957b. *Medical School Inquiry.* 85th Congress, 1st session. Washington, DC: Government Printing Office.

———. 1958a. *Automobile Labeling.* 85th Congress, 2d session. Washington, DC: Government Printing Office.

———. 1958b. *Unburned Hydrocarbons.* 85th Congress, 2d session. Washington, DC: Government Printing Office.

———. 1962. *Humane Treatment of Animals Used in Research.* 87th Congress, 2d session. Washington, DC: Government Printing Office.

———. 1965a. *Cigarette Labeling and Advertising.* 89th Congress, 1st session. Washington, DC: Government Printing Office.

———. 1965b. *Clean Air Act Amendments.* 89th Congress, 1st session. Washington, DC: Government Printing Office.

———. 1965c. *Drug Abuse Control Amendments of 1965.* 89th Congress, 1st session. Washington, DC: Government Printing Office.

———. 1969a. *National Commission on Product Safety Extension and Child Protection Act.* 91st Congress, 1st session. Washington, DC: Government Printing Office.

———. 1969b. *Review of Electronic Products Radiation Hazards.* 91st Congress, 1st session. Washington, DC: Government Printing Office.

———. 1971. *Consumer Product Safety Act.* 92d Congress, 1st session. Washington, DC: Government Printing Office.

———. 1973. *Energy Emergency Act.* 93d Congress, 1st session. Washington, DC: Government Printing Office.

———. 1974a. *Biomedical Research Ethics and the Protection of Human Research Subjects.* 93d Congress, 2d session. Washington, DC: Government Printing Office.

———. 1974b. *Controlled Substances Act Extension.* 93d Congress, 2d session. Washington, DC: Government Printing Office.

———. 1975. *Clean Air Act Amendments.* 94th Congress, 1st session. Washington, DC: Government Printing Office.

———. 1976. *Middle- and Long-Term Energy Policies and Alternatives.* 94th Congress, 2d session. Washington, DC: Government Printing Office.

———. 1977. *Impact of H.R. 6804 on H.R. 6831.* 95th Congress, 1st session. Washington, DC: Government Printing Office.

———. 1980. *National Automobile Research Act.* 96th Congress, 2d session. Washington, DC: Government Printing Office.

House Committee on Public Works and Transportation. 1990. *Development of High-Speed Transportation Corridors, Including Those Which May Utilize Magnetic Levitation Technology.* 101st Congress, 2d session (May 3). Washington, DC: Government Printing Office.

———. 1991. *High-Speed Rail Transportation.* 102d Congress, 1st session (October 16). Washington, DC: Government Printing Office.

House Committee on Rules. 1983. *A History of the Committee on Rules: 1st to 97th Congress, 1789–1981.* 97th Congress, 2d session. Washington, DC: Government Printing Office.

House Committee on Science, Space, and Technology. 1987. *High Speed Railroad Technology.* 100th Congress, 1st session (April 3). Washington, DC: Government Printing Office.

———. 1990. *H.R. 4549—the Magnetic Levitation Transportation and Competitiveness Act of 1990.* 101st Congress, 2d session. Washington, DC: Government Printing Office.

House Committee on Ways and Means. 1990. *Enemy Within: Crack-Cocaine and America's Families.* 101st Congress, 2d session (June 12). Washington, DC: Government Printing Office.

House Select Committee on Committees. 1973. *Committee Structure and Procedures of the House of Representatives: Working Draft of Report of the Select Committee on Committees.* 93d Congress, 1st session (December 7). Washington, DC: Government Printing Office.

———. 1974a. *Final Report, Committee Reform Amendments of 1974,* H. Rept. 93-916. 93d Congress, 2d session (March 21). Washington, DC: Government Printing Office.

———. 1974b. *Monographs on the Committees of the House of Representatives.* 93d Congress, 2d session (December 13). Washington, DC: Government Printing Office.

Hunter, Louis C. 1949. *Steamboats on the Western Rivers: An Economic and Technological History.* Cambridge, MA: Harvard University Press.

Idelson, Holly. 1992a. "House Gives Energy Bill Big Win; Lengthy Conference Expected." *CQ Weekly Report* (May 30): 1530–1532.

———. 1992b. "Miller vs. Dingell." *CQ Weekly Report* (May 23): 1438.

Jackson, John E., & David C. King. 1989. "Public Goods, Private Interests, and Representation." *American Political Science Review* 83:1143–1164.

"Japanese Make Significant Gains in Maglev Technology." 1989. *Research & Development* 31 (February): 64–66.

Jaroslovsky, Rich. 1990. "Turf Wars over Child Care Portend a Possible Legislative Mess." *Wall Street Journal* (February 9): A1.

Johnson, Haynes. 1991. "Washington Risks Irrelevance." *Washington Post* (November 29): A2.

Joint Committee on the Organization of Congress. 1945. *Hearings: Organization of Congress.* Washington, DC: Government Printing Office.

———. 1993. *Committee Structure.* 103d Congress, 1st session. Washington, DC: Government Printing Office.

Jones, Bryan D., Frank R. Baumgartner, & Jeffery C. Talbert. 1992. "Congressional Committees and Jurisdictional Dynamics." Paper delivered at the annual meeting of the Midwest Political Science Association, Chicago.

———. 1993. "The Destruction of Issue Monopolies in Congress." *American Political Science Review* 87:657–671.

Jones, Charles O. 1968. "Joseph G. Cannon and Howard W. Smith: An Essay on the Limits of Leadership in the House of Representatives." *Journal of Politics* 30:617–646.

Jones, Charles O., & Randall Strahan. 1985. "Crisis Response in Washington: The Case of Oil Shocks." *Legislative Studies Quarterly* 10:151–179.

Kahn, Gabriel. 1995. "Dreier, Frosh Take on Committee Reform." *Roll Call* (June 12).

Kaji, Joel T., & Michael Mintrom. 1995. "Selling Ideas: A Strategic Analysis of Policy Entrepreneurship." Department of Political Science, State University of New York, Stony Book. Typescript.

Kamen, Al. 1993. "Smoothing Bumps in Highway Jurisdiction." *Washington Post* (July 2): A17.

Kariel, Henry. 1961. *The Decline of American Pluralism.* Stanford: Stanford University Press.

Keefe, William, & Morris Ogul. 1981. *Congress and the Legislative Process.* 5th edition. Englewood Cliffs, NJ: Prentice-Hall.

Keller, Morton. 1977. *Affairs of State: Public Life in Late Nineteenth Century America.* Cambridge, MA: Harvard University Press.

Kiewiet, D. Roderick, & Mathew D. McCubbins. 1991. *The Logic of Delegation: Congressional Parties and the Appropriations Process.* Chicago: University of Chicago Press.

King, Christopher D. 1989. "Florida Rail Unit in Preliminary OK for Maglev." *Metalworking News* (July 3): 5–6.

King, David C. 1989. "Representation through Participation in Committee Hearings." Paper delivered at the annual meeting of the Midwest Political Science Association, Chicago.

———. 1990. "Congressional Committee Jurisdictions and Institutional Change: The 1946 Legislative Reorganization Act." Paper delivered at the annual meeting of the American Political Science Association, San Francisco, August 30.

———. 1991. "Congressional Committee Jurisdictions and the Consequences of Reform." Paper delivered at the annual meeting of the Midwest Political Science Association, Chicago, April 19.

———. 1992. "Committee Jurisdictions and Institution Change in the U.S. House of Representatives." Ph.D. dissertation, University of Michigan, Ann Arbor.

———. 1994. "The Nature of Congressional Committee Jurisdictions." *American Political Science Review* 88:48–62.

King, David C., Richard L. Zeckhauser, & Sven E. Feldmann. 1995. "Winning by a Little and Losing by a Lot on Congressional Roll Call Votes." Paper delivered at the annual meeting of the Midwest Political Science Association, Chicago.

Kingdon, John W. 1981. *Congressmen's Voting Decisions.* 2d edition. New York: Harper & Row.

———. 1984. *Agendas, Alternatives, and Public Policies.* Boston: Little, Brown & Company.

Kirschten, Dick. 1990. "Hyping the Big Quake." *National Journal* 22, no. 1 (January 6): 11–18.

Kirzner, Israel M. 1973. *Competition and Entrepreneurship.* Chicago: University of Chicago Press.

Koprowski, Gene. 1990. "Pittsburgh Examines Maglev Transportation." *Metalworking News* (March 4): 4–5.

Koszczuk, Jackie. 1996. "Regained Footing." *Players, Politics and Turf of the 104th Congress* (supplement to no. 12 *Congressional Weekly Report* [March 23]): 9.

Krehbiel, Keith. 1988. "Spatial Models of Legislative Choice." *Legislative Studies Quarterly* 13:259–319.

———. 1990. "Are Congressional Committees Composed of Preference Outliers?" *American Political Science Review* 84:149–163.

———. 1991. *Information and Legislative Organization.* Ann Arbor: University of Michigan Press.

Krehbiel, Keith, & Douglas Rivers. 1988. "The Analysis of Committee Power: An Application to Senate Voting on the Minimum Wage." *American Journal of Political Science* 32:1151–1174.

Kriz, Margaret E. 1992. "Poison Gamesmanship." *National Journal* (April 18): 930–933.

Kuntz, Phil. 1991. "Interior To Feel Firmer Touch after Udall's Gentle Hand." *CQ Weekly Report* (April 27): 1051–1053.

La Follette, Robert M. 1943. "A Senator Looks at Congress." *Atlantic Monthly* 174 (July): 91–96.

Levi, Edward H. 1949. *An Introduction to Legal Reasoning.* Chicago: University of Chicago Press.

Lewin, David I. 1992. "Setting an Agenda for Competitiveness." *ASAP* 114, no. 7: 85.

Lindblom, Charles. 1964. "Some Limitations on Rationality: A Comment." In Carl J. Friedrich, ed., *Rational Decision.* New York: Atherton Press.

Llewellyn, Karl N. 1960. *The Bramble Bush.* New York: Oceana.

Longley, Lawrence D., & Walter J. Oleszek. 1989. *Bicameral Politics: Conference Committees in Congress.* New Haven: Yale University Press.

Loomis, Burdette. 1988. *The New American Politician: Ambition, Entrepreneurship, and the Changing Face of Political Life.* New York: Basic Books.

Lowi, Theodore. 1969. *The End of Liberalism.* New York: W. W. Norton.

Maass, Arthur. 1983. *Congress and the Common Good.* New York: Basic Books.

McCaleb, Thomas S., & Richard E. Wagner, 1985. "The Experimental Search for Free Riders: Some Reflections and Observations." *Public Choice* 47: 479–490.

McConachie, Lauros G. 1898. *Congressional Committees.* New York: Thomas Y. Crowell Co.

McConnell, Grant. 1966. *Private Power and the American Democracy.* New York: Alfred A. Knopf.

McGough, Robert. 1991. "The Texas Cannonball." *Financial World* 160 (August 6): 20–22.

Madison, Christopher. 1984. "Strategic Value of Introducing Trade Bill May Be More Important than Passage." *National Journal* (January 14): 63–65.

———. 1990. "Dingell's Heat Wave." *National Journal* (July 7): 1655–1659.

"Major House Committee Reform Rejected." 1975. *Congressional Quarterly Almanac.* Volume 30. Washington, DC: Congressional Quarterly Press.

Maltzman, Forrest. 1992. "Committee-Chamber-Party Relations in the Post-Reform House." Paper delivered at the annual meeting of the Midwest Political Science Association, Chicago.

Manley, John F. 1970. *The Politics of Finance: The House Committee on Ways and Means.* Boston: Little Brown.

A Manual of Parliamentary Practice. 1856. New York: Clark, Austin & Smith.

March, James G., & Johan P. Olsen. 1989. *Rediscovering Institutions: The Organizational Basis of Politics.* New York: Free Press.

Maraniss, David. 1983. "Powerful Energy Panel Turns on Big John's Axis." *Washington Post* (May 15): A1.

"Markey Looks to Maintain Agenda in New Role." *Television Digest* 23, no. 49 (December 5): 3.

Marwell, Gerald, & Ruth E. Ames. 1979. "Experiments on the Provision of Public Goods: Resources, Interest, Group Size, and the Free Rider Problem." *American Journal of Sociology* 84:1135–1160.

Marwill, Philip. 1990. "Environment Turf." *CQ Weekly Report* (January 20): 151.

Masters, Nicholas A. 1965. "Committee Assignments in the House of Representatives." In Joseph S. Clark, ed., *Congressional Reform: Problems and Prospects.* New York: Thomas Y. Crowell Co.

Matsunaga, Spark M., & Ping Chen. 1976. *Rulemakers of the House.* Urbana: University of Illinois Press.

Matthews, Donald R. 1981. "American Political Science and Congressional Reform." *Social Science History* 5:91–120.

Mayhew, David R. 1974. *Congress: The Electoral Connection.* New Haven: Yale University Press.

Miller, Luther S. 1992. "1992 Outlook: Transit Hits the Bullseye." *Railway Age* 193 (January): 56, 59.

Mills, Mike. 1992. "Two Powerful Chairmen Duel to Shape the Bell's Future." *CQ Weekly Report* (June 27): 1866–1868.

Mintz, John. 1992. "Victory in Battle with the Bells: Brooks Wins Control of Turf for Regional Phone Companies." *Washington Post* (August 14): B1.

Morrow, William L. 1969. *Congressional Committees.* New York: Charles Scribner's Sons.

Moynihan, Daniel Patrick. 1989. "How to Lose: The Story of Maglev." *Scientific American* (November): 130.

Munger, Michael. 1988. "Allocation of Desirable Committee Assignments:

Extended Queues versus Committee Expansion." *American Journal of Political Science* 32:317–344.

Nadel, Mark V. 1971. *The Politics of Consumer Protection*. New York: Bobbs-Merrill.

Nakayama, Atasushi. 1995. "JAL First to Market with Maglev Train." *Nikkei Weekly* (August 7): 9.

Neustadt, Richard. 1965. "Politicians and Bureaucrats." In David B. Truman, ed., *The Congress and America's Future*. Englewood Cliffs, NJ: Prentice-Hall.

1990 Congressional Staff Directory. 1990. Mount Vernon, VA: Staff Directories, Ltd.

"Nixon Signs Comprehensive Bill to Regulate Pesticides." 1973. *Congressional Quarterly Almanac*. Volume 27. 1972. Washington, DC: Congressional Quarterly Press.

Ogul, Morris S. 1976. *Congress Oversees the Bureaucracy*. Pittsburgh: University of Pittsburgh Press.

Oleszek, Walter J. 1996. *Congressional Procedures and the Policy Process*. 4th edition. Washington, DC: Congressional Quarterly Press.

Oleszek, Walter J., Roger Davidson, & Thomas Kephart. 1986. "The Incidence and Impact of Multiple Referrals in the House of Representatives." Congressional Research Service, Library of Congress (July), 43, 46.

Olson, Mancur. 1965. *The Logic of Collective Action*. Cambridge, MA: Harvard University Press.

Ornstein, Norman J., ed. 1975. *Congress in Change: Evolution and Reform*. New York: Praeger.

Ornstein, Norman J., Thomas E. Mann, & Michael J. Malbin. 1992. *Vital Statistics on Congress: 1991–1992*. Washington, DC: Congressional Quarterly Press.

Peabody, Robert L., Susan Webb Hammond, Jean Torcom, Lynne Brown, Carolyn Thompson, & Robin Kolodny. 1990. "Interviewing Political Elites." *PS: Political Science & Politics* 23:451–455.

Perkins, John A. 1944. "Congressional Self-Improvement." *American Political Science Review* 38:499–511.

Peters, Ronald M., Jr. 1990. *The American Speakership: The Office in Historical Perspective*. Baltimore: Johns Hopkins University Press.

Polsby, Nelson W. 1968. "The Institutionalization of the U.S. House of Representatives." *American Political Science Review* 62 (March): 144–168.

———. 1971. *Congress and the Presidency*. 2d edition. Englewood Cliffs, NJ.

Polsby, Nelson W., Miriam Gallaher, & Barry S. Rundquist. 1969. "The Growth of the Seniority System in the U.S. House of Representatives." *American Political Science Review* 63:787–807.

Pope, Gregory T. 1988. "Supertrain." *Popular Mechanics* (June 1988): 78–89, 114.

Povich, Elaine S. 1994. "The Game's Afoot: Keep your Eye on the Health Bill." *Chicago Tribune* (February 6): C1.

Pressman, Steven. 1986a. "Beyond the Hoopla, Looking for Options." *CQ Weekly Report* 44 (November 22): 2936–2940.

———. 1986b. "Ex-Im Bank Measure Moves as Deadline Nears." *CQ Weekly Report* 44 (September 27): 2323.

———. 1986c. "Over Reagan's Protest, House Votes Trade Bill." *CQ Weekly Report* 44 (May 24): 1154–1158.

Price, David E. 1972. *Who Makes the Laws? Creativity and Power in Senate Committees.* Cambridge, MA: Schenkman Publishing Company.

———. 1979. *Policymaking in Congressional Committees: The Impact of "Environmental" Factors.* Tucson: Institute of Government Research, University of Arizona.

Pytte, Alyson. 1989. " House OKs Bomb-Detector Bill with Funding Compromise." *CQ Weekly Report* 47 (September 23): 2454–2455.

Ragavan, Chitra. 1994. "House Energy and Commerce Committee to Lose Influence." *All Things Considered.* National Public Radio, Washington, DC. Broadcast December 28.

Rauch, Jonathan. 1994. *Demosclerosis: The Silent Killer of American Government.* New York: Random House.

Reed, Thomas B. 1889. "Obstruction in the National House." *North American Review* 149:421–428.

Reich, Kenneth, & Jeffrey A. Perlman. 1991. "Maglev Line Hopes Vanishing in the Air." *Los Angeles Times* (May 5): A3.

Reid, T. R. 1980. *Congressional Odyssey: The Saga of a Senate Bill.* New York: W. H. Freeman & Co.

Ricci, David. 1984. *The Tragedy of Political Science.* New Haven: Yale University Press.

Rich, Spencer. 1993. "Senate Chairmen in Tug of War over Health Plan: Two Panels Battle for Jurisdiction—and Power." *The Washington Post* (November 24): A1.

Rieselbach, Leroy N. 1986. *Congressional Reform.* Washington, DC: Congressional Quarterly Press.

———. 1994. *Congressional Reform: The Changing Modern Congress.* Washington, DC: Congressional Quarterly Press.

Riker, William. 1980. "Implications from the Disequilibrium of Majority Rule for the Study of Institutions." *American Political Science Review.* 73:85–102.

———. 1986. *The Art of Political Manipulation.* New Haven: Yale University Press.

Ripley, Randall. 1978. *Congress: Process and Policy.* 2d edition. New York: W. W. Norton.

Ripley, Randall B. 1969. "Power in the Post–World War II Senate." *Journal of Politics* 31:465–492.

Robinson, George L. 1954. "The Development of the Senate Committee System." Ph.D. dissertation, New York University.

Robinson, William A. 1930. *Thomas B. Reed, Parliamentarian.* New York: Dodd, Mead.

Rohde, David W. 1991. *Parties and Leaders in the Postreform Congress.* Chicago: University of Chicago Press.

Roman, Nancy. 1994. "Dingell Panel Cuts Would Anger Heir to Chairmanship." *Washington Times* (November 16): A3.

Rovner, Julie. 1988. "Pepper Bill Pits Politics against Process." *CQ Weekly Report* 46 (June 4): 1491–1493.

———. 1990. "Rights Bill Linkage, Turf Spats Slow ADA Progress in House." *CQ Weekly Report* 48 (February 24): 600.

Roy, Roger. 1995. "Companies Vie to Get on Board Train Project." *Orlando Sentinel Tribune* (August 14): 12.

Rubin, Alissa. 1993. "Jurisdictional Power Struggle Slows Overhaul in Senate." *CQ Weekly Report* (November 27): 3274.

Rules and Orders of the House of Representatives. 1867. Washington, DC: Government Printing Office.

Samuelson, Paul A. 1955. "Diagrammatic Exposition of a Theory of Public Expenditure." *Review of Economics and Statistics* 37:350–356.

Schamel, Charles E., & Donnald K. Anderson. 1989. *Guide to the Records of the United States House of Representatives at the National Archives, 1789–1989.* Washington, DC: Government Printing Office.

Schattschneider, E. E. 1960. *The Semi-Sovereign People.* New York: Hold, Rinehart & Winston.

Schickler, Eric, & Andrew Rich. 1995. "Controlling the Floor: Parties as Procedural Coalitions in the House." Paper delivered at the annual meeting of the American Political Science Association, Chicago, August 31.

Schneider, Judy. 1995. "Committee Jurisdictions." In Donald C. Bacon et al., eds., *The Encyclopedia of the United States Congress.* New York: Simon & Schuster.

Schneider, Mark, & Paul Teske. 1992. "Toward a Theory of the Political Entrepreneur: Evidence from Local Government." *American Political Science Review* 86 (September 1992): 737–747.

Schneider, Mark, Paul Teske, & Michael Mintrom. 1995a. *Political Entrepreneurs: Agents for Change in American Government.* Princeton: Princeton University Press.

———. 1995b. *Public Entrepreneurs: Agents for Change in American Government.* Princeton: Princeton University Press.

Schumpeter, Joseph. 1942. *Capitalism, Socialism, and Democracy.* New York: Harper & Row.

Sciolino, Elaine. 1992. "Eccentric Still But Obscure No More, Texan Leads Inquiry on Iraq Loans." *New York Times* (July 3): A10.

Senate Committee on Environment and Public Works. 1989. *Benefits of Magnetically Levitated High-Speed Transportation for the United States.* Report prepared by the Maglev Technology Advisory Committee. 101st Congress, 1st session (August). Washington, DC: Government Printing Office.

Senate Committee on Rules. 1945. *Establishing a Joint Committee on the Organization of the Congress: Senate Report no. 42.* 79th Congress, 1st session.

Shakdher, S. L. 1974. *System of Parliamentary Committees.* New Delhi, India: Lok Sabha Secretariat.

Shepsle, Kenneth A. 1978. *The Giant Jigsaw Puzzle.* Chicago: University of Chicago Press.

———. 1986. "Institutional Equilibrium and Equilibrium Institutions." In Herbert F. Weisberg, ed., *Political Science: The Science of Politics.* New York: Agathon Press.

———. 1988. "Representation and Governance: The Great Legislative Trade-Off." *Political Science Quarterly* 103 (Fall): 461–481.

Shepsle, Kenneth A., & Barry R. Weingast. 1987. "The Institutional Foundations of Committee Power." *American Political Science Review* 81:85–104.

———. 1994. "Positive Theories of Congressional Institutions." *Legislative Studies Quarterly* 19:149–179.

Shifrin, Carole. 1979. "Kennedy Gains Support in Fight over Truck Bill." *Washington Post* (January 26): D3.

Shillinger, Kurt. 1995. "Efficiency-Minded Reformers Hit Snags." *Christian Science Monitor* (February 14): 1.

Shipan, Charles R. 1992. "Individual Incentives and Institutional Imperatives: Committee Jurisdiction and Long-Term Health Care." *American Journal of Political Science* 36:877–895.

Siff, Ted, & Alan Weil. 1975. *Ruling Congress: A Study of How the House and Senate Rules Govern the Legislative Process.* New York: Grossman.

Simon, Donald, 1977. "Senator Kennedy and the Civil Aeronautics Board." Case no. C14-77-157. John F. Kennedy School of Government, Harvard University.

Simon, Harvey. 1988. "Buying the Baretta: The Army's Dilemma." Case no. 848. John F. Kennedy School of Government, Harvard University.

Sinclair, Barbara. 1983. *Majority Leadership in the U.S. House.* Baltimore: Johns Hopkins University Press.

———. 1995. *Legislators, Leaders, and Lawmaking: The U.S. House of Representatives in the Postreform Era.* Baltimore: Johns Hopkins University Press.

Skaggs, Jimmy M. 1994. *The Great Guano Rush.* New York: St. Martins.

"Slight Change Expected in House Jurisdiction over Energy Matters." 1994. *Inside F.E.R.C.* (December 12): 1.

Smith, Hedrick. 1989. *The Power Game: How Washington Works.* New York: Ballantine Books.

Smith, Steven S. 1989a. *Call to Order: Floor Politics in the House and Senate.* Washington, DC: Brookings Institution.

———. 1989b. "Taking It to the Floor." In Lawrence C. Dodd & Bruce I. Oppenheimer, eds., *Congress Reconsidered.* 4th edition. Washington: Congressional Quarterly Press.

Smith, Steven S., & Christopher J. Deering. 1990. *Committees in Congress.* 2d edition. Washington, DC: Congressional Quarterly Press.

Stanfield, Rochelle L. 1988. "Plotting Every Move." *National Journal* (March 26): 792–797.

Starobin, Paul. 1988. "Parliamentarian 'Screwed Up': Jurisdictional Fight Stalls Drunken-Driving Bill." *CQ Weekly Report* (September 24): 2668.

Stewart, Charles, III. 1989. *Budget Reform Politics: The Design of the Appropriations Process in the House of Representatives, 1865–1921.* New York: Cambridge University Press.

———. 1992. "The Growth of the Committee System, from Randall to Gillett." In Allen D. Hertzke & Ronald M. Peters, Jr., eds., *The Atomistic Congress: An Interpretation of Congressional Change.* Armonk, NY: M. E. Sharpe.

Stratmann, Thomas. 1992. "The Effects of Logrolling on Congressional Voting." *American Economic Review* 82:116 2–1176.

Sukow, Randall M. 1992. "Rereg May Slim Down for Final House Bout." *Broadcasting* 122, no. 21 (May 18): 36.

Sullivan, Terry O. 1984. *Procedural Structure.* New York: Praeger Publishers.

Swinbanks, David. 1991. "Maglev Burns Out in Japan." *Nature* (October 17): 592.

Talbert, Jeffery C., Bryan D. Jones, & Frank R. Baumgartner. 1995. "Non-Legislative Hearings and Policy Change in Congress." *American Journal of Political Science* 39 (May): 383–406.

Teske, Paul, & Mark Schneider. 1992. "A Theory of the Bureaucratic Entrepreneur: The Case of City Managers." Paper delivered at the annual meeting of the Midwest Political Science Association, Chicago.

Riefer, Charles. 1989. *Congressional Practice and Procedure: A Reference, Research, and Legislative Guide.* New York: Greenwood Press.

Unekis, Joseph K., & Leroy N. Rieselbach. 1984. *Congressional Committee Politics: Continuity and Change.* New York: Praeger.

U.S. House of Representatives. 1964. *Clarence Andrew Cannon, Late a Representative from Missouri: Memorial Addresses Delivered in Congress.* 88th Congress, 2d session. Washington, DC: Government Printing Office.

———. 1867. *Rules and Orders of the House of Representatives.* Washington, DC: Government Printing Office.

———. 1975. *180 Years of Service: A Brief History of the Committee on Interstate and Foreign Commerce.* Washington, DC: Government Printing Office.

U.S. Public Health Service Office of Administrative Management. 1976. *History, Mission, and Organization of the Public Health Service.* Washington, DC: Government Printing Office.

Uslaner, Eric M. 1989. *Shale Barrel Politics: Energy and Legislative Leadership.* Stanford: Stanford University Press.

Van, Jon. 1992. "Why Maglev Won't Fly." *San Francisco Examiner* (August 9): E-14.

Victor, Kirk. 1995. "Mr. Smooth." *National Journal* (July 8): 1758–1762.

Walker, Jack L. 1977. "Setting the Agenda in the US Senate: A Theory of Problem Selection." *British Journal of Political Science* 7 (October): 423–445.

———. 1981. "The Diffusion of Knowledge, Policy, Communities, and Agenda Setting: The Relationship of Knowledge and Power." In John Tropman, Milan Dluhy, & Roger Lind, eds., *New Strategic Perspectives on Social Policy.* New York: Pergamon Press.

———. 1991. *Mobilizing Interest Groups in America: Patrons, Professions, and Social Movements.* Ann Arbor: University of Michigan Press.

"Waste Hauling Measures." 1990. In *1989 Congressional Quarterly Almanac.* Volume 45. Washington, DC: Congressional Quarterly Press.

Weimer, David L., & Aidan R. Vining. 1992. *Policy Analysis: Concepts and Practice.* 2d edition. Englewood Cliffs, NJ: Prentice Hall.

Weingast, Barry R. 1979. "A Rational Choice Perspective on Congressional Norms." *American Journal of Political Science* 23: 245–262.

Weingast, Barry R. 1989. "Floor Behavior in the U.S. Congress: Committee Power under the Open Rule." *American Political Science Review* 83:795–815.

———. 1992. "Fighting Fire with Fire: Amending Activity and Institutional Change in the Postreform Congress." In Roger H. Davidson, ed., *The Postreform Congress.* New York: St. Martin's Press.

Weingast, Barry R., & William Marshall. 1988. "The Industrial Organization of Congress." *Journal of Political Economy* 96:132–163.

Weingast, Barry R., & Mark J. Moran. 1983. "Bureaucratic Discretion or Congressional Control? Regulatory Policymaking by the Federal Trade Commission." *Journal of Political Economy* 91:765–800.

Weissert, Carol S. 1991. "Policy Entrepreneurs, Policy Opportunities and Legislative Effectiveness." *American Politics Quarterly* 19: 262–274.

Westefield, Louis P. 1974. "Majority Party Leadership and the Committee System in the House of Representatives." *American Political Science Review* 68:1593–1604.

Wilson, Woodrow. 1981 [1885]. *Congressional Government: A Study in American Politics.* Baltimore: Johns Hopkins University Press.

Work, Clement. 1990. "The Flying Train Takes Off: Maglev is Airborne, But American Business Is Not at the Controls." *U.S. News & World Report* (July 23): 52–53.

Wright, Gerald C., Leroy N. Rieselbach, & Lawrence C. Dodd, eds. 1986. *Congress and Policy Change.* New York: Agathon Press.

Young, Garry. 1994a. "Committee Gatekeeping and Proposal Power under Single and Multiple Referral." University of Missouri. Typescript.

———. 1994b. "Committee and Party Behavior under Single and Multiple Referral." Paper delivered at the annual meeting of the Midwest Political Science Association, Chicago.

———. 1994c. "Coordination and Legislative Organization: The Case of Multiple Referral." University of Missouri. Typescript.

INDEX

ABC News, 43
Addabbo, Joseph, 142
Adler, Madeline Wing, 165
Aid for Families with Dependent
    Children, 71, 98
Air Pollution Control Act, 53
Airport Trust Fund, 98
air transportation, 48
Albert, Carl, 99, 171, 172
Alexander, DeAlva S., 170
Ambrose, James, 142
American Political Science Association,
    3, 59, 164
Americans with Disabilities Act, 13, 101
America's Living Standards Act, 138
Ames, Ruth E., 167
Anderson, Donna K., 157, 160
Anderson, Glenn, 137
Anderson, P. W., 161
appropriations committees, 117
    exclusion from turf wars, 13–14
Archer, Bill, 73
Army Corps of Engineers, 127–128, 176
Arrow, Kenneth, 161
Arthur, W. Brian 161
Association of Legislative Clerks and
    Secretaries, 82
Axelrod, Robert, 167

Babcock, Charles R., 180
Bacon, Donald C., 168
Baker, Ross K., 160
Barclay, John M., 170
Baron, David, P., 150, 153
Barone, Michael, 158

Barry, John, 17, 146, 153, 155, 159, 180
Bates, Robert H., 167
Baumgartner, Frank, 2, 4, 109, 144,
    149–151, 159–161, 173, 180
Bayly, Thomas, 91
behavioralism, 3
Bianco, William, 167
Bibmer, Bruce, 151
Binder, Sarah A., 150
Birnbaum, Jeffrey H., 176
Bliley, Thomas, 43, 73–75, 77, 111
Boggs, Hale, 84
Bolling, Richard, 3, 100, 164, 169, 170
Bolling Committee, 3, 58, 63, 100
Bolling-Hansen reforms, 64, 100
Bonker, Don, 159
border cop, 2, 102, 113, 115
Boucher, Rick, 43
Breyer, Stephen, 17
Brown, Clarence, 167
Brown, George, 137–138, 140, 147
Brown, William Holmes, 21, 78, 80–81,
    84, 99, 109, 158
Budget and Impoundment Control Act
    of 1974, 117
Bullock, Charles, 155
Burdick, Edward, 82
Busbey, L. White, 171
Bush, George, 110
Byrd, Robert C., 164

Cannon, Clarence, 39, 62, 96, 97, 157,
    158
Cannon, (Speaker) Joseph, 58, 80, 87,
    95–96, 146, 171

Cannon's Procedure in the House of Representatives, 39, 47, 95, 157, 160
Cantril, Hadley H., 164
Carlisle, John G., 93
Carr, Robert, 126–127
Carter, James, 102
Cassidy, Robert, 176
Chitra Ragavan, 166
Chu, Paul, 125
Civil Rights Act of 1964, 16
Civil War, 92
Clapp, Charles, 155
Clark, Bennett C., 96
Clark, James B. (Champ), 88, 96
Clay, Henry, 89
Clean Air Act, 53, 139
Clerk at the Speaker's table, 8, 93–97
    see also parliamentarian
Cloud, David S., 152, 163, 166, 168
Clymer, Adam, 180
Coelho, Tony, 155
Cohen, Richard E., 179, 180
Collie, Melissa, 14, 101, 113, 152, 172
Committee of the Whole, 88
Committee on Congress, 59
committees
    ad hoc, 89
    as collective goods, 6, 20, 78–79
    institutional assets in, 27
    institutionalization of, 88–90
    and logrolling, 30
    and power, 18
    see also House of Representatives,
    Senate
common law jurisdiction, 7, 19, 33, 38, 41,
    51, 68
competitiveness, 119, 123–124, 138, 140
Congressional Information Service, 47,
    142
Congressional Research Service, 11, 108,
    118
Connolly, Paul, 166
Consumer Product Safety Act of 1971, 64
consumer protection, 17, 18, 48, 64, 123
Contract with America, 58, 71
Cooper, Joseph, 14, 101, 113, 152, 163,
    169, 172
Cordes, Coleen, 159, 179
Cowling, Maurice, 150
Cox, Gary, 3, 5, 149, 151, 153

Coyne, William, 130
Cranford, John, 151
Crisp, Charles F., 94
Crisp, Charles R., 94
Crotty, William, 150
C-SPAN, 1, 80, 98

Dahl, Robert, 150
David, Paul A., 162
Davidson, Roger, 3, 21, 73, 102–103, 149,
    154–155, 158, 164–165, 167, 170,
    172–175
Davis, Philip A., 152
Deering, Christopher, 47, 152, 160, 164,
    169
de la Garza, "Kika", 24
Department of Energy, 70, 127, 128, 137,
    176
Department of Housing and Urban
    Development, 110
Department of the Interior, 65
Department of Transportation, 117, 127,
    133, 176
Deschler, Lewis, 38, 80–84, 87, 94, 97,
    107, 120, 146, 158, 168–169, 173
*Deschler's Precedents of the U.S. House of
    Representatives,* 127, 160
Dingell, John, 12, 17, 34, 42–43, 54–55,
    68–70, 73, 77, 81, 110, 111, 113–114,
    117, 120, 146, 158–159, 165–166, 173
Dion, G. Douglas, 150, 155, 167, 170
distributive politics theory, 4, 5, 18, 29–31,
    75, 124
Dodd, Lawrence C., 154, 160, 164, 169
Doig, Jameson, 160
Dole, Robert, 153
Domenici, Pete, 17, 153
Dopfer, Kurt, 161
Downey, Thomas, 173
Dreier, David, 56–58, 70–71, 73–76, 166
Drug Enforcement Agency, 65

Eilperin, Juliet, 151, 168
Eisenberg, Melvin A., 158
Eisenhower, Dwight, 66, 101
Elster, Jon, 167
England, David E., 155
Environmental Control Act, 71
Eulau, Heinz, 140, 152, 179

Evans, Lawrence, 3, 70, 104, 149–151, 165–166, 172–173
Export-Import Bank, 13

fair trade, 141–142
Family Farm Act, 99
Federal Environmental Pesticide Control Act of 1972, 106
Federal Insecticide, Fungicide, and Rodenticide Act of 1947 (FIFRA), 106
Federal Trade Commission, 44, 117
Fenno, Richard, 12, 25, 151–152, 155
Ferejohn, John A., 150, 153, 156
Fess, Lehr, 97
Fields, Jack, 76
Finnegahn, David, 2
Fiorina, Morris, 31, 153, 156
Florio, James, 44, 110, 173
Foley, Thomas, 1, 11, 13, 84, 108, 117, 155
Follett, Mary Parker, 94, 170
food inspection, 75–76
Francis, Wayne, 22, 154
Freeman, Donald M., 150
Froke, Christopher J., 155
Froman, Lewis A., Jr., 149

Gais, Thomas L., 180
Gallaher, Miriam, 164
Galloway, George, 36, 59, 157, 163, 164, 170
Gamm, Gerald, 22, 150, 154, 169
Garner, John Nance, 83
General Agreement on Tariffs and Trade, 13
Gifis, Steven H., 151
Gillett, Frederick, 97
Gilligan, Thomas, 25, 151, 156
Gingrich, Newt, 1, 8, 12, 56, 58, 70–71, 73, 83, 104, 138, 141, 147
Glass-Steagall Act, 76
Goldston, David, 112
Gonzalez, Henry, 110
Goodwin, George, Jr., 150, 156
Gould, Stephen Jay, 51, 161
Greenstein, Fred I., 158
guano trade, 91–92

Hall, Richard, 26, 152, 155, 173, 177, 178
Halleck, Charles, 85, 96

Hamilton, Alexander, 88, 163
Hamilton, Lee, 24, 56–57
Hansen, Julia Butler, 63
Hansen Committee, 63, 65
Hardeman, D. B., 168
Hardin, Russell, 167
Hargrove, Edwin, 160
Harlow, Ralph V., 169
Harris, Orren, 43, 55, 153
Hatfield, Mark, 153
Hayes, James, 129–130
Healey, Jon, 152
Henderson, David, 95
Henning, Charles, 164
Highway Trust Fund, 67, 98
Hinckley, Barbara, 155
Hinds, Asher, 62, 95, 158–159, 162, 164, 169
Hinds Precedents of the U.S. House of Representatives, 95–96, 158
Holmes, Oliver Wendell, 33, 120, 156
Hook, Janet, 151, 163, 166, 168
House of Representatives, U.S., committees
Administration, 61
Agriculture, 16, 17, 22, 24, 30, 35ff., 39, 41, 71, 73, 75–76, 99, 106, 113, 115, 123–124, 142, 174
Appropriations, 26
Armed Services, 110, 128, 133–134, 142, 174, 176
Banking, 12, 17, 22, 62–63, 66, 74, 76, 99, 101, 110, 111, 115, 123–124, 126–127, 133–134, 142, 174, 176
Budget, 117, 174
Commerce, 2, 7, 9, 12, 16–17, 19, 22, 24, 34–35, 39, 41, 42–55, 57, 63, 66, 68–70, 73–77, 99, 101, 103, 106, 108, 110–117, 120–122, 126–128, 132–134, 142, 145, 155, 157, 158, 159, 162–165, 173–176
District of Columbia, 22, 134, 174
Education, 18, 35–36, 54, 65, 71, 155, 174
Finance, 11
Foreign Affairs, 24, 63, 91, 92, 115
Government Operations, 174
Government Reform and Oversight, 26
Health, 17

House of Representatives (*continued*)
Interior, 26, 65, 116, 119, 133–134,
175–176
International Relations, 33, 36, 103
Judiciary, 16, 17, 22, 35, 65, 76, 99, 108,
110, 116, 117, 157
Labor, 11
Merchant Marines and Fisheries, 26,
40, 41, 57, 71, 99, 109, 157, 162, 175
Natural Resources, 44, 71, 74, 76, 140,
160, 166
Oversight, 22, 112
Post Office and Civil Service, 26, 71,
174
Public Works and Transportation, 17,
39, 48, 63, 66–67, 74–75, 99, 117,
121–122, 126–127, 132–134, 137,
165, 169, 174–176
Rules, 13, 21, 70, 84, 87, 95, 98, 100,
134, 144–147, 174
Science, 17, 22, 24, 43, 53, 65, 74–75,
111, 116, 119, 124, 126–127,
133–134, 137, 161, 175–176
Small Business, 22, 71, 119, 175
Standards of Official Conduct, 22, 71,
127, 174
Veterans Affairs, 22, 71, 174
Ways and Means, 17, 19, 22, 26, 36,
41–42, 51, 63–64, 70–71, 73,
91–92, 98–99, 104, 109–110, 114,
127, 133–134, 141–142, 155, 163,
173–176
House Rules Manual, 19, 29, 49, 64
Houston, George, 91, 170
Hunter, Louis, 162

Idelson, Holly, 152, 160
Infant Mortality Awareness Day, 101
information theory, 4, 6, 18, 31–32, 139,
144
institutionalism, 3
insurance regulation, 12, 17
Intermodal Surface Transportation
Efficiency Act of 1991, 126
iron triangles, 144, 180

Jackson, John E., 175
Jaroslovsky, Rich, 179
Jefferson, Thomas, 89
Jeffrey, Christina, 83

Johnson, Bob, 82
Johnson, Charles, 8, 80, 83, 99, 108, 147
Joint Committee on the Organization of
Congress, 3, 57, 59, 70, 99
see also jurisdictional reform
Jones, Bryan, 2, 4, 109, 144, 149, 150,
159–161, 173, 180
Jones, Charles O., 166, 171
jurisdiction,
definition of, 1, 11–13, 16, 18
history in political science, 2–6
importance of, 15
stability of, 14–15
jurisdictional ambiguity, 39
definition of, 18, 42
new issues and, 18, 32, 42
jurisdictional change, theory of, 19–32
and expertise, 32
hypothesis relating to jurisdictional
proximity, 24
and institutional assets, 27
and motivations of legislators, 25–26
operationalization of, 122–124
and policy entrepreneurs, 22–29
and the role of parliamentarians,
28–29
and self-selection onto committees,
26–27
summary, 6
test case, 124–136
jurisdictional fragmentation, 6, 9, 40–41,
55, 68, 77, 115, 119, 138–147
benefits of, 144–145
costs of, 140–144
jurisdictional proximity, 29, 32, 40–41
see also jurisdictional change, theory
of
jurisdictional reform, 7, 56–77
1946 Legislative Reorganization Act,
36, 45, 49, 56–63, 95, 99, 140
in 1974, 58, 62–67
in 1980, energy, 58, 67–70
in 1995, 1, 3, 56, 70–77, 101, 113, 140
rational problem solving model, 58

Kahn, Gabriel, 163
Kaji, Joel, 160, 176
Kamen, Al, 152
Kariel, Henry, 180
Keefe, William, 150

Keller, Morton, 170
Kennedy, Donnald, 110
Kennedy, Edward M., 11, 43
Kephart, Thomas, 102, 158, 172
Kiewiet, Roderick, 152
King, Christopher D., 175
King, David C., 155, 165
Kingdon, John W., 153
Kirzner, Israel M., 159
Kolm, Henry, 124
Kolter, Joe, 129–130, 177
Koszczuk, Jackie, 151
Kovenick, David M., 164
Krehbiel, Keith 5, 25, 29, 31, 150–156, 167
Kriz, Margaret E., 153
Kuntz, Phil, 160

Labor and Industry Coalition on International Trade, 114
La Follette, Robert, Jr., 59, 164
Legi-Slate (database), 128
Legislative Reorganization Act of 1946, 5, 34–36, 45, 49, 56–63, 95, 99, 140, 169
Levi, Edward, 38, 158
Lewin, David, 179
Lindblom, Charles, 164
Llewellyn, Karl N., 156
Lodge, Henry Cabot, 92
logrolling, 15, 30
Longley, Lawrence D., 174
Longworth, Nicholas, 83
Loomis, Burdett, 160
Lowi, Theodore, 180

Maass, Arthur, 4, 150
McCaleb, Thomas S., 154
McCarran-Ferguson Act of 1945, 112
McConachie, Lauros, 91, 170
McCormack, John, 84, 153, 164
McCubbins, Mathew, 3, 5, 149, 151–153
Madison, Christopher, 159
Magnetic Levitation Transportation and Competitiveness Act of 1990, 133
magnetically levitated trains (also, "maglev" technology), 6, 75, 121–122, 124–126, 175–176
Malbin, Michael J., 156, 164, 179
Manley, John F., 154
Mann, Thomas E., 156, 164, 179
Marannis, David, 158

March, James G., 150
Marine Hospital Service, 51
Marshall, William, 30–31
Martin, Joseph, 85
Marwell, Gerald, 167
Marwill, Philip, 153
Mayhew, David R., 155
Medicaid, 98
Medicare, 71, 98, 141
memoranda of understanding, 19, 34, 108–109
Michel, Robert, 83–84
Miller, George, 44
Miller, Luther S., 176
Mills, Mike, 174
Mills, Wilbur, 19, 170, 180
Mintrom, Michael, 159–160
Mintz, John, 152
Monroney, Mike, 58–59
Moran, Mark J., 156
Morin, Richard, 180
Morrow, William, 12, 143, 151, 158, 180
Moss, John, 64
Moynihan, Daniel, 11, 43, 126, 175
Mrazek, Robert, 129–130, 133, 179
Munger, Michael, 154, 156, 158

Nadel, Mark V., 165
Nader, Ralph, 52
Nakayama, Atasushi, 176
National Aeronautics and Space Administration (NASA), 53, 137
National Planning Association, 59
National Science Foundation, 49
Natural Gas Policy Act, 68
Neustadt, Richard, 143, 180
Nightline, 42
Nussle, Jim, 83

Office of International Trade and Tourism, 65
Office of Management and Budget, 125
Office of Technology Assessment, 125, 130
Ogul, Morris S., 150, 173
oil embargo of 1973, 119
O'Leary, Michael K., 164
Olsen, Johan P., 150
Olson, Mancur, 154
Omnibus Trade Act, 115, 139, 141

Ornstein, Norman J., 156, 164, 179
Ostenso, Grace, 111

Panitz, Raphael, 111
parliamentarian, 7–8
    history, 96–104
    as institutional guardian, 22, 78–88
    see also referral process
Patterson, Jerry, 68, 173
Pena, Frederico, 126
Pentagon 71, 125, 142
Pepper, Claude, 146–147
Perkins, John A., 164
pesticide regulation, 16
Peters, Ronald M., 93, 95–96, 168,
    170–171
Peterson, Mark A., 180
Pierce, Franklin, 91
Pines, David, 161
Pitts, William R., Jr., 83
Poage, W. R., 106
policy entrepreneur, 22–25, 40–45, 111,
    128–129
Polsby, Nelson, 2, 149–150, 164, 171
Pope, Gregory T., 175
Powell, James, 121, 124
Pressman, Steven, 152, 174
Price, David E., 160
Public Health Service, 51, 53
Pytte, Alyson, 152

Rauch, Jonathan, 145, 180
Rayburn, Sam, 83, 159
Reagan, Ronald, 110, 143, 153
Reed, Thomas Brackett, 58, 93–95, 170
Rees, Tom, 97
referral process, 7, 21, 86, 98, 105
    in countries other than the U.S., 29–30
    history of, 7, 85–104
    multiple referrals, 100, 101–104,
        113–116
        additional initial, 113, 145
        joint referrals, 101–102, 113
        sequential referrals, 100, 102–104,
            113, 115
        split referrals, 102
    referral precedent, 7, 9, 35, 37–38, 107
    see also parliamentarian, weight of the
        bill
Reid, T. R., 17, 153

Ricci, David, 150
Rich, Andrew, 5, 37, 73, 151, 157
Rich, Spencer, 13, 151
Rieselbach, Leroy N., 163, 173
Riker, William, 159, 167
Ripley, Randall, 150, 164
Rivers, Douglas, 153
Robinson, George, 62, 169
Robinson, William A., 170
Roe, Robert, 137
Rohde, David W., 151
Roman, Nancy, 166
Roosevelt, Franklin, 59, 163
Rostenkowski, Dan, 17, 73, 81, 114, 146,
    155, 168, 171
Rovner, Julie, 152
Roy, Roger, 175
Rubin, Alissa, 151
Rundquist, Barry S., 164

Samuelson, Paul A., 154
Schamel, Charles E., 157, 160
Schickler, Eric, 5, 37, 73, 151, 157
Schneider, Judy, 118, 154, 174
Schneider, Mark, 43–44, 159, 160
Schott, Richard, L., 160, 164, 169
Schumpeter, Joseph, 159
Sciolino, Elaine, 173
Securities and Exchange Commission, 54,
    76
Senate, U.S., committees,
    Appropriations, 153
    Agriculture, 33
    Budget, 153
    Commerce, 16
    Finance, 11, 36, 153
    Labor, 11
    Public Works, 17
Shakdher, S. L., 156
Sharp, Phil, 75
Shepsle, Kenneth, 150–152, 154–156,
    169
Shillinger, Kurt, 163
Shipan, Charles, R., 149, 180
Siff, Ted, 167, 171
Simon, Donald, 153
Simon, Harvey, 180
Sinclair, Barbara, 81, 167
Skaggs, Jimmy M., 170
Smith, Hedrick, 143

Smith, Steven, 18, 47, 152, 153, 160, 164, 180
Smock, Raymond, 83
Social Security Act, 65, 98
Speaker of the U.S. House of Representatives, 7, 12, 27, 86, 93–96, 104
Staggers, Harley, 43, 66, 75, 159–160, 165
Stanfield, Rochelle L., 158
Starobin, Paul, 152
statutory jurisdiction, 7, 19, 33–38, 41, 45
Stewart, Charles, III, 154
Strahan, Randall, 166
Stratmann, Thomas, 153
subcommittees, 27, 110, 118–119
Sullivan, Terry O., 160
Swinbanks, David, 176

Talbert, Jeffrey, 4, 109, 149–151, 161, 173
task forces, 28, 34, 141
Teske, Paul, 43–44, 159, 160
Thevenot, Wayne, 178
Tiefer, Charles, 17, 86, 116, 153, 158, 169, 173–174
Torricelli, Robert, 129–120
Toxic Control and Substances Act, 106
trade, 42, 114
Trans-Alaska Oil Pipeline, 75, 140, 166
Travel Bureau, 65
turf
    see jurisdiction
turf wars,
    definition, 13
    and institutional assets, 28
    strategies for winning, 8, 105–120
        amend public laws, 105–107
        argue for multiple referrals, 113–116

cite referral precedents, 107–109
gain expertise, 109–112
Turner, James, 112

Udall, Morris, 44, 160
Ujifusa, Grant, 158
Underwood, Oscar, 96
Unemployment compensation, 98
Uslaner, Eric, 68, 70, 166

Victor, Kirk, 163
Vining, Aidan R., 154

Wagner, Richard E., 154
Walgren, Doug, 179
Walker, Jack L., 165, 180
Walker, Robert, 75
weight of the bill, 6, 8, 85, 96, 98, 120
    see also jurisdictional proximity, referral process
Weil, Alan, 167, 171
Weimer, David L., 154
Weingast, Barry, 5, 30–31, 150–151, 154, 156, 174
Weissert, Carol, 44, 160
Welfare, 71
Wilson, James, 112
Wilson, Woodrow, 14, 139, 151
Wolf, Frank, 179
Work, Clement, 176
Wright, Jim, 17, 146

Young, Cheryl D., 169
Young, Don, 76, 166
Young, Garry, 172

Zorack, John L., 158, 167, 173

DATE DUE

GAYLORD			PRINTED IN U.S.A.